THE INEVITABLE ALLIANCE

Additional Praise for *The Inevitable Alliance*:

"*The Inevitable Alliance* is a learned and provocative contribution to ongoing debate about the future of transatlantic relations. Basing his study on a unique conceptual framework, Parsi offers an analysis that is theoretically rich as well as relevant to the key policy issues of the day."—Charles A. Kupchan, Georgetown University and Council on Foreign Relations, author of *The End of the American Era*

"Parsi offers us a grand synthesis on the state of the world since the Cold War, and of transatlantic relations since Iraq. The book is written with passion, formidable range, and intellectual acuity. In reaching a seemingly conventional endorsement of the need for sound transatlantic relations, but from an unusually critical and radical direction, his is a highly original contribution that deserves our close attention"—Ian Clark, Professor of International Politics, University of Wales Aberystwyth, UK

"Amid the current cacophony of voices expressing arrogance, resentment or discouragement, Professor Parsi comes forward with a uniquely positive message. His attempt to reconcile American hegemony, multilateralism, and European identity is both bold and realistic. His call for the unity of the West in a plural world deserves the widest audience"—Pierre Hassner, Directeur Emeritus Centre d'Etudes et de Recherches Internationales (CERI) Paris

The Inevitable Alliance

Europe and thc United States beyond Iraq

Vittorio Emanuele Parsi

THE INEVITABLE ALLIANCE

Original title: *L'alleanza inevitabile: Europa e Stati Uniti oltre l'Iraq*
Copyright © 2003, 2006 EGEA-Università Bocconi Editore

Translated by Catherine Bell

First published in 2006 by
PALGRAVE MACMILLAN™
175 Fifth Avenue, New York, N.Y. 10010 and
Houndmills, Basingstoke, Hampshire, England RG21 6XS
Companies and representatives throughout the world.

PALGRAVE MACMILLAN is the global academic imprint of the Palgrave Macmillan division of St. Martin's Press, LLC and of Palgrave Macmillan Ltd. Macmillan® is a registered trademark in the United States, United Kingdom and other countries. Palgrave is a registered trademark in the European Union and other countries.

ISBN 1–4039–7022–X

Library of Congress Cataloging-in-Publication Data

Parsi, Vittorio Emanuele.
    [Alleanza inevitabile. English]
    The inevitable alliance : Europe and the United States beyond Iraq / Vittorio Emanuele Parsi.
        p. cm.
    Includes bibliographical references and index.
    ISBN 1–4039–7022–X
        1. European Union countries—Foreign relations—Iraq.
    2. Iraq—Foreign relations—European Union countries. 3. European Union countries—Foreign relations—United States.
    4. United States—Foreign relations—European Union countries.
    5. United States—Foreign relations—Iraq. 6. Iraq—Foreign relations—United States. I. Title.

JZ1570.A57172613 2006
327.4073—dc22   2005054976

A catalogue record for this book is available from the British Library.

Design by Newgen Imaging Systems (P) Ltd., Chennai, India.

First edition: May 2006

10 9 8 7 6 5 4 3 2 1

Printed in the United States of America.

To my mother, Fiorenza, and in memory of
my father, Brigadier General Antonio Maria Parsi

The Brain—is wider than the Sky—
For—put them side by side—
The one the other will contain
With ease—and You—beside—

The Brain is deeper than the sea—
For—hold them—Blue to Blue—
The one the other will absorb—
As Sponges—Buckets—do—

The Brain in just the weight of God—
For—Heft them—Pound for Pound—
And they will differ—if they do—
As Syllable from Sound

                         Emily Dickinson

To the Muses,
who only know the hidden thoughts

CONTENTS

Acknowledgments   xi

Introduction to the English Edition   1

1   From the End of History to the End of the World   11

2   Force, Law, and International Order   61

3   The Remains of the West   125

Notes   169

Bibliography   187

Index   197

ACKNOWLEDGMENTS

For several years now in the first week of May a small group of friends, European and American scholars, have had the good fortune to meet in a splendid Tuscan villa to converse freely and privately about the transatlantic relationships. Thanks to G. John Ikenberry and Michael Mastanduno's hospitality, the days spent in "Villa Le Balze," Georgetown University's residence near Fiesole have been unique occasions for intellectual nourishment and comparison of ideas. Those days also increased mutual and direct awareness among many of the authors quoted in the pages that follow through frank and at times ruthless discussions, but always in an atmosphere of friendship and in the attempt to understand reciprocal positions. These pages have been written in that spirit.

The idea for this book began to germinate at the beginning of July 2002 but it then took shape very quickly starting from the last war against Saddam Hussein. All this would not have been possible without the help of a dear friend and intelligent colleague, Annalisa Galardi. My sincere thanks go to her for having shared the effort in making this work as accessible as possible to a less restricted public than normal.

The book has been consistently reviewed and updated for the English version, making use of the advice and encouragement of John Ikenberry, Matthew Evangelista, and Michael Cox, whom I thank for their critical contribution. My deep gratitude to Lorento Ornaghi, my master and friend. Gianmarco Festini gave a significant contribution to the publication. My assistants Alessandra Amato, Serena Giusti, Andrea Locatelli, and Michela Mercuri relieved me of a large part of the most tiring tasks regarding the conversion into English from the Italian text and also the updating of data. Catherine Bell did an excellent job with her translation, managing to solve many problems. Obviously all the claims herein remain my sole responsibility. The last "thank you" goes to my wife Teresita and to my girls Malvina, Lavinia, and Costanza, for the support and comprehension that they have yet again accorded me.

Introduction to the English Edition

"No important problem in the world can be resolved without the joint efforts of the United States and Europe; no problem is unsolvable when we confront it together." These few, simple words taken from the appeal endorsed by some leaders from the "old and new Europe" in mid-June 2003 close this book. It is right that these same words are the first that the reader encounters in order to make the basic argument explicit right from the outset: the union of the West is not only the indispensable condition for the security of Europe and the United States, it is also the precondition for any potential democratic peace for the world.

What is the actual state of transatlantic relations? Why do the multilateral institutions and the selfsame international law seem to have fallen so badly into disgrace? Are the defense of freedom and the security of democracies worth more than peace "without ifs and buts"? What chance does democracy have of winning Muslim countries over to its cause? These are some of the questions that this book tries to answer, with the realization that every answer must be sought within the values of the culture that condition our hierarchies and our preferences. In writing this I have tried to keep a distance from both simplistic pamphleteering and also from an excessively academic treatment, aiming to express a middle-ground position, or rather a position of rationality in the midst of much extremism that has been seen in recent years.

The point of departure is the acceptance of the hegemony of the United States: not only as a simple matter of fact but as a scenario which is by far more preferable than the balance of nuclear terror that preceded it. This conviction does not however lead us to sympathize with that sort of "satisfied unilateralism." In a highly successful article a few years ago, Robert Kagan outlined the metaphorical description of a strong Martian America and a weak Venusian Europe, divided on almost all fronts starting from the image of the world in which they live: a Hobbesian hell for the former and a Kantian paradise for the latter. In actual fact, pluralism, far better than weakness explains how

Europe is different from the United States. Its disunity is the first cause of its weakness and not vice versa.

The objective to be reached is therefore to create a stronger and more influential Europe to make it more united, even if the forms of this "unity" may be different from those conjectured in the past decade. This does not mean that a more united Europe must also be a Europe which is less friendly with the United States. Nor does it mean that the breakdown of Atlantic solidarity is obligatory to build a more solid European identity. The smart-alec rhetoric by the bards for "Europe-a civilised power" is frankly intolerable. Europe's destiny should be to "balance" the power of the United States and to rebuke the pitiable observations that have been read, heard, and denied in recent times. It is remarkable that those who challenge the idea of "exceptionalism," which is so evident in American political culture, fuss so tirelessly in trying to oppose a form of European supremacy. At times it seems as if we are witnessing the construction of an enormous self-deception, in which a considerable part of the European managerial class tries to hide itself and its own irrelevance as regards the decisive choices made in international politics. It is indeed better to forsake the specular clichés of a muscular America and an old, cowardly Europe that force us to look through the distorting lenses of mutual prejudice, in which the "arrogance of force" is opposed by the "arrogance of weakness."

Americans and Europeans would do better to reflect upon how alike they are even in the "complementary" mistakes they make. In the face of the peace-keeping issue, both of them move in a perspective in which both derive a partial and diametrically opposed training. The Americans claim that the idea of a multilateral government of the international political system inspired by the principle of democracy is nonsense, when the majority part of governments do not keep count of that principle. The Europeans reply that the procedure of a multilateral management of the world will gradually lead the individual nondemocratic governments toward democracy. The former pretend not to see that, at least for now, multilateralism has been poorly implemented even with regard to those selfsame European democratic allies, and that the instrumental but continual recourse to force jeopardizes the end result of *a peaceable world because it is democratic*. The latter skirt the central issue of the necessity to use force in order to safeguard the principles in which they believe and seem to be unconcerned by the concrete tools that can be used in order to reach the final goal of *a democratic world because it is peaceable*.

This book is divided into three chapters. The first is dedicated to the transition phase we experienced between the end of the cold war and September 11, 2001. Starting from the real reasons that enabled the combined development of the balance of Soviet-American terror and the hegemony of the United States through almost half a century, the attempt is made to explain why the end of the bipolar system did not open up that season of peace for which so many had hoped and expected for so long. The second chapter starts from the fragmentation of the previous international political system into several subsystems, each one inextricably linked to the others mainly by violence. By means of an analysis of the Iraqi campaign, a series of conceptual pairs are considered that are today subjected to continual prodding almost as if they were logical "duellers": democracy and sovereignty, peace and security, and legitimacy and legality. Finally, the third chapter analyzes thoroughly the Euro-American relationship, placing emphasis on the novel aspect represented (at least potentially) by the European Union and, while fending off the facile temptation for anti-Americanism and a European genesis for secession from the West, there is an attempt to define the real challenges that the Union will have to overcome in order to even hope to assert itself in the international scene.

The question as to what kind of multilateralism is possible and indeed worth wishing for today, or rather as to how it is possible to institutionalize a system that would be in any case unipolar, is the leitmotif that permeates the book. For a large part of the Bush administration's first term we experienced a paradoxical situation: we lived in a world in which the dominant power did not seem to concern itself unduly with the aspects of legitimacy of its own power. The consequences of a power that swaggered as if it believed it was "enough for itself" was without question devastating. The United States' power stopped being regarded as benign and reassuring, not only by public opinion, which, according to some surveys, deem the United States the most dangerous player in the international political scene, but also by a considerable percentage of the European political class. In particular, following the war in Iraq, the United States has run the risk of being perceived as a *free-rider* in the international political system—which is perhaps the worst image it could project from the point of view of a *leader*—and although it has tried to ensure the leadership not only of its own allies but of the system in its entirety, at the same time it is considered to be the one that threatens the supporting columns of the system: rules, institutions, and expectations.

But there again, even if we consider the issue and benevolently give credit to the Americans' reasons, it seems obvious that the United States has entered a vicious circle in the crisis of legitimacy, so it exercises ever more power—in some ways it must do so—which is, however, detected as being less and less legitimate. The crucial question for the future of the stability of that system is this: how can it get out of this vicious circle and initiate a virtuous circle?

With the "Bush administration's change of course," perhaps defined rather too hastily, the United States has supplied its own answer to the problem. In his inaugural address for the second term, President Bush took steps to enunciate clearly the principles in the name of which hegemony is exercised. The continual reference to the values of liberty and democracy and to the universality of these principles shows there is an attempt to double back to the basics of the legitimacy of a great democratic power, to call again on and redefine a platform of values without which even the premise for the sharing of policies and associated agenda would falter: not only the fight against terror and the enemies of democracy, but active support for the promotion of liberty. It is, however, not enough to evoke the shareable and shared principles of democracy if they are not followed up by means of multilateralism, which must not be understood as a "good in itself" but rather as an "instrumental good." Multilateralism is standard practice for democracies; it is the procedure of political action typical of democracies; it is the way to define the objectives and is also the best way to reach them.

The president's journey in Europe at the beginning of 2005, preceded by that of the Secretary of State Condoleeza Rice, clarified the American position: the time has come to leave behind the bad taste that was left in the mouth as regards the way upon which war was embarked in Iraq and to find the path that leads to Atlantic cooperation. It has been meditated upon at length whether this return to singing the praises of multilateralism was a sort of authoritative retraction of the political line held up to then by the United States. Someone even went so far as to talk of a sort of "homage" that Bush's imperial presidency was bound to render to the moral authority of Europe. Frankly, such considerations seem pure nonsense. Much more unimaginatively, the fact is that the situation has changed and a different situation requires and permits a different strategy. To wage war on Iraq the United States could not but act unilaterally, inasmuch as the opposition from countries like France and Germany was invincible. In order to realize the far more ambitious plan contained in the "agenda of liberty" expounded in the speech that inaugurated the second term, America has to find a multilateral agreement with its European allies. In this sense President Bush neither contradicted himself nor retracted his own political progress, but he even put into practice what his predecessor Bill Clinton's secretary of state had claimed on more than one occasion: "the United States acts multilaterally when it can, unilaterally when it must." In short, rather than a change in strategy, we are dealing with the return to the possibility of multilateral action after the necessity for unilateral action has run dry.

From Europe's point of view, even if we consider the issue in the most benevolent way imaginable, a logical contradiction continues to amaze us. Europe criticizes the United States sometimes in the name of the most cynical realism (accusing the Americans of being dangerously naive and simple-minded) and at other times in the name of the most unbridled idealism (charging the United States with immoral politics). But, either the Americans are more cynical than we are, and so they have to correct their politics in an idealistic way, or they are more naive than we are, and so they have to correct their politics in a concrete way. It is certain that they cannot make mistakes at the same time in the two directions. As a European, this is what strikes me most about the criticisms that are thrown at the United States by Europe, also because this ambiguity is a serious problem as regards the redefinition of the alliance; on the part of Europe there is a total lack of clarity. Do we regard the relationship with the United States in an essentially defensive way, emphasizing the need to identify a common enemy as we did during the cold war? Or are we willing to consider the transatlantic link as a proponent relationship between democracies that have a global agenda, global responsibilities to be carried out together, but that in its principles and final aims cannot be an object of political bargaining? It is essential that this junction is cleared, because only if the second choice is chosen unflinchingly can the agenda of support for liberty be shared effectively by all.

The issue surfaces conspicuously in the never-ending debate on multilateralism. Multilateralism is often confused with a return to multipolarism, an unlikely hypothesis to conjecture, at least for the next twenty years. We can argue whether this is a "classical" unipolar world with a single dominant power, or whether it is an "a-polar" world, in which not even the greatest possible concentration of power manages to ensure order in the international political system. Reflecting on the multilateralism that is possible today, it makes little sense to think of the historical precedent of the concert of European powers put to the test in the nineteenth century. That was indeed an authentic multipolar system in which no player, not even Great Britain, was sufficiently powerful to decide alone, to impose its own vision and try to realize it. In that world it was necessary to try to decide together: when this transpired there was peace; otherwise there was war. In a multipolar world, multilateralism was the bound method; it did not necessarily guarantee peace but without it war was a certainty. This was the European tradition theorized by the so-called realism that led to two world wars in twenty-five years, the first of which was all in all the fruit of errors of calculation and of conspicuously mistaken intuitions.

What is certain is that a multipolar world with so many powers balancing each other is not only not imminent, but in the event that it should be so, it is not even desirable. If multipolarism has to be achieved through the growth of the international political importance of China "just as it is"—authoritarian—and Russia "just as it is"— yesterday Yeltsin's, today Putin's, tomorrow who knows whose, but nevertheless illiberal—it is far more preferable to live in a world badly unipolar like today's. Besides, even if someone were convinced that a similar multipolarism was preferable, he would have to consider, however, that it is not within Europe's capabilities to compete to realize it. As the lesson of the Iraq war has taught us, whoever thinks of bringing Europe to greater cohesion with an anti-American vision, albeit in good faith, ends up losing that small amount of unity which has been achieved so far. On such a decisive question as the war in Iraq, Europe was divided according to the fracture lines determined by the legitimate sovereign choices made by the national governments. What remains today of the "Franco—German axis," the engine of European construction, is clearly visible: as happened about fifty years ago, at the time of the failure of the European Defence Community, once again, last June France launched a missile that sank the hopes of a more cohesive Europe which were pinned on the Constitutional treaty. Old Europe, rather than allow equal dignity to the new Europe, chose to drown itself.

In effect, it is since the 1990s that America has found itself in a position of unique strategic supremacy, so as to make people talk of a "uni-polar order" of the international political system. No American president has ever intended or intends to renounce this supremacy, which represents the fruits of the victory in the cold war. Those same 1990s saw America begin to move toward a unilateral approach on the principle issues of security, even if it assumed the appearance of a unilateralism which was more superficial than concrete. The gym in which American unilateralism trained was the Balkans of the 1990s, reaching its apotheosis in the Kosovo crisis, when in Rambouillet Madeleine Albright "summoned" the European allies to force them to "share" the American decision to send an ultimatum to Milosevic's Serbia. In the previous years the United States had sampled chronic weakness (first political rather than military) of the European states;

they had gradually proven to be unreliable partners in the realization of a responsible, effective multilateralism. In the months when the Kosovo crisis escalated, the United States had also ascertained how Russia's intractable opposition and, in a different way, China's could in fact be ignored without facing significant consequences.

American unilateralism is thus the fruit both of a "temptation" tied to an unprecedented supremacy, and to the conviction that it is not possible to "extract" from the international political system (in fact from its partners) the resources of authority, capacity, and the will necessary to guarantee security: its own and also collective security. Today, because of the security crisis which was so blatantly declared with September 11, the European partners, on condition that they do not act misleadingly, are able to show their American ally that it is precisely the unipolar order of the international political system that makes it necessary to have a multilateral approach. To go back to the effective concept of the "a-polar" system: without multilateralism, the unipolar system is transformed into its degenerate form of a-polar system, where the concentration of power in the hands of the hegemon, however big it may be, cannot stop the progressive entropy of collective security and that of the selfsame hegemon. Vice versa, multilateralism in no way tarnishes the American supremacy that makes the system unipolar, but rather it makes it functional for the security of the hegemon and indeed of the entire system. The multilateral way of working makes available those resources of authority, capacity and the will that can only come from sharing and which again confer legitimacy to the power of the hegemon, inverting that vicious circle from which we started. For this to happen it is however necessary that both sides of the Atlantic are willing to learn from the mistakes of the recent past and return to favoring the path of cooperation between countries which are extremely dissimilar in power and capacity, but are incredibly alike in the liberal institutions that govern them, tried and tested over almost fifty years of Atlantic Alliance.

In this regard it is necessary to demand and ensure the utmost frankness, starting from the declarations in principle and of the principles that in international politics count just as much as concrete interest. Today it is crucial to think of multilateralism in a new way, defined first and foremost as a work procedure, as a method that enforces precisely those principles—of the promotion of freedom and the spread of democracy—which on the other side of the Atlantic have been declared for the first time so vehemently by the administration of George W. Bush. This means then not spoiling everything in the name of that European syndrome that is said to be made up of retreats and weakness in the political arena even more than by diplomatic and military tools. It is about abandoning once and for all, as too often happens with us Europeans, being masters of rhetoric and cynicism. It means being realistic and idealistic at one and the same time, able to see things for what they are and still continue to believe that politics is above all tomorrow's supreme creative capacity and not merely the administration of today.

Only if the European Union ceases to be so isolationist and turned in on itself, will America be induced to take up again the road of Western partnership. Whoever attributes the unilateral turnaround of American politics to George W. Bush and the "neo-conservatives" commits a glaring blunder. As we have seen this was basically already decided by President Bill Clinton as an answer to a structural change in the international political system. It was Madeleine Albright, Bill Clinton's Secretary of State, who commented during the Kosovo crisis: "If we are forced to use force it is because we are America. We are the indispensable nation." Events of September 11 simply heightened and hastened a choice that had already been made.

Despite the fact that America's unilateralism has never diminished, the partnership with the West remains the mainstay for any order that wants to maintain both the conditions of well-being in democracies and the solidity of those principles like individual liberty, democratic legitimacy, and market economy which up until now only the West has been able to represent and protect, albeit imperfectly and continually subject to endless improvements. It is this oneness of the sharing of values and principles that creates the "inevitable alliance" of mutual interest between Europe and the United States.

For the time being at least, the only multilateralism possible is that between Europe and the United States; it is the only acceptable multilateralism if what spurs us on is not any old order or an "equally shared" order, but a correct order. Multilateralism in itself is not a value. Multilateralism becomes an objective to reach when it is the tool whereby those principles of liberty are affirmed, principles which cannot be subject to bargaining. As the other states gradually give their full support to these values, the growth of multilateralism will become morally compulsory. It is not a problem of race or culture: it is simply a question of principles on which the order must be built. For over half a century Japan has belonged completely to those group of states that recognize unconditionally the principles of democracy and liberty. The same is true for those giants in the south of the world that have embarked upon the road toward democracy and liberty: from India to the new South Africa to Brazil. It is the difficult path to an "assembly of democracies." Alongside the sharing of values there must also be the will and capacity to share the responsibility to guarantee the overall security of the international system. As long as America is the only one to take on this responsibility, any discussion about greater multilateralism risks being a purely rhetorical exercise. Here it is up to Europe to step forward by virtue of its wealth and its history. Only if we know how to be a reliable and credible partner in this task and if the amount of security that we can guarantee to the international system increases significantly, will we be able to hope to secure more weight in the decision-making processes—including those to do with war and peace. This is the only alternative both to an exasperated American unilateralism and to the unsustainable legalistic pretence of the equality of all states.

CHAPTER 1

From the End of History to the End of the World

No More Enemies?

On November 9, 1989, practically with their bare hands, and without any resistance from the *Vopos*, tens of thousands of citizens from East Berlin smash up "the Wall," that horrendous scar of cement, barbed-wire, and watch-towers, that all-too-tangible symbol of the permanent, irreversible division of Europe for almost thirty years. In its own rough and apparently temporary way, that wall, erected in one night in 1961—almost like a malicious mushroom which sprouted on the wounds of Europe,—in a single, far more joyful, even if just as incredible, evening, collapses. And its collapse marks the beginning of the end of Soviet rule over the peoples of central-eastern Europe. In a short space of time, all the Communist regimes that from 1945 to 1948 had been established by Moscow in the areas occupied during the Second World War are to fall one after the other, for the most part without bloodshed.[1] The USSR abandons the field (completely unpredicted by all analysts, scholars, and the intelligence network), and on the wave of enthusiasm for the rediscovered unity of Europe, strong optimism spreads about the fact that history has reached a sort of conceptual terminus, that the last great battle between the "powers of good" and the "evil empire" has been won and that nothing can hinder the progress of the development of liberal democracy and market economy now that the last, most dangerous, ideological enemy has been routed.

The enthusiasm with which many embraced the notion of the "end of history" is a typical blunder of a totally Eurocentric concept of history, paradoxically the fruit of a Japanese-American political scientist, Francis Fukuyama, who works in the U.S. State Department. "Have we in fact reached the end of history? Are there, in other words, any fundamental 'contradictions' in human life that cannot be resolved in the context of modern liberalism that would be resolvable by an alternative political-economic structure?": This was the main question that Francis Fukuyama asked.[2] In reality, in a very short time we will have to take painful note that the end of the opposition between democracies and Communist regimes will herald the beginning of another quite different story, one in which the threat of the safety and well-being of the "rich, powerful West" will no longer come from one of its "ribs," even if on the frontier as was Russia, and neither in the name of a philosophy, Marxism, which was also a child of modernity. No. This time, for the first time since 1683, when the Turkish armies were defeated at the walls of Vienna, the challenge is to come from a really "different" world. The collapse of the Soviet Union is to cause all the *puppet states* of the Russian empire to fall into disarray and will transform some of its ex-provinces into free zones and bases for fundamentalist terrorism of Islamic origin, which scarcely a dozen or so years after the demolition of the wall, will be successful in carrying out a mortal attack in the heart of the world's economic and political power. In truth, in his article, Fukuyama had addressed the problem of "the rise of religious fundamentalism in recent years within the Christian, Jewish, and Muslim traditions," but his thoughts concluded with the observation that in the "contemporary world only Islam has offered a theocratic state as a political alternative to both liberalism and communism. But the doctrine has little appeal for non-Muslims, and it is hard to believe that the movement will take on any universal significance."[3]

It is, above all, because of the concatenation of events subsequent to the end of Soviet communism that we realize how the inevitable obsessive attention paid to the East–West conflict obscured for us the fact that for almost half a century this was just one of the political fault lines on the planet, even if it was the main one. Of course, it was a fracture so sharp and jagged with nuclear missiles as to eclipse all the others, starting with the problem between the northern and southern hemispheres. But now its decline has let other quite differently opposed forces come out of the shadows, besides everything else conceptually far more complicated to identify, analyze, and categorize. Indeed, as this book demonstrates, the fact that that fracture was completely within the Western world guaranteed at least three consequences. In the first place it re-established all the other most disparate and plural dividing-lines that were crossing the planet in its various peripheries. In essence, it supplied a "core" to the system—a certain unity. Second, the fact that the East–West fracture had its geographical, cultural, and political heart in Europe permitted Europeans to maintain their own centrality in the international political system: the European states were no longer the exclusive dominators nor the key figure in the system that they had created at Westphalia in 1648. However, they compensated for that evident loss of the importance of the "relationship" factor, while maintaining an extraordinary importance of "position." Moreover, if Europe no longer counted such a great deal as regards the area of concentration of the main world powers, it remained the main arena for the cold war. Third, the Berlin Wall enabled the governments and public opinion of Europe to avoid seeing that the reality of the dominant relationship, both benevolent and almost "constitutionalised," in John Ikenberry's words, as is the case in the current relationship between the United States and its Western allies, matched the reality and rhetoric of the balance of terror between the two superpowers within the transatlantic reality.[4]

One of the reasons for the crisis today in the transatlantic relationship stems from the little importance that the United States confers on Europe in its global strategy. If it is true that the "Americans view Europe as relatively more important than Asia and as a potential ally in addressing a wide range of challenges,"[5] it is also just as certain that the United States' *grand strategy* "has gradually shifted its focus away from the relatively trouble-free zone known as Europe, to more pressing regional problems in the Middle East and Asia. . . . Naturally, this does not mean that Europe has become insignificant, but it does point to the fact that it has lost its once central position in US eyes. To this extent, the pro-European moment has passed."[6]

A target for facile and small-minded ironies, the concept of the "end of history" regains its pro-European capacity today, now that so much history has passed right before our very eyes since Francis Fukuyama's article hailed the new era. Sadly, it must be recognized that it has been a history made up of wars from the Gulf to the Caucasus, from the Middle East, to Afghanistan, to Iraq, to the myriad African disasters that come to pass with hardly a mention. It is a history, let us not forget, that saw war and extermination hit the center of Europe for almost a decade in former Yugoslavia. Fukuyama was right when he warned that the end of the cold war represented something quite deep and definitive, not attributable to yet another stage in the fight for dominance between rival powers, which dragged on for almost fifty years. It is true that with the end of communism and the crumbling of the USSR, history did end in a certain sense: an era was concluded that had begun in 1648 with the peace in Westphalia and the end of religious wars in Europe. The origin of the international political system dates back to this event. This system was founded on the sovereignty of a multiplicity of states and no longer on an imperial universalistic design, and we can trace back to that moment the notion that an order based on the acceptance of plurality is possible. Contemporaneously, that same date also marks the start in politics of the triumph of modernity over pre-modernity: it is the starting point for the separation of politics and religion, church and state that is to characterize quite significantly the political adventure to be embarked upon by the West in the centuries to come. It will allow us to formulate a conception of political modernity interpreted as progressive laicization. Liberalism, just as much as Marxism, is a child of that laity and of the "Divine right" that had signaled the humanization of politics and its distancing from any trace of transcendence, in order to anchor it well and truly to humanity.

The end of the cold war is the "end of history" because it is the end of the confrontation between two systems that had managed to incorporate all the other fractures within them, and in so doing they had fooled themselves into thinking that they could "integrate the world," in the dream of modern, cultural European tradition. Long before the end of the USSR, it is possible to sense how Marxism, just as much as capitalism allowed diversity and plurality in the world to be confined within a scheme in which even the enemy was not really particularly "different." Certainly, as explained in the lucid analysis expounded by the ingenious, original conservative Raymond Aron, the bi-polar system revealed itself to be not uniform as regards ideological values: communism and liberal democracy were not only incompatible, they were in fact mortal enemies, destined to wage war until defeat or triumph.[7] Besides, although the West and the communist world did not share the "equivalent of the bonds of common culture among European powers in earlier centuries," they did have "a heritage of ideas in common such as progress, rationality and the centrality of Man".[8]

As subsequent events have shown, even in a violent way, the perception of living in a world in which no mortal enemy would rise up to threaten the safety and well-being of the West and its own conceptual fundamentals of "political rationality," was extremely misleading. Rather more than in an era characterized by the growth of democracies and the expansion of the market area, by greater international security and an increased respect for basic human rights, we are under the impression that we have entered a new "era of uncertainty." From the euphoria at the end of the cold war that ushered in the last decade of the century, we have arrived today, through an infinite series of wars, to face a new, more terrible enemy. From the confidence of a world united by market rules and the principles of democracy, we have plummeted to the disheartening realization that we live in a world which is more harshly divided by cultural, religious, and economic factors, even before political factors, at least as far as the term is understood in the liberal western tradition. As the decade slips by from the fall of the Berlin Wall to the collapse of the Twin Towers and then to the last Iraqi war, we have an increasingly disturbing and unprecedented sensation, which is less and less exorcisable within the classical models of modern Western thought. That sensation is that "the notion of expectation does not go hand in hand with transition, although they should be inextricably linked," so that "the same transition becomes a bridge to nothing."[9] In truth, a similar sensation recurs in the twentieth century associated to those real periods of crisis that the century experienced beginning with the First World War, so much so that these words written in 2000 could have been perfectly suitable in describing the final phase of the Great War. "The undetermined risk is the central predicament of the present. It is a risk that from the complexity of the world a single individual immediately ascends."[10]

Almost scornfully, the history that Fukuyama had predicted in his "dialectic conclusion" is not over just because of that Islamic fundamentalism which was so underestimated by the American scholar. Even if the different phases of the war against Islamic terrorism should prove to be greater and swifter successes that might have been imagined, from the military point of view, what leaves us perplexed is the feeling that the United States is fighting without a suitable strategy. Paradoxically, re-enforced by the easy victory over Saddam Hussein and the never-ending bloody "post-war" that ensues,[11] one detects a feeling of doubt that America is incapable of exploiting politically her military successes gained on the field, and that she has passed from holding a strongly advantageous position as regards the enemy, to one of extremely dangerous vulnerability. Because of the objective role of leadership that the United States holds, the whole Western world despite itself is involved in a colossal and continual succession of fault-line wars, able to give body to that "clash of civilizations" hypothesized by Samuel Huntington as the most plausible scheme predicted for the post–cold war conflicts: "The clash of civilizations will dominate global politics. The fault lines between civilizations will be the battle lines of the future."[12] It is clear how, if realized fully, a similar nightmarish scenario would provide Bin Laden or his rivals or successors with an extraordinary propagandistic opportunity to convince the Muslim masses (already alienated from the global economic system and the political state process) of the anti-Islamic nature of yet another "Western crusade." And yet, although it is perfectly aware of the obviousness of this and with the same logic behind the antiterrorist campaign, in Iraq, an increasingly limited Western coalition (noticeably reduced to the United States and Great Britain) has wound up *forced to fight*, because of the lack of even the slightest hint of a strategy in which war was a possible choice and not the only means of combating terror. As has been controversially observed, "A foreign policy that is both immoral and unsuccessful is not simply stupid, it is increasingly dangerous to those who practice or favor it."[13] Despite the two great wars that overpowered Nazism and Communism to the detriment of myriad numbers of military interventions throughout the world, and also incurring hefty economic, human, and political costs, the "United States has more determined and probably more numerous enemies today than ever, and many of those who hate it are ready and able to inflict death and destruction on its shores."[14]

To understand the reasons for this absence or lack of an outlook that does not entirely foresee a sort of permanent conflict with the Muslim world, we have to start from the recognition that we are in fact atoning for the lack of a new "grand strategy" on the part of the various American administrations that succeeded each other from 1991 up to the present day. Quite apart from the excessive amount of rhetoric that has been applied to the West's victory in the long cold war, and despite the evidence that the bi-polar system and its balance of terror has declined, taking with it the idea of an order as stable as it was "balanced," it seems that the United States has not yet set about formulating a convincing explanation about the new situation of global hegemony, portraying the present (more or less effective) order of the system. At bottom, it would seem that different administrations in Washington have been long convinced that the weakening of the rival superpower (in the substantial absence of a credible global challenger) requires nothing other that the extension throughout the planet of United States hegemony (already pertinent to the West and sizeable chunks of east Asia), quite apart from the fact that the operational rules and the pillars on which that hegemony was founded are useful and effective even outside the Western political community. Frankly, whether we consider the stability of the order to have been founded on the balance between rival powers or on the hegemony (more or less constitutionalized) of one sole great power, what we tend to forget is that the totality of our categories has never been put to the test in a situation in which the threat of security or the diffusion of power emerged from the "Northern hemisphere" (i.e., from an exceedingly enlarged notion of the West). Balance, alliances and peaces, hegemony, institutions, and cooperation have always had Europe and its new, stronger offshoots as a reference point. When we have had to tackle rivals or hostilities hailing from countries outside our European culture, in truth our only response has been war. It is from this conceptual gap that we must start, in order to make sure not that war is excluded from the world (this would be mere dangerous utopia) but rather that it becomes again a possible political choice and not a necessity for survival, the continuation of politics with other means and not its abdication.

So, confronted with this war, the Iraqi campaign risks being only the third round (after the war in Afghanistan and September 11), it is well nigh useless to assign dogmatic explanations that date back to Westphalia, in which the principle of sovereignty was sanctioned internationally, that should have put an end to the bloody season of religious wars. We could forget that those were, in fact, above all, as Carl Schmitt says, *civil religious wars*, while the knife-edge along which we are dangerously running is that of a *war between religions*. We could forget, above all, that the birth of the international political system almost coincides temporally with the end of the Ottoman threat in Europe. From the second half of the seventeenth century, the slow Turkish withdrawal from Europe begins, a movement parallel to the rapid assertion of international society in the European states. European expansion throughout the world takes place at first in the form of colonialism, and then in the form of decolonization, which leaves the Western world in a position of absolute supremacy. But there is not a trace of "multiculturalism" in the fabric of institutions and rules that the West designs to keep the world together. It is just as useless to evoke Westphalia today, when the threat arrives mainly from nonstate players, like the terrorist network led by Osama Bin Laden. We are in fact in the presence of an event which is so revolutionary that it becomes useless to consider the criterion of guaranteed reciprocal destruction—a logical hypothesis for that balance of terror that made Aron write of an improbable war (but which facts have proven to be "impossible," at least as much as peace could be, given how the USSR dissolved)—since it is not a state that threatens atomic attack on New York or London.

There are, in fact, two unprecedented distinctive characteristics in the contemporary international political system. The first, and also the most obvious, is that ours is a unipolar system, as regards the distribution of power: in other words, we only have one powerful state, and that is the United States. The second, just as unprecedented, is the end of the coincidence between political rivals, economic rivals, and the threat to security. It is this split that rocks the system's proverbial boat. In America, when considering who could be a possible challenger to its power in the medium–long term, China immediately comes to mind. Right or wrong as it may be, there is a real obsession in the United States about the fact that, sooner or later, China will challenge America over the problem of Taiwan or Korea or demand a greater role in Asia. As Joe Grieco observes, "During the latter part of the cold war, from the late-1970s to the mid-1980s, the United States and China were moving toward the construction of a balancing coalition against the Soviet Union. Since the end of the Cold War, however, America's ties with China, while not adversarial, have become more strained (and have become so in spite of a boom in two-way commercial and financial ties), with each looking at the other as a future potential rival."[15] Even more directed toward this worry are the pages dedicated to China in John Mearsheimer's latest book, that give a precise idea about the "yellow fever" that runs through the American analysts. According to Mearsheimer, China will sooner or later make it clear that American interference in Asia is unacceptable, in a sort of Asian edition of the Monroe doctrine ("America for the Americans!"), and at this point an intensification of contrasts would be inevitable and the outcome uncertain, since, what "makes a future Chinese threat so worrisome is that it might be far more powerful and dangerous than any of the potential hegemons that the United States confronted in the twentieth century."[16]

If we move from the political to the economic field the scene changes. In terms of economics and trade, there is no doubt that the European Union (EU) is the United States' rival. With a Gross Domestic Product (GDP) which is basically identical to the United States' and holding an important slice of world trade, the EU is considered to be America's real economic challenger. Overseas, there are those who, like Robert Gilpin, fear that such a danger will rise to traumatic dimensions and warn of the risk to world stability that the creation of exclusive economic zones might entail. "For more than four decades, the international political order has supported the development of a liberal world economy and encouraged both mutual security and mutual prosperity. Today, that order is changing in many ways. A regionalized world economy would threaten the security and well-being of America's allies as well as those of the United States." If a regionalized global economy made up of mutually exclusive trade blocks should replace the current unified, multilateral world economy, Gilpin concludes, it could quite easily lead to a "regionalized international political system, and this could undermine the foundations of world peace" because a "regionalized world is likely to be unstable both politically and economically."[17] Others, like Henry Kissinger, dare to support the usefulness of the construction of a colossal area of free trade—the Transatlantic Free Trade Area (TAFTA)—capable of integrating the EU and NAFTA (North American Free Trade Agreement). And lastly there are others who see the progressive separation between Europe and America's destiny as irretrievable. They make a close analogy with what happened to the Roman Empire with the Western and Eastern partition. This is Charles Kupchan's theory: the separation between the United States and Europe is now inevitable, precisely because of the unification process of the latter, which will have structural consequences on the international political system and which will be no less important than were those that were generated by the first German unification in 1870. Europeans and Americans will only have the choice whether to have a consensual separation or a bitter divorce, and America has to exploit the time remaining by exerting its supremacy over the world in order to "devise a grand strategy for the transition to a world of multiple power centers now, while it still has the luxury of doing so."[18]

Finally, if we look at the military threat, the protagonist is Islamic terrorism, borne of fundamentalism, as became quite clear to all after September 11: "The enemy is clearly Osama Bin Laden and his Islamist sympathizers and collaborators, as well as terror-supporting states,"[19] even if this does not mean in the slightest, that the entire Islamic world should be considered the "enemy." Indeed, it is in this very world that intellectual figures have emerged over the last decades who, without denying their own religious background, rather referring explicitly to Islamic values, have contributed to creating "new concepts and vocabulary" which are essential "for creating new perceptions of global interaction . . . reacting against the jihad view of the world. They have been especially important in defining the terms of intercivilizational dialogue from an Islamic perspective."[20]

The really innovative fact in the system is that he who threats security is neither the main political challenger nor the main economic rival. This not only has far greater consequences but is also far less reassuring than the pluridimensional structure designed by Joseph Nye. Above all, it highlights a certain weakness in the "soft power" concept that seems to have become the new magic word for the expression "politically correct." In Nye's opinion, besides all the "hard power," that is, "military power and economic power," there is "soft power" that consists of "getting others to want what you want" and which "rests on the ability to set the political agenda in a way that shapes the preferences of others": in other words, soft power "is the ability to entice and attract. And attraction often leads to acquiescence or imitation."[21] The concept in itself does not really seem so revolutionary if we remember the old "hegemony" already defined by Antonio Gramsci. Nye himself acknowledges this when, quoting the Sardinian scholar's example, he notices that "the ability to establish preferences tends to be associated with intangible power resources such as an attractive culture, ideology, and institutions."[22] In short, the soft-power concept seems vague, at least just as much as Nye's switching use of hegemony: he oscillates between two quite different interpretations without deciding on one or the other. Now hegemony "means being able to dictate, or at least dominate, the rules and arrangements by which international relations are conducted"; now the same word "is defined more modestly as a situation where one country has significantly more power, resources or capabilities than others," so that "it simply signifies American preponderance, not necessarily dominance or control."[23] At times there is still the doubt that with this term we elude ourselves. We believe that we can evade the problem of the growing uncertainty that implies there might be a slightly less traumatic clash between basically antagonistic models of values and principles, like those embraced by fundamentalist Islam (perhaps it would be enough to say "rigorous") and Western civilization. That is, there is the question as to which "cultural and political hegemony" is possible when two civilizations or cultures, bearers of their own soft power, confront each other. But the real problem of soft power is that it is useless in the fight against fundamentalist terrorism and its followers, inasmuch as for them "Western habits, Western morals, Western art, music, and television are seen not as freedom but as temptations."[24] In other words, the soft power is useless as regards those who programmatically do not want to become "like us." Niall Ferguson's approach is much more encouraging. While he sees the profile of an American empire, he looks into the hypothesis that the international political system has become "apolar," a world of "generalized impotence," in which "the great powers of today ceased to be magnetic, losing their powers both to attract and to repel, abandoning the 'Bismarckian model of the balance of power,' in which the international relations resemble the interplay of magnets, with the growing powers attracting satellites as if they were iron filings, sometimes joining together, but more often repelling each another".[25]

If we look at the nature of the players that the dominant power faces in three different areas—politics, economics, and security—we see that even this is different. China is in fact a state. In many aspects—considering the most classical and conservative view of the functions, role, and prestige of the state—today China shows more "stateness" than can be seen on average in Europe and even in America. The European Union is still a very uncertain entity and is certainly unique: it is more than a mere organization of states, but it is not yet a federation nor is it a confederation. It does not have a real foreign policy and as regards common security, it has not advocated the whole sovereignty of its member states. However, it "mints its own coins." As is well known, it is this second point that eventually makes Washington lose sleep. Certainly, however, the EU is of a territorial public nature. Al Qaeda, which has been adopted as the icon of new globalized fundamentalist terrorism,[26] is not a state, a public individual, neither has a currency or any of the attributes of sovereignty, nor is a legal entity like a multinational (e.g., Microsoft, just for the sake of mentioning one). It does, however, exist, and it represents a further increase in the re-privatization of wartime violence, when not a veritable "privatisation of politics."[27]

So, there are different challengers in the different arenas (politics, economics, and security) and challengers of a different nature (states, territorial public individuals, and "private" terrorist groups): this is the general picture of the current "age of uncertainty." Defining the present an "age of uncertainty" may be a rather too cushy ploy, to paint an evocative picture of a general state of mind fed by financial collapses and speculative bubbles, chronic wars and indescribable massacres, global terrorism and unprecedented threats.[28] The bipolar division of the world and the horrendous scar that was the Berlin Wall are behind us now, but they have been replaced by a system that seems increasingly fragmented and noncommunicative, even when not in the brutal conditions of terrorism or war. The areas of conflict and tension have increased, just as the number of those "black holes" on the world map ("failed States") has increased exorbitantly. Starting from these considerations, the crucial question that we must inexorably pose is this: has the international political system entered a phase of accentuated discontinuity as regards its operational rules, behavioral procedures of its main players, the nature of these players, and the type of threats?

The Two Peaces in the Cold War

In the months following November 1989, the stable bipolar system of the cold war ceased to exist, due to desertion on the part of one of the main protagonists. The ways in which it collapsed permit us to look at the years 1945 to 1989 in a completely different light. That whole period coincided with the bipolar order, characterized both by many years of peace at its core and by an extenuating conflict on the outskirts, fought with iron and fire, but won without a single shot being fired in its main arena, Europe, which was the only place that the decisive match could be played. The "long peace of the Cold War" in truth was a veritable deconstructive great war in the international political system. It was a general conflict of widespread dimensions, from which emerged what analysts, theoreticians, and players in the international political scene had widely claimed to be impossible: a *new unipolar order* dominated by the United States, and more that ten years after the start of this era no global challenger has as yet appeared.

The cold war thus turned out to be a "hegemonic war" or a "constituent war"[29]: it was at least the result of a "major war" that led to that American dominance which is even today void of credible global challengers. Now, however, America seems to be paying a high price for having reached this result without having to resort to arms against the Soviet Union, its systemic adversary. Just because of the fact that the cold war was a major war, a great war fought, however, for the most part without military intervention, it seemed sterile, incapable of giving life to a real constitutive peace. So, yet again, as always happens and must acrimoniously be admitted, only a victory gained bloodily on the battlefield is able to transform the power of the dominator to *legitimated authority*. No local or regional war, no matter how important and maybe even won on the battlefield (an objective which still has to be reached in the case of the last war in Iraq), can replace this lack of legitimacy.

Discussions over the imperial nature of post–cold war America have been ongoing for over a decade. It is in Michael Hardt's and Antonio Negri book *Empire* that the term "empire" moves beyond the confines of specialized literature. On publication, *Empire* becomes the *livre de chevet* for practically all of the left-wing who are disorientated in various ways having been left an orphan by the communist myths and anti-imperialist struggle, overwhelmed by the collapse of the USSR and China's conversion to a sort of "Asian chimera," where the most unrestrained and wild capitalism lives alongside the guiding rule of the Communist Party (and the Popular Army). It is of little importance that Hardt's and Negri de-territorialized empire with no core is different and of far more daring construction than the "American Empire" that has filled library bookshelves throughout the world over recent years. Hardt's and Negri book was in fact an extraordinarily innovative answer to the theoretical and interpretative crisis of the concept of state sovereignty, that globalization seemed to have definitively highlighted during the 1990s. However, despite Antonio Negri insisting on the radical difference between "his" empire (a network, with no center and de-territorialized) and the American empire theorized by some of the gurus in the Bush administration, a certain overlapping of the two concepts is transparent with rebellious spirit in some of the pages in Hardt's and Negri book: "Every juridical system is in some way a crystallization of a specific set of values, because ethics is part of the materiality of every juridical foundation, but Empire—and in particular the Roman tradition of imperial right—is peculiar in that it pushes the coincidence and universality of the ethical and the juridical to the extreme: in Empire there is peace, in Empire there is the guarantee of justice for all peoples . . . And in order to achieve these ends, the single power is given the necessary force to conduct, when necessary, 'just wars' at the borders against the barbarians and internally against the rebellious."[30] Even though the "theoretic stature" of the two texts is incomparable, a similar fortune for a certain part of the "free-falling" Left compared to modernity and post-modernity befell Naomi Klein's *No-Logo* a few years later. This became in its turn the "Bible" for those who seemed unable to resign themselves to having to endure the triumph of the global market economy, along with the defeat of communist ideology.

The stir caused by Negri and Hardt's thesis and the suggestion made by their words which penetrated unrestrictedly, so to speak (to an even greater number of people than those who read the book), ended up, however, obscuring a fact that was abundantly clear to everyone. It is that the neo-imperialist hegemony of the United States was by no means anything new in the post–cold war times. On the contrary, the neo-imperialist power was the keystone in the American strategy of postwar pacification of what we today call "The West" (the political not completely coinciding with the cultural West). Such a strategy, elaborated in the 1940s with the war still in progress, proposed a rather ambitious immediate objective: to prevent the European powers, which in slightly more than twenty years had dragged the world into two devastating conflicts, from repeating the very same mistake. If the objective was already in itself ambitious, the strategy to carry it out was even more so. It started from the idea that the peace balance proved itself to be not only too fragile but also extremely difficult to pursue: so difficult to pursue that it was a sort of accelerator in the race toward the breaking-up of any balancing, once the system had begun to settle on the slippery slope of instability. In short, if the attempt to pursue peace by means of the balance between the great powers had led to war, this represented a part of the problem and not a part of the solution.

To remedy this, America proposed "putting together" under its own protective umbrella the players who had failed so sensationally in their attempt to be reciprocally balanced. So it was necessary to move from a peace of balance to a hegemonic peace of which the United States would be the originators and guarantors. The consequence of a similar approach in economic terms implied the participation of ex-rivals in an open economic system, in which those economies were made interdependent on each other and also structurally linked to the American economy. In the event of prolonged periods of economic crisis, this would prevent the different national systems being able to opt for protectionist strategies, rightly considered concausa of military political conflicts.

The initial project did not yet include Japan and China (at that time not communist), and at the same time it was not conceived from an anti-Soviet viewpoint. The cutting of relations with Moscow due to the acquired awareness of the aggressive and tyrannic nature of the communist regime, joined to the inclusion of Japan, took over starting from 1945 and led to the second pillar of the American grand strategy in the cold war: curbing communism. Evidently, even America would gain in the "exchange" proposed to the Europeans. In economic terms, the enormous increase in production capacity that America had developed during the war would have stable market openings. The dollar, adopted even in an official capacity as the currency of reference in the new world economy, would seal the integration between the different economic systems. In political terms, moreover, the United States ensured both a stable network of alliances and an outpost in Europe: both of these are to have vital consequences for decades. It is in fact with regard to the Soviet Union and the threat constituted by Communism that the Americans "resign themselves" to a peace of balance with Moscow and its satellite states, virtually restricting hegemonic peace to Western confines. This situation, however, was conceived only after the painful recognition that no serious partnership agreement would be possible with the USSR that would be able to integrate the Soviet economy and that of Eastern Europe into the new international system. As is well argued by John Ikenberry in his book *After Victory*, the "settlement that followed the Second World War was both the most fragmented and most far-reaching of any postwar settlement in history," and even if the war "did not end with a single comprehensive peace settlement . . . the United States and its allies brought about history's most sweeping reorganization of international order,"[31] by means of the creation of a fabric of institutions that had never been so rich as regards either quantity or quality.

The Second World War was indeed concluded with two distinct agreements even if, as this book illustrates, they are certainly linked. The first, made between the Soviet Union and the United States, brought about bipolarism and the cold war. The second, that involved America, the countries in Western Europe and Japan, led to the formation of a series of complex security, political, and economic institutions which all together created a "security community" (as the definition coined by Karl Deutsch in 1950),[32] that is, an area where war as a tool to resolve controversy is in no way considered a hypothesis. The intra-Western *hegemonic peace* was one of the most institutionalized in history while the *peace of balance* between the East and West was one of the most militarized. The cold war did not create cooperation between the democratic states; rather it reinforced it because the latter were already cooperating before they began to realize the irremediably threatening nature of the Soviet Union.[33] The relationship between the two diverse positions, between hegemonic peace and peace of balance,[34] should not however lead us to confuse them, nor to mix the profoundly different logics that shaped them. The confusion between these two forms of peace that lived side by side (and with which the Western citizens have lived) for almost half a century, is one of the main sources of misunderstanding in the current phase of international politics and the Manichaean confrontation between the "law of force" and the "rule of law," was one of the principal causes for the dispute within both the European Union and the United Nations Security Council.

Apart from being quite different in origin, the peace of balance and hegemonic peace have profoundly different rationales. Peace of balance implies the idea that the arena to which it is applied is an "anarchical" environment in itself, that is, characterized by the absence of any ordained political authority. In such a context, security—survival itself—of states is entrusted to the relative force. The balance between the relative force of different players (or the coalitions of players) is the necessary condition and the primary source of order and peace. The only way to pose a limit on the excessive power of one single player (or a coalition of players) is to oppose them with a coalition of states, a temporary liaison to contrast the growing power that threatens the balance, stability, and peace. This concept, to be quite clear, is the one that led Great Britain to mobilize eight coalitions against Revolution and Napoleon's France, and that also put an end to this temporary alliance (even if it did last from 1791 to 1815) shortly after the end of the Congress of Vienna. Often recalled as being the precious tool that created European peace throughout the nineteenth century, in reality, the peace of balance worked in Europe within a wider context of enormous asymmetry of power and an increasingly imminent regional hegemony. In other words, on one hand France, Russia, and Germany alternately assumed the role of growing power, the other states joining forces against the rest. The equilibrium in the nineteenth-century system of European states was really possible only insofar as it was the demonstration of a *local balance of power*, in which one power that was an absolute power (void of credible challengers) on a global level—Great Britain—from its status of superiority acquired the resources to carry out the role of *re-balancer*[35] in Europe.

The concept of hegemonic peace, on the contrary, starts from the idea that international politics is a succession of orders imposed on the political system by the leading states. Rules and rights are determined and implemented only thanks to tools of power of the dominant state (or coalition states). Respect for order, stability, and peace is guaranteed by the resources of the dominant state that range from military strength to market access and from technological sophistication to financial means. So, hegemonic peace is as stable as the solidity of its power over the other states. It is important to underline, as does, Robert Gilpin—one of the most scrupulous scholars in this matter—that the tools of which the dominant state may make use also include prestige and ideology, thanks to which it is possible to perpetuate hegemonic order. It is obvious that the authority of the dominant state and the conservation of that hegemonic order lie in the surplus of power at the disposal of the leading state, but it is also just as obvious that the means by which this hegemony is carried out vary from case to case. The United States and the Soviet Union gave life to two rival powers during the cold war. But while Soviet power was based on direct, coercive supremacy of the leading state over minor states, American power was objectively less oppressive and violent, held together also by interstate relations in which reciprocity, institutionalization, and consensus played an important role. Without ignoring the importance of the asymmetric distribution of power, it reduced the probability of dire consequences. As John Lewis Gaddis observes: "The history of American grand strategy during the Cold War is remarkable for the infrequency with which the United States acted unilaterally, as well as for top-level resistance to the idea of preemption and its related nuclear era concept, preventive war."[36] It could not be better put.

In *hanging sovereignty*, that is, in sovereignty which remains an effective privilege only for the two superpowers, the paradox of the bipolar system lies hidden; if on one hand it emphasizes the nature of security as had happened never before, on the other it takes away the capacity to exert security from almost all the other states, which in that particularly crucial domain have to be subjected to the greatest limitations as regards their ostensible sovereignty. The degree to which it is limited varies consistently from block to block, but what the West has in common with the Communist world is the fact that the national governments are basically deprived of choice in terms of political security; these are, on the contrary, subjected to the final decision of the two superpowers (even if, it must be stressed, there are different levels of consensus). In historically unprecedented international systems, the hegemon players in the coalitions had the tendency to manage collective defense directly, depriving the minor allies of their own security policy.[37] But it was the rigid structure of the bipolar system of the cold war—the irremediable gap created by the nuclear arsenal of the two superpowers and the hierarchical strength of the system—that made the limitations of sovereignty of minor states a condition from which it was well nigh impossible to recover.

If, by virtue of the central role that ideology played in structuring the international political system, it managed to determine the "institutional form" of the central states of the system, for these peripheral ones things were quite different. They were linked to the bipolar scheme and its logic by means of the creation of "international patronage" of one or the other block, dominated by the main worry of security of the patron-state. The link to the client-state was of a two-fold nature: it was set up at state level (between the peripheral and the central state) and also at an elite level (here too between peripheral and central state). The client-state—thanks to the relationship that tied it to the patron-state—obtained protection, access to the international political system, mitigation of the consequences of its political and economic inferiority, and above all, protection against the internal enemies of the powerful elite. The patron-state, in its turn, obtained three advantages: an increase in its own security zone; continuing access to economic resources that would otherwise be inaccessible or accessible in a non-exclusive manner; reinforcement of an international system that guaranteed, strengthened, and perpetuated its position of pre-eminence. In this way the international client-states contributed to the expression of the international political system, stabilizing and conferring on it an order founded on hierarchy as regards access to the resources of power.[38]

AFTER DESERT STORM: AMERICA—POWER
WITHOUT RIVALS

The Second Gulf War[39] of 1990–1991 seemed to endorse that a "New World Order" founded on security, liberty, and justice might really be possible. Following Iraq's aggression on its neighboring emirate Kuwait, on August 2, 1990, President George Bush (the elder Bush) managed to form a coalition of over fifty states to free Kuwait and restore its sovereignty. The importance of the military success that crowned the allied coalition[40] and the speed with which it deployed its ground attack during operation *Desert Storm* (January 17–February 8, 1991) were incredible. But even more astonishing was the indisputable success that had smiled upon the United States, which had even been able to enlist in its coalition a reasonable number of Arab and Muslim states and to obtain the total backing of the Security Council for the operation—the result was that it was all carried out under American military command but also under the UN flags.

The Soviet Union had not yet been dissolved; Gorbachev was still firmly in his saddle. No one could have imagined that within such a short space of time the First Secretary of the Soviet Union Communist Party would be forced to disappear dolefully from the scene, after a failed coup d'état, which marked simultaneously the rise of Boris Yeltsin to the head of the new Russia, the end of Communism and the same self-dissolution of the Soviet Union. No one, not even Bush and his new staff of advisors could bring into account such an incredibly revolutionary series of events, so much so that Bush's speech on the "New World Order" given to the two Chambers of Congress assembled in a joint session in September 1990 contained an offer to the Soviet Union, asking it to participate in the new order characterized by the strengthening of the role of the United Nations in order to facilitate cooperation between states and greater respect for international regulations. The Second Gulf War was the most definitive sign that the cold war was over for good. But it was also the starting point for an era of hope, perhaps of illusions, and it supplied the irresistible temptation for the United States—it seemed there was no possible realistic alternative: to transform the success gained after the long cold war and the victory in the war against Iraq into a permanent situation. As for the capacity to formulate a grand strategy suited to its time and suitable to make the acquisitions of the two-year period (1989–1991) permanent, Bill Clinton's years were "lost years."[41] Not only among the political class but also within the scientific community, the conviction had spread "that the international system had become so benign that the United States no longer faced serious security threats of any kind. Paradoxically, the success of the American grand strategy during the Cold War encouraged this view."[42] The Clinton administration drew from this perception and from believing in the Fukuyama thinking "the idea that if the progress toward political self-determination and economic integration was assured, then the United States need only, as national security adviser Anthony Lake put it, 'engage' with the rest of the world in order to 'enlarge' those processes. The hegemony by consent the United States had won during the Cold War would simply become the post–Cold War international system."[43]

The United States was able to seize the opportunity to reform the world and make it better, that is, more in compliance with those values of liberty, democracy, and market that are considered at one and the same time universal and American values. "Boys! Tonight America asks us to charge Iraqi Kurdistan to make the world a better place!" This sentence delivered during the operation *Iraqi Freedom* by the commander-in-residence of the American parachute regiment in Vicenza expresses simply but incisively how the faith in the universal goodness of certain values is united with the profound conviction that it is in American political culture that it can best be accomplished. Who knows if that official realized that he was summarizing in one sentence the analysis made by Samuel Huntington ten years previously in 1993. At that time Huntington pointed out (and the events in the years to come were to make him one of the most heeded but also badly interpreted and contradicted analysts in the world) that not only was America the only superpower able to control the world, but that any failure on her part would simply have made the world a worse place. The United States, in any case, could vindicate this lonely leadership because it was the only superpower whose identity was based on universal political and economic values.[44] These were the 1990s, in which it seemed that nothing could seriously thwart the beginning of a new even greater American century, to the extent that "for most American policy makers during those lost years, the United States was the only real actor in the international system. If we did the right things, good consequences would follow and our intentions would prevail. The international system was not just unipolar, it was monothelete—there was only one effective will operating in the world, the will of the United States."[45]

It has often been noted that the values of democracy and liberty are considered as a sort of contradiction. On one hand they manage to go beyond the mere affirmation of principle only when a concrete juridical system, a state with its constitutional order, recognizes and protects them. It is only within the limited walls of the *polis*, of the political community, that those rights become concrete attributes of citizenship. At the same time, however, their strength and capacity to leave their mark on the whole system depends on the fact that, as principles, they are universal, valid everywhere, and applicable to anyone. It is the innate character that is attributed to these rights that necessitates their universality. It is their concrete preservation that necessitates that they are limited within specific systems. And it is precisely this that causes problems for us. Such opposition or dialectics, if it is preferred, has always existed, but the new fact is that with the end of the balance of terror, with the end of the blocks and the collapse of what seemed to be the last sworn enemy of freedom, the reduction of contradictions seems possible and somehow even inescapable. It is possible because it cannot be seen who, and in the name of what, could oppose a similar prospect. It is inescapable because in the absence of an enemy able to atomize us by pressing a button, it would appear to be an incomprehensible choice to refuse to fight (not necessarily militarily) for the triumph of universal values that only particular historical conditions had obliged to be satisfied with a particular legitimacy (in the West). It is a shame that coherent direction of the progress of humankind toward liberal-democracy and modernity incorporates values that, according to some and far from being in a minority (within the fundamentalist wing of the Muslim world, just to be quite clear), are considered to be without question negative values, as Roger Scruton underlines without beating about the bush, as regards the problematic relationship between Islam and democracy: "In short, the emergence of secular politics from the prophetic community is a sign not of civilized progress but of moral decline."[46]

The American political triumph of the Second Gulf War perhaps marks the apex of the "unipolar moment," as is defined by a brilliant neo-conservative author in an article that appeared in the prestigious journal "Foreign Affairs" in 1991, when totally unexpectedly and in contrast with all the most reliable theories, the collapse of Soviet–American bipolarism did not lead to a multipolar readjustment of the system but simply to a reorganization around the only surviving superpower. Charles Krauthammer concluded his remarks: "Our best hope . . . is in American strength and will—the strength and will to lead a unipolar world, unashamedly laying down the rules of world order and being prepared to enforce them."[47] This unipolar moment was made possible to a great extent not only by the fact that America is a *net exporter* of the cultural, political, and economic values with which we view the world, but also by the much more prosaic fact that it possesses an unequalled military force. The then president of the European Commission Romano Prodi commented in an interview given at the end of the European Summit in Athens in April 2003: "I remember at the time of Kosovo when the Americans chastised us Europeans for spending the equivalent of 60% of the US budget on defense while having less than a tenth of their operative capacity."[48] That interview was indicative of the state of mind that permeated the air at the Summit; it was not rhetoric to define it "historic," because it sanctioned the expansion of the Union itself, the addition of ten new member-states. However, it did take place right after what appeared to be the Anglo-American victory in Iraq, after a conflict that had bitterly divided European governments and which had above all added a greater dose of bitterness to the expression "economic giant, political dwarf and military worm"—more and more often the European Union's main limitations were pointed out. But that interview also alluded to the need to balance the United States's excessive power, a hypothesis that was not only unrealistic—since "the allied impulse in response to US unilateralism or bullying should be binding rather than balancing"[49]—but also indicative at showing how times had changed compared to the cold war and how Henry Kissinger was correct in remembering: "During the Cold War, European integration was urged as a method of strengthening the Atlantic partnership; today many of its advocates view it as a means of creating a counterweight to the United States."[50]

The United States has spared no expense for defense, and extremely efficient expense at that, even though not totally free of waste and corruption, considering that the Pentagon has opened an internal investigation after realizing it had paid 1,000 dollars for each coffee machine installed on board the flying super-fortresses. It has a strength which is incomparable to its peers, and is far more advanced than at any time in history, if it is true that the British Empire in its day was content to own a fleet that was equal to those of the two pursuing powers put together, while today the tonnage of the whole world's fleets would not be able to compete with the total fleets of the United States of America. Not to speak of the qualitative aspect. Just to give one figure, at the moment the United States deploys thirteen large aircraft carriers (each one about 300 metres long), apart from the helicopter carriers and the Marines support ships, all unfailingly equipped with take-off pads. This is what gives substance to the "unipolar moment" of the international political system, that

American power seems "unrivaled." As William Wohlforth shows with great attention to detail, in 1995 the United States spent 298 billion dollars compared to Russia's 43, France's 42, Great Britain's 39, Japan's 37, Germany's 35, and China's 14. Five years later, in 2000, so before the Twin Towers and the Afghan and Iraqi campaigns (with an unchanging dollar) the United States spent 281 billion dollars, compared to Russia's 44, France's 40, Japan's 36, Great Britain's 36, Germany's 33, and China's 23. If we total these figures, it means that the six countries that spend most on defense in the world only accumulated 208 billion dollars in 1995 as opposed to the United States' 298, and in 2000 only 213 billion dollars compared to the United States' 281 billion. Of course, America has military commitments all over the planet, while none of the other countries on the list is a global power, and at most can aspire to the role of "regional challenger of the United States."[51] But it is also true that the cost of duplication makes the relationship between the United States and its followers more favorable for the former than the latter.[52]

These are the figures that make it possible to talk of an American Empire, and of a unipolar system, since in this type of system there is a concentration of power in the hands of the strongest state, which is so overwhelming as to make any counterbalancing prohibitively expensive. Once a system has reached this threshold, we move to a condition in which stability is no longer guaranteed by balance, but if anything, by a further concentration of power. We move from the possibility of a *peace of balance* to *hegemonic peace*. Other data reinforces the perception of an America which is ever more capable of pursuing ambitious objectives—this would have been unimaginable only a few years earlier.

In the last three centuries, no great power has had the same capacity in economic and military terms as the United States at the end of the last millennium. Devoting only 3–4 percent of its GDP to military expenditure, the United States generates 55 percent of the whole military expenditure of the planet. This is a much lower percentage than in previous years, when its budget reached 5 percent in the days of George Bush senior; it exceeded 6 percent with Ronald Reagan and stayed around 8 percent in the harshest years of the cold war and during the Vietnam War.[53] Not only this. If we look at qualitative detail, the imbalance in the United States' favor is even more noteworthy, with 80 percent of the whole expenditure in R and D in the defense sector of the seven strongest nations. And there is more: America also counts for 43 percent of world economic production, 40 percent of high-tech production and 50 percent of the whole expenditure in R and D. America is the first power in history that has managed to be at the same time a great naval and commercial power (as was imperial Great Britain) and a great land power (as was Napoleon's France or Germany).[54] As is obvious, recognition and appreciation of this enormous gap tends to favor jumping on the winner's bandwagon on the part of the minor powers, and in so doing they implicitly accept its role as hegemon. The satisfaction that America must have felt and France's humiliation when in the mid-1990s, Paris requested to enter again the integrated military structure of the Atlantic Alliance, which it had left slamming the door at the time of General de Gaulle, causing, among other things, the move of the General Headquarters at Fontainbleu (near Paris) to Brussels and Mons. All the more reason to understand America's disappointment in the events that have taken place over the last two years, to find Paris again in the guise of leader of a "coalition of the unwilling" that cannot be defined a counter hegemonic alliance; but certainly it is the most worrying form of internal "faction" that has ever been experienced in the West in almost half a century of United States hegemony.

NYC, 9/11: Asymmetric War and Preventive War

The American dream of a new world order collapsed along with the Twin Towers, one sunny morning in mid-September. When America woke up, shocked and alarmed, it found itself in a nightmare, having passed from the end of history to the end of the world. A handful of terrorists, coming what's more from "allied" countries like Egypt and Saudi Arabia, bombarded New York and Washington, causing a veritable massacre of innocent lives in the most devastating attack to take place on American soil since the war with Great Britain in 1812. This time, too, as had happened at Pearl Harbor in 1941, America woke up to find itself at war, desperate to return the blow inflicted on them by these new enemies, and yet dramatically aware that while it is capable of defeating any country that gets in its way, it is also vulnerable to the hit and run attacks of terrorism. Niall Ferguson comments: "One consequence of 9/11 was to shatter forever the illusion that Americans could retreat to enjoy the fruits of their productivity behind a missile defence shield, leaving the benighted countries of the world to take their own perdition."[55] Where are our enemies? Where are they hiding? What kind of war do we need to prepare for to prevent the "indispensable nation" becoming the "indefensible nation"? But there is yet another question that the Bush administration posed the morning of the "day after," when they began to take stock of the material damage sustained and the tragic death toll and when, above all, the world asked holding its breath for various reasons, what America would do to restore the credibility of the planet's only superpower?

The question that we imagine was asked by Donald Rumsfeld, Colin Powell, Condoleeza Rice, Dick Cheney, Paul Wolfowitz, and George W. Bush, is simple and direct: Why, on a quiet, peaceful september day, was the enormous military force that the United States has at its disposal rendered useless in the defense of not an obscure naval installation at the end of the world during a peripheral conflicts but New York City? The answer to this question must be just as simple and direct: it didn't work because strength, all the strength in the world is worthless without a suitable doctrine for its use. Strength is like a gold mine in the vast field of international politics. It is of course an extremely important resource, but for it to be transformed into an effective tool, it needs to be supplied with a doctrine suited to its time and the changing threats. It is absurd to think that, at a time when the lethal threat to the "lonely superpower"[56] can be made by a handful of terrorists, who, at the most, need the support of some obliging state, the old doctrines of the massive nuclear retaliation or gradual escalation reprisals can still be useful.

In the speech given by President George W. Bush at the Military Academy in West Point, the "Bush doctrine" is clearly set out: "The gravest danger to freedom lies at the perilous crossroads of radicalism and technology . . . For much of the last century, America's defense relied on the Cold War doctrines of deterrence and containment. In some cases, those strategies still apply. But new threats also require new thinking. Deterrence, the promise of massive retaliation against nations, means nothing against shadowy terrorist networks with no nation or citizens to defend. Containment is not possible when unbalanced dictators with weapons of mass destruction can deliver those weapons or missiles or secretly provide them to terrorist allies . . . and our security will require all Americans to be forward-looking and resolute, to be ready for pre-emptive action when necessary to defend our liberty and to defend our lives."[57]

George W. Bush's speech recalls surprisingly another stirring speech given by Abraham Lincoln during the Civil War when he concluded his second Annual Message to Congress, on December 1, 1862 like this: "The dogmas of the quiet past are inadequate to the stormy present. The occasion is piled high with difficulty, and we must rise—with the occasion. As our case is new, so we must think anew, and act anew.

We must disentrall ourselves, and then we shall save our country."[58] The theory necessary for the strategy decided upon by George W. Bush had already been formulated several years prior to this, under the name "pre-emptive war doctrine"; Paul Wolfowitz, Undersecretary of State for Defense during the administration of George W. Bush was responsible for this. All that remains to be done is to decree that the moment has come that makes that theoretical formulation appropriate. The idea that the threat is prevented before being crushed is certainly no novelty in American foreign policy: the use of force, also employed preventatively can be found easily throughout the history of the Union.[59] But it has never constituted a central element in the doctrine of American foreign policy since the United States ceased to be a world of its own, isolated from other nations. This is particularly true since the United States became one of the major powers in the international political system. As a consequence of the attacks on September 11, 2001, "a nation that began with the belief that it could not be safe as long as pirates, marauders, and the agents of predator empires remained active along its borders, has now taken the position that it cannot be safe as long as terrorists and tyrants remain active anywhere in the world."[60]

John Lewis Gaddis establishes a direct relationship between the surprise attacks and the changes in the concept of doctrine for national security. So, the first great surprise attack suffered by the United States in 1814 (the fire in Washington by agency of the British) reinforced the idea that the Republican experiment could survive only if guaranteed by a concrete "empire of liberty." This was the origin of the strategy of John Quincy Adams, "of seeking control over the North American continent by unilateral means where possible, through pre-emptive action where necessary."[61] Until the 1930s this was the type of security policy favored and pursued by the United States by means of continental hegemony, ideological example and exploitation of trade opportunities. In 1941, the attack on Pearl Harbor pushed the United States to search for a new doctrine, still under the impression that empire and freedom could coexist. "The military and economic strength of the United States would be employed now, not just to dominate North America or even the Western hemisphere, but to restore an international balance of power in which democracies would be secure."[62] Since the end of the Second World War, the United States found itself at the head of an informal empire of global size. The shock of September 11 pushed the Bush administration, originally one of the most isolationist since the Second World War, to convince itself that "surviving authoritarian regimes, even if feeble or failing, can breed terrorists capable of attacking the United States with devastating results on its own soil. The Bush administration, therefore, has called for yet another expansion of the empire of liberty: it can no longer respect the sovereignty of *any* State that harbors terrorists; it must pre-empt such threats wherever they appear; it will extend democracy everywhere."[63]

One may agree or disagree with Gaddis' theory, or with some of his claims, like those in which he considers Roosevelt's American politics oriented toward the pursuit of the balance of power, when it could be said he was pushed to assert a benign hegemony on an international system molded as much as possible on American principles. What is certain is that the September 11 attack is the concrete, striking expression of how quickly the scenario regarding security had changed since the end of the cold war. We were well and truly out of the old bipolar system in which the geopolitical environment was by and large predictable, in which communism was the main danger to American security, and to which the United States replied by means of the tool of permanent alliances (NATO, first and foremost), in which it was "naturally" the leading power of the West, and the UN was an organization which was invariably paralyzed (on the really central issues for collective security) by interlocking Soviet-American vetoes. The new contest regarding security is on the other hand complex and highly uncertain. It is a world in which nationalism and religious fanaticism substitute Communism as the source of danger. The United States has to build temporary ad hoc alliances, to contrast the threat wherever it rises and manage to transform, each time, its own status of sole military superpower into a real global leadership. All this, however, takes place having to compete (at least in cramped style) with a more dynamic UN compared to the cold-war days, when the use or avoidance of the right of veto by the Security Council ended up being more and more burdensome from a political point of view.

Still on the issue of tuning the defense tools to suit the new threats, the Bush administration is convinced that the international laws that regulate resorting to war must also be reviewed, so that they are enforceable.[64] The risk is that we loiter in a sterile, stubborn system of defense regulations that are no longer suitable for the new type of threat that democracies have to face, and this only results in the spreading of negative prejudice on the usefulness of international law. A perfect example is the "Guantanamo prisoners," captured in Afghanistan during *Enduring Freedom.* The law permits only two possibilities: to treat them as criminals (so put them on trial) or consider them prisoners of war (and send them home when the war is over).

It is easy to claim that neither of the two categories is applicable to militants from a terrorist organization captured after bloody shoot-outs thousands of miles from the American borders. If they were to be considered criminals, they should be guaranteed the right to the usual legal procedures in the American system—at least until the introduction of the controversial "Patriot Act"—and for each of them precise charges should be issued and personal responsibility for each criminal act singled out. Their arrest could even be judged "illegal" and expensive pools of lawyers, handsomely rewarded by Al Qaeda itself, could raise infinite procedural exceptions or object to the legitimacy of American tribunals performing the trials. If, on the other hand, the prisoners were considered "prisoners of war," the international conventions on the matter (endorsed by the United States) should be applied to them. Above all, however, in a relatively short time after the end of hostilities, they should be released and sent to their homelands. What guarantee would the United States have that these "soldiers from an army with no State," once freed, would not recommence their fight against it? None. The problem is that in reality it is a matter of individual combatants and groups of criminals belonging to the army of an organization (Al Qaeda) which has never stipulated either a surrender or peace with the government of the United States and has no intention of doing so in the future.

It is no coincidence that the concept "threat" or even the more generic notion "risk," come back to the center of theoretical contemplation on the new security scenario. Robert Keohane and Celeste Wallander claimed that the viability of NATO depends precisely on its capacity to change from an organization totally dedicated to facing the Soviet threat to a flexible structure, charged with the task of managing the risk in Europe.[65] As far as Stephen Walt is concerned, he has substituted the concept "strength/power" with "threat" in order to explain the anomaly—from the point of view of the strictest realist orthodoxy—created by the fact that for over a decade there was absolutely no attempt by other powers, Western or not, to counterbalance the progressive emergence of American hegemony. It is not power in itself that the states would try to counterbalance, but only that power that is perceived as "threatening" in terms of "offensive capabilities and aggressive intention," so that rather than a theory of *balance of power* it makes more sense to talk of a *balance of threat*.[66] During these years, to tell the truth, different "anti-USA diplomatic relations" have been announced and even ostensibly displayed. We have had the "European troika" made up of France, Germany, and Russia even during the war in Iraq, the "special relationship" between

Germany and Russia, the "strategic triangle" between Russia, China, and India or the "strategic partnership" between Russia and China. But all "these arrangements reveal their rhetorical as opposed to substantive character," since real *balancing* "involves real economic and political costs, which neither Russia, nor China, nor indeed any other major power has shown any willingness to bear."[67] On the basis of this, it is nonetheless obvious that for the United States the question of its own capacity to be accepted as a benevolent power, or rather to defend the legitimacy of its own supremacy is decisive.[68] What John Ikenberry mentioned just before the disaster on September 11 still holds true, that is, that despite the divisions of the last two or three years the "dominance of the United States . . . has not triggered the type of counter hegemonic balancing or competitive conflict that might have been expected." There is in fact much less. Despite "complaints about the American abuse of its hegemonic position, there are no serious political movements in Europe or Japan to call for a radical break with the existing Western order organized around American power and institutions. Indeed there is evidence of an ongoing demand for American leadership."[69] It is a leadership that one would wish to be or more simply that one presumes to be "benevolent," but which is challenged today even by the democratic allies of NATO. This benevolence was not, nor is, the fruit of any communicative ability, but derives from the presence of an elite that share determined values, liberal in the broadest sense, both in Washington and in the allied capitals; it also comes from the circumstance that these societies make themselves rich in the shadow of American hegemony. But not all the governments and political groups that are "compelled" to live within American hegemony share the liberal values nor do they benefit from the political and economic advantages that Europe, for example, has enjoyed and continues to enjoy. So, if it is true that different from what happened to the hegemonic powers of the past, the United States "is not using its power to conquer new territory it is surely enriching itself, other states are growing rich along with it while maintaining their sovereignty . . . As the world was forcefully reminded on September 11, 2001, many actors want no part of these increasing returns [to acquiescing to U.S. power] and perceive anything but benignity and restraint when they observe America. These actors tend to be the same actors who reject political liberalism".[70] As is obvious, however, the success of the liberal elite in the countries that lie within American hegemony and the fact that similar elite can continue to share with Washington the "benevolent" perception of the power of the United States depends also on the possibility to sense old opponents (communism) and new ones (the fundamentalist terrorist) as common rivals.

> What is clear is that after September 11, as before, American military primacy owes a great deal to the congruence between the purpose to which the United States puts its power and the purposes of elites in so many states that could, if they chose, help to challenge that primacy. So long as the United States uses its power in ways consistent with the goals of those elites, those states should eschew counterbalancing, and U.S. primacy should endure. America is indeed a benign superpower. But benignity is in the eye of the beholder; and to the benefit of the United States, the balance of world power is in the hands of actors who behold a benign America precisely because America's ideological enemies are theirs as well.[71]

This explains quite simply just why it is crucial for the United States to defend the legitimacy of its own superiority in a far stronger fashion than any other great power or empire had been required to do in the past inasmuch as "Balancing behaviour will be less likely if foreign elites hold positive images of the United States, share similar outlooks on most global problems, and in general regard U.S. preponderance as benevolent, beneficial, and legitimate."[72] This also supplies the reasons for the gravity of the dissension between Western countries, extremely dangerous precisely for the preservation of the "legitimacy" of American hegemony.

The transition after the cold war marks a change between two different threatening scenarios. In the world of the cold war, there was basically one threat, or at least traceable to one main source, the Soviet Union. It was a clear threat, open, aimed at the very survival of the United States, sensitive to deterrence and revolving around Europe. The risk of nuclear escalation was high and foresaw the use of strategic nuclear weapons. After the cold war and as 1989–1991 was gradually left behind, the threat changed: it was no longer attributable to one particular challenger. The threat, or rather, threats that are prevalently aimed at the United States are hidden, unclear and as a result not immediately identifiable, deducible or sympathised with by its partners. To complicate the picture it must be added that we are dealing with threats which are not very, if at all, sensitive to deterrence, prevalently to be found outside Europe, with a low risk of escalation, although the use of nuclear or chemical-bacteriological weapons by terrorist groups can indeed be foreseen. It must be acknowledged that it had already been sensed that the scenario had changed during the Clinton years, if only in the general optimism of the Clinton era. Antony Lake, National Security Advisor to Bill Clinton for a long time, had pinpointed a new set of dangers, expressed clearly in a public speech given at the George Washington University on March 6, 1996: (1) the enemies of peace in the Middle East; (2) old and new threats such as ethnic or religious violence; (3) aggression by rogue states; (4) the spread of weapons of mass destruction; (5) terrorism; (6) organized crime; (7) drugs trafficking; (8) environmental destruction.[73] The United States' main task was to prevent these risk factors, totally manageable if dealt with one by one, but jointly capable of provoking terrible chaos. The basic axis in the "Lake doctrine" was the transition from containment to enlargement, so that the particular role of the United States in the world consisted of defending, enlarging, and reinforcing the community of democratic nations, and in this task the ideals and interests of the United States coincide.[74] But there is a certain superficiality and lack of determination in the search for a suitable strategy when confronted with this premature situation.

Given that the geopolitical scene and the type of threat that the United States faces have changed so radically, it follows that there is a real need for a new, different doctrine regarding the use of force. During bipolarism various theories were developed that were founded on the assumption that an open, head-on war between the two super-powers was in fact impossible, because it would have meant the extinction of mankind and of almost every other form of superior life on the planet. The strategy of *Mutual Assured Destruction* (MAD) was pure dissuasive doctrine, regarding the *non use of force*, because it showed that whoever launched a precise, destructive attack against his opponent would not survive long enough to "enjoy the spoils of war": it was the so-called balance of terror, the demise of which in November 1989 was one of the reasons for the most incredible enthu-siasm that hailed the end of the cold war, on the part of generations of citizens who had grown up in the shadow of the wall and the night-mare of nuclear death. The real doctrine in the use of force, the only force possible in that context of "blocks," predicted a war of attrition in that central European theater and a proxy war, carried out wherever possible, that is, where there was conflict on the uncertain frontiers of the relative gray areas belonging to the Soviet and American "client-states." Above all, in the war of attrition the use of high technology was predicted. Not only that: for the deterrence to be effective, the military tool had to be visible and "exposed to the risk of an attack by the enemy power," so that it was clear that any direct attack would trigger a destructive reaction. Also, to reassure its own allies as to

Washington's political will to honor the contractual agreements within the permanent alliances, it was vital that massive American ground forces, heavily armored, were deployed in bases outside the United States' territory, in a scenario of advanced deployment which was able to count on the logistic support of its host nation.

In the new context, it is obvious that everything has changed regarding security. The doctrine of the use of force, described at the beginning of the 1990s by the American Secretary for Defense Les Aspin, is based first and foremost on the American capacity to lead decisive attacks at key targets. It is because of this that the "smart weapons" sector has become so highly developed. It is of course tied to the aims of foreign policy, of communication and to help limit the collateral damage in possible conflicts or even in simple military operations, but above all it aims at making attacks on strategic and tactical objectives effective. Data available on the use of "precision guided munitions" (PGM) by American forces in the campaigns during the 1990s are astounding. During *Desert Storm*, when they appeared for the first time in the media, PGMs counted for about 7 percent of all the ammunition employed. During the massive air raid on Kosovo (*Allied Force*, March–June 1999) 35 percent of all the ammunition employed by the allied forces was comprised of PGMs. In the two short air raids against Iraq (*Desert Strike*, September 1996 and *Desert Fox*, December 1998) the percentages jumped to 100 and 72 percent.[75] Other sources limit their assessments to single bombs dropped by American bombers and fighter planes and they compare *Desert Storm*, *Allied Force*, and *Enduring Freedom* (the war in Afghanistan). According to this data the percentage of the employment of "smart bombs" by American forces is steady and high, with figures respectively of 89, 80, and 99 percent.[76] Rather than reinforcing the number of clients (more or less reliable) able to conduct wars by proxy against the United States' enemies, it becomes a priority to concentrate all efforts on direct reinforcement. The new doctrine in the use of military force provides for integrated use of high, medium, and low technology, and great effort to make the United States' power seem even more substantial, effective and complete. It must be placed back within national boundaries and it must be able to count on its own strength for logistic support and for long-drawn-out struggles. The strategic importance of traditional allies has consequently diminished and accordingly their ability to put pressure on Washington.

There again, precisely what happened in Afghanistan, and more particularly with Bin Laden's terrorist group, warned the United States to mistrust these makeshift comrades-in-arms who, in the long term, have often proved to be an extremely poor investment. A sort of "legend" had grown up around the black prince of fundamentalist terrorism, about the CIA's role in supporting its militia during the Soviet occupation of Afghanistan. The explanation is attributable to one of the tritest and stupidest platitudes—American stupidity—thanks to which the left just as much as the truly right-wing conservatives in Europe love to avoid coming to terms with their own marginal role in the great international political choices.[77] As one can never tire of saying, no "stupid idiot," no matter how powerful or rich he is, can manage to govern the world for over half a century. In retrospect, what seems to us to be the mistake, that is, the financing of Islamic militia in Afghanistan, was totally logical and rational during the cold war, within those proxy wars that the great powers fought against each other. It should be superfluous to remember that the Afghan disaster was one of the concauses that led the Soviet Union to implode. Without American support for the Afghan *mujihaedin* the USSR would probably have collapsed much later (maybe it would still be there). To think that there are absolutely rational choices, quite apart from the context within which they are made, is simple illusion; or rather it belongs to a finalistic vision of history somewhere between Hegel and Divine Providence. There is little indication that there were no more idiots in the CIA or in the Pentagon than are statistically present in every complex organization (from companies to ministries, from the media to political parties, to universities): and it is a fact that the United States started to buy up again, at elevated cost, the deadly *Stingers* (land-air missiles slewn over the shoulder) from the various leaders of Afghan guerrilla forces, as soon as it became obvious that Gorbachev was about to send the Red Army home.

The adoption of the doctrine of preventive war is an answer to the new type of "asymmetric warfare" launched by Bin Laden and his terrorist organization.[78] Two colonels from the Chinese Popular Army, Quiao Liang and Wang Xiangsui, described back in 1999 with chilling clairvoyance the existence of "non-state organisations, the mention of whose names make the West tremble. These organisations, all with a military imprint, are generally led by a cause or an extremist belief; let us think, for example, of the Islamic organisations that pursue a holy war, the white militia in the United States, the Japanese Aum Shinrikyo and, more recently, terrorist groups like Bin Laden's, which blew up the American embassies in Kenya and Tanzania. Undoubtedly, the various monstrous, crazy acts carried out by these groups are the factors which most probably spark off contemporary wars."[79]

Moreover, right from the beginning of the 1990s, we witnessed a proliferation of military attacks by private organizations or military acts in which the classical territorial players (nations) were flanked by subjects somehow retraceable to the military tradition (suffice to remember the long Balkan war). The two Chinese colonels continued: "Just when modern technology is modifying weapons and the battle-field, at the same time the concept of participants in war fuddled. From now on, soldiers will not have the monopoly of war. Global terrorist activity is one of the derivatives of the tendency for globalisation pro-moted by technological integration. Nonprofessional fighters and nonstate organisations are posing an ever-increasing threat to sover-eign states, making these fighters and organisations increasingly difficult for any professional army to combat. Professional armies are in fact gigantic dinosaurs compared to such adversaries and in this new era they lack the strength proportionate to their size. On the contrary, their opponents are rodents with a most extraordinary capacity for survival, able to use their sharp teeth to bedevil the best part of the world."[80]

The government in Washington did not procrastinate in reacting to the declaration of war issued to America by Al Qaeda, pinpointing the Taliban in Afghanistan as the military target to hit. Much has been written on the imbalance of the military force of the two warring parties; as for the undeniable military success of the campaign, we need only remember here that the irreversible internal crisis of the Soviet Union was triggered in the Afghan mountains, and that Afghanistan itself is several thousand miles from the United States. More importantly on the wave of the incredible tide of emotion and indignation evoked by the attacks on September 11, George W. Bush managed to mobilize well-nigh global support for the war against Afghanistan, the govern-ment of which, quite apart from anything else, admitted to supplying hospitality to Osama and his organization, was unpopular to a large extent with Muslim governments (with the important exception of Pakistan and Saudi Arabia, historical allies of America in the Islamic world), including the Iranian theocratic regime.

Immediately after September 11, NATO, for the first time in its history, invoked Article 5 of the North Atlantic treaty, which stipu-lates: "The Parties agree that an armed attack against one or more of them in Europe or North America shall be considered an attack against them all"; it authorizes the exercising of the right to self-defense guaranteed by the Charter of the United Nations. This is the strongest sign that each of the United States' partners had well under-stood the historical significance of the attacks on September 11. But it is also the clear counter-evidence that none of the Western allies had any intention of not giving full solidarity to the injured superpower. Perhaps slightly less predictable were the expressions of consolation that arrived from Putin's Russia, the first to call Washington to express his condolences to his ex-enemy. Maybe there was also a touch of hope that the West's attitude toward war in Chechnya might change. Even more importantly, very shortly afterward, Vladimir Putin offered Russian assistance in the United States' campaign against Afghanistan: not only did they pass information to the American secret services, above all they permitted America to use the ex-Soviet military bases in Uzbekistan and other republics in central Asia that belonged to the USSR. They proved to be of decisive importance for the swift success against the fundamentalist terrorists (a veritable Foreign Legion of terror) who had an ally in the Taliban militia. Attempting to link the Chechen war to the war on terror, Putin seemed to believe that the security of his country not only "was not put at risk by the long-term presence of the U.S. military bases along its periphery," but indeed that "those bases contribute to the effort to break up an international terrorist network that threatened Russia," or rather "served Russian security interests."[81] China itself, the most conservative custodian of the orthodoxy of the principle of sovereignty, decided to be benignly neutral toward a war that was taking place close to its Western borders.

FAILED AND ROGUE STATES

By no means paradoxically, on the strength of the all-encompassing confrontation between East and West, the post–Second World War period had permitted the perpetuation of the pretence that the sovereignty of all states was formally equal, even while denying it with a previously unknown peremptoriness. Never as in that period, when most of the international and supranational institutions which still exist today were born, had the contrast between the logic of power and the logic of right been more obvious. In the course of time the truly solid sovereign states were reduced to a handful: those extremely powerful ones able to govern the world (the United States and USSR), or those powerful enough to *shut off* the world (as did Communist China until the rapprochement with Nixon and Kissinger's America), and those so poor and wretched as to be cut off despite themselves from the rest of the world and its rulers. These were also the years in which, alongside the process of de-colonization, the number of states which were formally sovereign grew excessively, reducing the specific importance of Western democracies (in the assemblies where there was one vote per head) and consequently the principle of formal equality of states. De-colonization was in some ways a devastating process, which theoretically would be able to break the monopoly of European tradition in culture, rules, and above all in the standard practice of the international political system. However, it ended up being drained of its revolutionary capacity. Although the potentially "de-structuring" North-South divide wound up fossilized within the East-West bipolarism, a myriad of "paper states" only formally sovereign, were born from the debris of the colonial disaster. This caused an increase in confusion and in the distance between the world as it is and its formal juridical representations.

The greatest changes came after 1989; the most decisive break with the framework that had begun to take shape at Westphalia and that had been gradually perfected in the course of over three centuries. While globalization seemed to be the decisive opening for the creation of a network that was finally able to include the whole world—mainly by economic and technological means—an increasing segmentation of the international political system into a series of secondary systems and, even more significantly, systems in which the "stateness" is often only a façade. The same operational rules and the main concepts, on which those rules rest, seem to diversify depending on the subsystem to which they belong. For the first time since 1648, when the international political system began its slow expansion from its primitive European nucleus, it seems to undergo a contraction.[82] It is a haphazard withdrawal that leaves behind sensational "black holes," those "collapsed" or "failed states" which supply (not randomly) the necessary "reserves" in which transnational fundamentalist terrorism (Islamic) can organize itself undisturbed in the shade (we will painfully discover this with the first African attacks by Al Qaeda).[83] If it is true that in the cold war "irrelevant" places in geopolitical terms did not exist, in the new post–cold war unipolar system everything has changed. First of all, nonintervention on the part of one of the two superpowers in a crisis area was unimaginable, because it would have given a "gratuitous" advantage to the enemy; now any participation is calculated on the basis of strategic relevance per se of the area in question. Not by chance were collapsed states not left to fend for themselves during the long Soviet-American conflict. Even decidedly discredited figures like Bokassa (the self-proclaimed emperor of Central Africa) or Idi Amin Dada (the Ugandan tyrant) both suspected of cannibalism toward their opponents, found in Washington and Moscow, or at least in Paris, an interested protector.

Perhaps Somalia best exemplifies how the change of scene from the cold war to the following era radically changed for the new unstable states in Africa and Asia; they were given a chance not to be left to their own fate. In the cold war years, under the dictatorship of Siad Barre, Somalia changed sides three times, each time gaining economic and political advantages in terms of aid and regime stability (which rarely had any effect outside the limited entourage of the president and his clan). A few years after they had achieved independence, the country abandoned the West, and rented out the harbor installations in Berbera to the Soviet Union. After about a decade, following the poor military assistance received from Moscow during the Ogaden war (instigated by Siad Barre against Menghistu's Ethiopia, another Soviet client-state), he threw himself back into American arms, who embraced him warmly. Very significantly after *Desert Storm*, the world realized that in the meantime Siad Barre had been ousted from his precarious throne and that Somalia had been left to fend for itself against gangs and clans, who had destroyed any trace of sovereignty, causing an appalling humanitarian emergency.

On the wave of the success of that conflict and under strong pressure by the Western media (particularly CNN, which was one of the greatest players in that crisis, managing to agree upon the landing time of the Marines on the beaches near Mogadiscio), America and the United Nations launched the operation *Restore Hope*. This was one of the first "humanitarian operations" and was divided into two parts. The original intention was to escort the convoys of food aid and to protect volunteers in the humanitarian organizations. This was subsequently combined with the political intention to restore state sovereignty in Somalia.[84] It ended in total disaster: America suffered an incredible political failure and its own military power was humiliated when the American Special Forces ended up in a trap that led to the shooting-down of a helicopter, the killing of several soldiers, and the hasty retreat of the other Rangers, forced to leave the bodies of their own comrades-in-arms on the field. The scene of the slaughtering of the American corpses by ferocious crowds, well-orchestrated, spread around the world and forced Bill Clinton to bring the American contingent swiftly home. The American departure marked the end of the mission, which had seen several other fierce battles, one of which was a veritable slaughter of civilians carried out by the Pakistani contingent, as well as a violent ambush on the Italian contingent who paid their sad contribution of human casualties at "check point *Pasta*." It is important that the "Somalia lesson" was internalized by the Clinton administration so much so that it became the focal point of Anthony

Lake's meditations. According to him it is dangerous to believe that the United States can build other nations when they staying on the scene for a long time; once the conditions for peace have been made it must leave the local players the task of completing the process of building democracy.[85]

Restore Hope was indeed a parenthesis in Somalia's gradual drift toward the category of ex-state. In the following years, other countries, particularly in Africa, suffered the same fate: from Uganda to Rwanda, from Liberia to the Ivory Coast to Congo-Zaire. For a long period of time, both the United States, the only real supplier of security in the international political system, and the international community by means of its institutions (mainly the UN), no longer intervened, or did so tardily, at most permitting improvised and ineffective regional coalitions or even some ex-colonial power to deal with the matter.

The Taliban's Afghanistan can be considered an even more sensational case of failed state left to its own devices for years; it is an even more striking example than the scenario following the Soviet–American bipolarism of the cold war. To understand why, we need to consider three factors. The first is of great symbolic value: the Afghan war, led by Brezhnev and his successors, was one of the concause that accelerated the fall of communism and the end of the Soviet Union. The same theatre, which some five years previously had been deemed so important as to force Moscow to undertake a long, disastrous war, now became basically insignificant. The second factor that must not be underestimated is the geographical position of the country. Even though Afghanistan no longer borders Russia, since the central Asian republics were made independent, it is however adjacent to an important strategic area for Moscow, wedged as it is between Pakistan, Iran, and China, that is to players of significant importance for the balance of the Middle East and Asia. But not even this is considered sufficient to take on the re-establishment of an order or sovereignty which is responsible for what happens in its territory.

The third factor is precisely this: responsibility toward the international community, that should have led to this last "let's do something" for Afghanistan. What was happening within Afghanistan was well-known and well hidden by the "theology students" republic, believed to be the upholders of an extremist, fanatically religious, obscurantist state, even by theocratic Iran. Quite apart from the real bloody civil war between the Uzbek and Tagik tribes in the north and the Pastun tribe in the central south area, the other "war" being waged was common knowledge; it was the war that the regime had started not against a "minority," but against the majority of its own citizens: women, who were even forbidden to study. It was well known that Afghanistan was one of the main international producers of opium and cocaine, which reached the western markets by the Tashkent-Moscow-Berlin route.[86] It was also known that Afghanistan was one of the ideological centers for Islamic fundamentalism and for the military *jihad*, which had gathered proselytes in Algeria, Sudan, Kyrgyzstan, and Pakistan. The destruction of the two huge statues of Buddha, removed all doubt about the intransigent madness that inspired the Taliban government. These were splendid works of art that preceded the Islamization of the country and despite strong international pressure, they were blown up being considered idolatrous images. It was also known that Afghanistan was host to the bases and structure of Bin Laden's terrorist organization, so that after the attacks on the American embassies in Kenya and Tanzania, causing a total of 500 deaths, Bill Clinton had Afghanistan bombed (as well as Sudan) as a warning and in retaliation. In short, for years it was widely known that Afghanistan was a "black hole," where not only did deplorable acts for any civilized conscience take place, but it was also extremely dangerous for the outside world in terms of ideological threat, narco-criminal threat and terrorist threat. Before deciding that a similar collapsed state is too dangerous to be tolerated by the system, it is necessary to wait for a while. A serious terrorist attack and similar sequence of attacks like the one carried out by Al Qaeda first on the World Trade Center on February 26, 1993 (miraculously there were only 6 deaths and 1000 injured) and then the bloodshed of the American embassies in Africa ("only" 300 deaths), the attack on the *USS Cole* at the end of Bill Clinton's second term of office—all of this was not enough. We have to wait for September 11, 2001, the devastation in New York and Washington, and the subsequent refusal by the Taliban to hand over their guest and master Bin Laden: only then does the idea develop that the Afghan anomaly needs to be eliminated.

At this point we understand better how the division that ran through the West—interpreting this term from the external point of view, so including the Russians among the Westerners—was what permitted the whole system to remain united, connecting every corner of the globe, no matter how distant, in a complex game, a world game in which no place could be considered strategically "insignificant." The "great divide" within the Western world of liberal political and Marxist philosophies, the great internal break toward modernity, were in reality what permitted even in a violent, hierarchical, and in many ways superficial way, to keep united what was not. Indeed, with the end of the cold war, the "natural harmony of interests" and visions loosens within the Western communities which, while becoming richer as more players take part, finds itself deprived of an unambiguous means of interpretation and action. Representative of this is the increasing divarication between Europe and the United States in their attitudes and behavior toward international politics, and the role that force plays in such an environment. Some believe that the divarication is so great as to jeopardize the self-same transatlantic solidarity, with every crisis that the West is called on to manage or simply to face. The increasing of differences and diffidence between Europe and the United States brought the American political scientist Robert Kagan to argue that there is a "Venusian" Europe as opposed to a "Martian" America, a sort of educated version of the diatribe against "old Europe" hurled by Donald Rumsfeld (United States Secretary for Defense) on the eve of the operation *Iraqi Freedom*.[87]

With the outbreak of the Second Gulf War (1990–1991) and then with the progression of Islamic fundamentalism, there was, however, a far more striking fracture: the one between "the West and the rest." Only the pressurized lid of the cold war and its global contraposition and zero sum game had held it at bay on the backdrop of the international arena. The complexity caused by the largely compressed nature of the plurality of concepts in politics exploded with unexpected force and, more importantly, with a violence exacerbated by the fact that in the Arab and Muslim world decolonization and national independence, as much as the illusion of national Arab and not anti-Islamic socialism, were viewed as failures tied to the nature of the importation of both liberal and Marxist doctrines.

> The overwhelming majority of Muslims now live in independent states, which have brought no solutions to their problems. The bastard offspring of both ideologies, national socialism, still survives in a few states that have preserved the Nazi Fascist style of dictatorial government and indoctrination, the one through a single all-powerful party. These regimes too have failed every test except survival, and have brought none of the promised benefits. If anything, their infrastructures are even more antiquated than others, their armed forces designed primarily for terror and repression. . . . . Meanwhile the blame game—the Turks, the Mongols, the imperialists, the Jews, the Americans—continues, and shows little sign of abating. For the governments, at once oppressive and ineffectual, that rule much of the Middle East, this game serves a useful, indeed an essential purpose—to explain the poverty that they have intensified. In this way they seek to deflect the mounting anger of their unhappy subjects against other, outer targets.[88]

These are tough comments by the well-known, highly esteemed British scholar of Middle East problems Bernard Lewis. But the words that come from inside the Arab world from those who have experienced first hand those conditions sound even more bitter. As was observed by Ali Ahmad Said Esber, a Syrian poet of among the most important in the Arab world, in exile in France since 1985, Arab culture "should work towards its refoundation," so that "the previous cultural experiences, all for one cause, are not repeated: for Palestine, for Arab nationalism, for socialism and liberation from colonialism etc. All of this passed for the cause of Arab unity, or rather, that experience which, with its Fascist connotations on one hand and clerical on the other, was the reason for our defeats and our decadence."[89] And so, not surprisingly, such plurality and diversity having been so long compressed, no longer limit themselves to demanding a sort of right to co-existence in the name of the particularity of their own culture. Rather, they push toward demanding the right to break the totally "Western" unity of the same international political system: they do this even at the cost destroying the foundations, resorting to ever more spectacular terrorist acts, those truly asymmetric new wars that accompany the dawn of a millennium that was supposed to commence under the sign of "universal perpetual peace." Recalling Michael Novak's words, the authoritative Catholic American intellectual greatly heeded by the White House (just like Bernard Lewis), an international war has been clearly declared. "Its perpetrators called it an international jihad, aimed not only against the U.S. but the entire West, indeed, against the whole non-Islamic world. . . . No major moral authority had any difficulty in recognizing that a war to prevent this new type of terrorism is not only just but morally obligatory."[90]

THE WAR ON TERROR

The threat of new international terrorism of global dimension is probably what best connates the current phase of transformation in the international political system. The long wave of consequences generated by the attacks on September 11, 2001 is in well underway. If we look at such a transformation with the humility imposed by the hecatomb from which it originated, there is all the more reason for acknowledging the difficulty of predicting with reasonable certainty not only when it will tire itself out, but actually what direction it will end up taking. Since September 11, the terrorists have gained several undeniable successes: they have opened war on three fronts with the United States (internal, Afghanistan, and Iraq); they have sharpened the contrasts and suspicions between the Islam and Western worlds; they have rekindled the Israel–Palestine conflict; they have impaired the unity of the West dividing them on what should be an appropriate response to their actions; they have endangered the solidity of law and international institutions; they have shaken up European public opinion with respect to their own governments; they have worsened our style of life; they have inflicted more bloodshed, causing thousands of victims in the Far East, Oceania, the Middle East, South America, Europe, and North Africa.[91] And, what is even more serious, they have made more proselytes and have basically escaped our hunt for them.

Since the day of the attack on the Twin Towers, we have been living in a sort of *planetary state of emergency*, a continual transitoriness that seems to have been able to nullify one of the greatest acquisitions of the end of the cold war and the defeat of Soviet Communism: the idea that we would live in a generally safer world, much more like the international community imagined by Immanuel Kant in his *Perpetual Peace* rather than the anarchic arena described rationally by Thomas Hobbes. It is not like this. If it is not a foregone conclusion that the future that awaits us will be dominated by the conflict between civilizations or by religious wars, similar dreadful scenarios risk being more probable if we do nothing to ward them off. Terrorism and the reaction to it are the possible triggers for these disastrous predictions. In order to fight and beat this new treacherous enemy, for a start it is necessary to acknowledge that we still know too little. The knowledge question is fundamental in order to find the right strategy to beat it.[92]

When tackling the question of terrorism, the transitoriness of the object of study shows itself in the difficulties that are encountered in defining what it really is, and if what we are facing today has characteristics which are so novel as to justify imposing radically new strategies. As is known, no one likes to call himself a "terrorist." It is necessary to go back in time to the Jacobin phase of the French Revolution to find an apologia consistent with the concept of terror and politics which was aware of terror. On February 5, 1794 at the height of the reign of "Terror," Maximilien Robespierre remarked: "The mainspring of popular government in revolution is virtue and terror: virtue, without which terror is deleterious; terror, without which virtue is impotent." Let it be clear: long before and long after Robespierre and Saint Just's rule, political power resorted to terror to consolidate its hold on society. At bottom, the infinite lists of proscriptions at the time of the Roman dictator Silla, were also a terrorist tool. In the dark centuries of Europe and after the Counter-Reformation and the wars of religion, accusations against not only potential political opponents but also against mere nonconformist elements in society (for example heresy, apostasy and witchcraft) were often dealt with by terrorist means. The practice of state terror to force society to comply definitively with its own violently innovative design is to be the domain of totalitarian regimes—from Nazism in Germany to Communism in the Soviet Union. And one only needs to gaze over the European borders to understand how in its Asian version (in Pol Pot's Cambodia, the Cultural revolution in China and Kim's North Korea), Communism was able to resort to terrorist campaigns of such vast entity, and yet concentrated in time, as to make the reign of "Terror" in 1792–1794 seem relatively calm and secure.

The "terror of the totalitarian state" sets three targets: to revenge its enemies, intimidate those who might become enemies and free society from subjects whose survival makes the triumph of the revolution impossible. As is well known, in the case of totalitarianism, it is a matter of a "revolution from above," triggered by revolutionary elite and by a totalitarian state against society. As Hannah Arendt had sensed, if illegality is the essence of tyranny, terror is the essence of totalitarianism. And yet, if we look at the action of international terrorism of the fundamentalist kind, one of the first elements that strikes us is the deep similarity of action with that of the totalitarian and terrorist state. With the attacks of September 11, 2001, Al Qaeda wanted: (1) to take vengeance on the United States, punishing it for its Middle-East policies; (2) to intimidate Western societies and those in the Islamic world that view the fundamentalist project with suspicion; (3) to announce the purification of Islam through the programmed elimination from the political and social Muslim scene of the renegade "friends of the West." In all, if terrorism has intrinsically a "totalitarian" nucleus, expressed basically by its self proclamation, the new Islamic terrorism exasperates it to the point that it takes the form of a sort of "totalitarianism without state."

What exactly is a terrorist action? When can we speak of terrorism and not of simple crime or guerrilla warfare? I believe that a good starting point is given by this definition: a terrorist action is qualifiable as such when it is an intrinsically criminal action, carried out for political ends and brought about in the style of military strategy. Paraphrasing Clausewitz, it can be observed that the terrorist act takes the form of a clash between a "live force" (the fiery group, attacker, suicide bomber) that moves within a military political design and a defenseless mass, and which acquires a political profile (involuntarily and unawares) only the moment in which it becomes the object of terrorist violence. Terrorism in military terms is the negation of the clash, because it impedes self-defense on the part of the victim and it does not seek the concentration, attrition, and the destruction of the enemy live force. Terrorism aims more particularly at paralyzing the enemy's will to fight through the barbarous killing of innocent victims. But there again, in the terrorist's view no one is innocent and in a cynical fanatical notion of reality—the same murderous, devastating act is put forward first and foremost as a communicative act.[93]

The workings of the process of terror are revealed effectively by the three phases into which they can be broken down: to gain attention through a spectacularly sanguinary act, to force the counterpart to interpret the message launched by the terrorist (that is to "work" on the political agenda drawn up by the terrorist), and to get a reaction that remains imprisoned between the dilemma of whether to fight or escape. But how is terrorism to be fought? Undoubtedly, we are faced with a complex phenomenon that knows how to exploit the gray area that lies between peace and war, so that they oblige us to face one of the many dilemmas that are posed on the road to fighting terror. To recognize the terrorist as a "political enemy" or *hostes*, to say it in Carl Schmitt's words,[94] and automatically permit him to achieve his first success or consider the terrorist a simple *inimicus*, a bandit, and limit oneself to fight with the only weapons that are licit in times of peace? Indeed, the limbo of Guantanamo and Camp X-Ray is born of that shilly-shallying between the horns of the dilemma. The blurred image of those men in orange overalls behind barbed wire and metal fences, their wrists and ankles tied, stumbling, supported by two marines in camouflaged uniforms, should have been a warning to Islamic terrorism; in fact in Camp X-Ray, "the United States risks involuntarily putting on show its own fear. It is the involution that an aversive phenomenon like the one that contributed to the massacres of September 11 can provoke in a democratic and Western society par excellence . . . Guantanamo has been changed into a sort of metaphor of the force and impotence of the victors. It is a stage of suffering on which ambiguity and the difficulty to define a 'war non-war' have spread and increased in size. What has emerged and been accentuated is the insufficiency not only of the bombardments and intelligence, but also of the laws that the West has tried to impose on the world to make some basic concepts of any conflict respected. And if that were not enough, the insufficiency has not strained relationships between the United States and its enemies, but between Washington and its allies, in first place the Europeans."[95] The "potential damage" created by Guantanamo is nothing compared to the real set-back of image suffered by the United States in the sad story of abuse and humiliation inflicted on Iraqi prisoners in the prison Abu Ghraib.

We know that for the number of victims, the magnitude of the damage, for the fact that the attack did not only hit the land but also the institutions and symbols of the United States, the American administration believed that the attacks on September 11 would reveal themselves a veritable act of war, even though they were executed by a nonstate player. Thanks to the enormity of the attacks, bin Laden intended to transform his personal *jihad* against America into a "holy war" for the liberation of the Islamic world from "Christian and Zionist" oppression. Behind the will shown to provoke the immediate and total withdrawal of the United States from the Middle East chessboard, it is legitimate to suppose that there is a more detailed plan. A necessary element of this was to force America to be more greatly involved and more visible within the *Dar-al-Islam*. Only by securing the direct intervention of the United States in the area and transforming a terrorist attack into the spark for real guerrilla warfare, aimed at draining American military forces, could their objective become reality: the objective of a general insurrection against Arab and Islamic "Kings of apostasy" and "accomplices" of the United States.

In some ways it could be alleged that Osama bin Laden acted not so very differently than did Gavrilo Princip in Sarajevo in 1914: to hit the superpower blamed for the misery of one's own nation (yesterday the Austro-Hungarian Empire and the Slavs, today the United States and the Arabs) in order to force a reaction that leads to a general outburst. If one can sympathize with this hypothesis, then the American reaction to go to war, first in Afghanistan and all the more so in Iraq, did the terrorists a great service, because it contributed to the realization of the scenario pursued and planned by them. This would have been impossible without the United States' active cooperation. On the other hand, if terrorism is characterized by the will to flee from the confrontation and to strike defenseless masses in the shade, then accepting the provocation and transforming a "terrorist war" into "guerrilla warfare" seems a risky strategy but is not necessarily doomed to fail. On the contrary, opening a theater of operations in which the terrorist group is under the illusion that it can instigate insurrection and subsequently crush it coincides with forcing the enemy to come out of the shadows into the light of day, to face that confrontation in an open field where the differential between the firing power of the two parties involved is completely spread out. As long as suitable means are set aside for such a purpose and as long as the end result is not to fight the "right war in the wrong place." As was remarked by Wesley Clark when the post–Iraqi war situation had not yet reached its worst phase: "By July 2003, many Americans were still questioning whether they were safe at home. The conquest of Iraq was complete, but there was growing appreciation that the occupation would require tens of thousands of troops, more than $100 billion, and several years to be successful. Are we any safer today than we were on September 10, 2001? That is the fundamental question for Americans concerning the global war on terror."[96]

As can be seen, not even knowledge about the enemy and his most hidden intentions is able to dictate an a priori effective strategy. We are all aware that steadfastness is the only way to defeat terrorism. In particular, if we think again about the terrorism that caused bloodshed in Italy during the 1970s, the Italians better than anyone know that there is no alternative—one cannot yield to the blackmail of terror. But it is just as well known how narrow the course of action is; effective repression of the armed cells must not end up enlisting new recruits under the terrorists' flag, due to excessive violence employed to combat it. The dilemma to resist or flee is further complicated: how can we accept the challenge brought by the terrorists without lending them a hand with their preordained scheme? In what way can a military reaction be avoided without seeming to flee from the terrorists?

Since September 2001 the United States, the only global superpower to survive the cold war, has declared war on terror without zones, boundaries, or time limits. Since the massacres of September 11, they have learnt the lesson that not even America is safe in the face of an enemy who is determined to inflict devastating damage knowing that they could face extremely tough reprisals. The whole armory of the United States was useless, as was its overwhelming, historically unparalleled military supremacy. As well as this, there was a complete absence of credible global challengers for its political leadership and was assisted by a vibrant, reactive economy despite the heavy federal deficits and incredible foreign debts. A group of ten or so people managed to cause more victims and destruction on American soil than had happened in over forty years of bitter and total discord with the mortal enemy, the Soviet Union. Four teams of suicide bombers armed with paper-cutters were enough to bring the end of the world to the shores of the Atlantic in the United States. Paradoxically, that act carried out with such crude weapons is to open the floodgates to a real American obsession regarding weapons of mass destruction, the search for which becomes the official reason for the war against Saddam Hussein. In truth, the massacres on September 11 should have proved that, if anything, the will to provoke mass destruction is far more determined than the possession of this or that technology.

They should have induced a more articulate revision of the concept of power in international politics today, not necessarily in the direction undertaken by Joseph Nye (of a *soft power* analytically distinct from a *hard power*), but at least just as original.

There has been great debate, and it will continue for a long time to come, as to whether such a barbarous, unbelievable act can justify the American demand to bring into question the formal and informal laws that regulate the relationships between states and international political life. Indeed, the morning after the September 11, Washington let it be known that the concept of sovereignty would be seriously reviewed. Hit in their own jealous and proud sovereignty, the United States decreed that they would disregard the sovereignty of others any time they believed it was necessary to safeguard their own national security. This was certainly nothing new—suffice to think of the retaliation following the terrorist acts ordered during Clinton's presidency on Iraq, Afghanistan, and Sudan, or of the bombardments on Libya and Lebanon at the time of President Reagan. But for the first time this limitation of the sovereignty of others, comes to be transformed by a conscious break with normality, an exception linked to the exceptional nature of a particular situation, to a point of attack for the redefinition of "normality" suited to the times in which the unheard-of was made reality. This is where the permanent, global state of emergency was born, and in which we have been living for over four years.

The leader of the international political system basically reported the need to modify the rules of that same system, the moment they proved to be completely ineffective to protect its own security. From here was developed the doctrine of preventive war (proven to be extremely dubious as regards efficacy, but also not challenged by any theoretic formulation or by any alternative policy).[97] Included was the transition to the employment of categories which are basically new (revolutionary or revisionist, if it is preferred) to interpret the real state of international politics, like those of the "rogue states" and "failed states." From that moment the classical ad hoc alliances are favored (the *coalition of the willing*) compared to the permanent and institutionalized political, military alliances fostered and created by the United States. These had been one of the great novelties during the cold war and the idea is reinforced that the progressive march from an international anarchic arena to a pluralist international community had met with a sudden disruption, if not a veritable "about-turn."

It should really go without saying, that although there is no sense in placing the attacks and the reaction to these attacks on the same ethical plane, there is no doubt that even the way in which the reaction was expressed resulted in strengthening the devastating impact produced by the terrorists from the point of view of the consequences on the international system. Paradoxically, the moment in which they revealed themselves so surprisingly ineffective, the exclusive faith in the military is reinforced and it becomes the only reliable bastion for security. To those who object that precisely September 11 proved the vulnerability of a security system which relies almost exclusively on military means, the reply is given that in order for it to be effective, this tool must be put in a suitable condition to be able to carry out its assignments in an appropriate way. A doctrine is needed for the use of force suited to the times, which substitutes the one adopted during the cold war. A doctrine needs to be formulated that enables the threat to be stopped before it is planned, and it must legitimise politically the need to root out terrorists wherever they may be hiding, striking out contemporarily at the regimes that offer them protection. And lo, the "Bush doctrine" was born, the foundation stone of the *War on terror*, which integrates the doctrine of pre-emptive war within a highly ambitious political plan that aims to substitute hostile despotic regimes with allied democracies. Little does it matter if, in order to do this it is necessary to challenge the international institutions to highlight their insufficiency and even to put at risk their political survival, even more so if it is believed that they are an objective hindrance to victory over terrorism. In the words of the liberal intellectual Benjamin Barber, "there is nothing partisan in this new doctrine. In its 2000 Party platform, the Democratic Party suggested that an evolving international environment called for a new doctrine of 'forward engagement,' that would 'mean addressing problems early in their development before they become crises, addressing them as close to the source of the problems as possible, and having the forces and the resources to deal with these threats as soon after their emergence as possible.' Forward engagement is not preventive war, but it is not exactly traditional self-defence either."[98] When considering the doctrine of pre-emptive war, surfing comes to mind; the threat, just like the wave must be tackled as it is taking shape if it is to be dominated.

Whether one agrees or not with what seems to be the main preoccupation in the American offices of George W. Bush's administration, the fact is that it is subsequent to this preoccupation that the world finds itself having fought first the Afghan conflict and then the Iraq war. Having managed to strike the global superpower so savagely, and having pushed it to react with determination, terrorism has succeeded in imposing itself as the main discriminating element in the discussion and construction of the international political system.

The novel fact that we have to face is the global dimension of hyper-terrorism which counteracts American hyper-power. Much irony has been used when debating whether it is possible to declare war on a way of behavior rather that on its authors. The truth is that we are at war with the propagators of an ideology that deliberately distorts and redirects Islam to strike in its name Arab and Islamic governments and societies, just as much as Western governments and societies. As Roger Scruton writes, "Terrorism is not, after all, an enemy, but a method used by the enemy. The enemy is of two kinds: the tyrant dictator, and the religious fanatic whom the tyrant protects. To act against the first is feasible, if we are prepared to play by the tyrant's rules. But to act against the second requires a credible alternative to the absolutes with which he conjures. It requires not merely to believe something, but to study how to put our beliefs into practice."[99] On the other hand it is difficult not to notice how the powerful symbolism and forceful meaning of the *jihad* dominate modern Muslim politics and society in a hitherto unknown way. The era that began with the collapse of the Twin Towers has been defined the "era of terror." It follows those years in the 1990s which, while by no means free of cases of bloody disarray (just think of the Balkans, from Bosnia to Kosovo), seemed on the whole definable through the concept of globalization. The era of the "Great G" has perhaps come to an end, or else, and this is more probable, it has settled down. In so doing, it has fueled global terrorism, which is without one main leader, but the advocates of which are united in their objective: to stop what *we* call globalization and *others* consider to be simply yet another form, maybe more refined but also more persuasive, of Westernization. Fighting terrorism also means understanding the causes that fuel a phenomenon characterized by such loathsome methods. It means trying to understand how on earth it is exercised, prevalently, though not exclusively, by groups that adhere to Islamic fundamentalism. It cannot simply be a problem of different levels of economic development or unequal distribution of wealth, given that there are societies which are far poorer and disadvantaged but do not produce a phenomenon like this type of terrorism. Suffice to consider that there is no international terrorism coming from the most desperate areas of "black Africa." If anything it is the ensemble of wealth and its unequal distribution, through corruption, abuse, and political frustration, modern technology and fanatical backward ideology that produces the mixture that fuels fundamentalist terrorism: "There is however, a powerful economic dimension to the crisis in the Arab world. The problem is wealth, not poverty."[100] Unpleasant and even disturbing it may be to admit, "improving the quality of life, fighting against illiteracy and spreading secularisation, reducing the pockets of poverty, opening efficient hospitals and psychiatric services, . . . will *not* eliminate the question of radical religious extremism on which the terrorist organisations count".[101] At the very least, this alone is not enough, since the "countries that give the greatest contribution to the suicide terrorism of Al Qaeda are Saudi Arabia and the Gulf States, the richest in the Islamic world and the average terrorist is neither poor nor underprivileged nor uneducated. It would seem that what torments Muslim societies, is rather the problem of "denied dignity" and frustration from "insignificance of status." Fundamentalist terrorism offers the false solution of "curing" with violence the contradiction of a grandiose past and the miserable present in which these societies continue to lose themselves.

CHAPTER 2

Force, Law, and International Order

ONE WORLD, MANY SYSTEMS

It really can be argued that the old, united international system is breaking up into different subsystems, each one of which is destined to coexist and is regulated by different operational laws and behavior. Despite the fact that the transatlantic relationship is going through a critical phase of readjustment, there can be no doubt that it is still possible to consider the West an international subsystem, highly institutionalized and peaceful, and founded on democracy and the market. It is a veritable security community, free from the prospect of internal war or aggressive regulation of possible contrasts, in which the different members share at least the interest to cooperate for reasons of common security. So far, this security has only been threatened from outside and it has been guaranteed by the supremacy of the United States, so that within the West it is out of place to complain of the need for a balancing of the American power. Evidently problems may arise only when the "minority partners" in this community believe that the hegemonic power, following any unilateral initiative external to the West, jeopardizes the collective security of the community—that is, if it "imports insecurity" from outside. It is precisely this which, at least in part, and according to some observers, has been transpiring since the Third Gulf War.

A good example showing how opinions have changed toward the United States is Germany. The "pacifist" behavior of Schroeder's Germany during the Iraqi conflict is inexplicable both from a merely idealistic point of view and in terms of simple pre-electoral cynicism. Schroeder is certainly no "absolute pacifist" and he is certainly not anti-American: Germany took part in the Kosovo conflict (not "authorised" by the UN Security Council) and sent German soldiers to fight in Afghanistan after September 11. It was that very same Germany that coordinated the NATO contingent in Afghanistan and

Germany was, and still continues to be, America's most important strategic ally in Europe. But, there again, after the Second World War, it was America who repeatedly guaranteed not only the security of Germany's borders, but also the democratic reliability of its new institutions. It did so by pushing for German re-armament, by letting Germany join NATO in the 1950s and, more recently during Helmut Kohl's chancellorship, by actively encouraging immediate reunification of the eastern Laender and East Berlin with the Federal Republic; it even had to conquer resistance from Germany's European partners, Paris and London included. Almost just as certainly, admitting that Schroeder is endowed with a good share of cynicism, a necessary quality and common to every political leader, he cannot be so unscrupulous and foolhardy as to jeopardize the consolidation of the German presence in the West, which goes back to Bismarck's day, just to satisfy the pacifistic mood of public opinion and win the difficult round of elections in 2002. What seems to have guided the Chancellery strategy were perhaps two slightly less contingent reasons. The first has to do with the eternal question of the security of German borders. To the west, for over half a century, the Rhine border is one of the most open and safe that has ever been known. And not only this. France, rival that it was, has become Germany's most important European ally. To the east, a severely weakened Russia and much less of a neighbor geographically (Poland, Ukraine and Belarus separate it from Germany), is Germany's main creditor. Relations between Moscow and Berlin have never been so good, at least since the 1920s, the time of the Rapallo Treaty, when the Weimar Republic and the newly born Soviet Union were both on the edges of the systems of European states: one because it was heir to the defeat of Kaiser William's Empire, the other, inasmuch as it was a Communist revolutionary regime. Today for the first time in history, while German borders run no risks, Germany is the possible leader of the old continent, even if this leadership encounters understandable (and increasing) resistance. At this point it is to be imagined that Schroeder and his advisors have asked this simple question: "What enemies does Germany have?" The answer could be more or less this: "None, apart from the ones procured by the United States."

The second thought comes precisely from this excess of American initiative (as seen from Berlin, at any rate) and highlights an ambitious objective: to put an end to American protection of German democracy. A Germany with no "natural enemies" obviously has far less interest in American protection. But a Germany that offers itself as a champion of the "anti-war front", opposing itself to its ex-guarantor, its institutions by nature democratic and nonaggressive, achieves a sensational victory not so much over America, as history itself. Since its birth, Germany has had to reckon with the problem of "Prussian militarism." The whole of highly institutionalized and pacific Europe has frequently had to endure the consequences of a phenomenon which, precisely because it was badly managed by German state institutions, ended up involving it in continual explosions of aggression. In changing itself from a "military power" to a "pacifist power," Germany achieves two important results. On the one hand, it releases itself from American protection, something that it can only manage to do without rousing apprehension in Europe, by means of the choice of the peace option as opposed to the war option favored by the United States. On the other hand, it conquers and strengthens in terms of cultural discernment a hegemony that had eluded it twice in the twentieth century (having pursued it by military policies), and that in the last forty years it had limited to mere economic fact. This project is not pursuable in a predictable way. It obviously provokes jealousy and worry among the allied Europeans: from Great Britain to Italy to Poland. These fears and worries, on top of that, become greater the more the German leadership tries to assert itself by distancing itself from Washington. The "Paris-Berlin axis" and the "French-German engine" do not only worry the Americans, but also many Europeans.

Alongside the Western system that we have just looked at, it is possible to identify two other subsystems; they are all united by the characteristic that "internal peace" and the nontoleration of war as a tool to resolve controversy sound more like declarations of principle rather than effective practices or realistic expectations. According to Henry Kissinger,[1] for example, Asia is the subsystem which best recalls Europe in the nineteenth century, where war between strategic rivals (China, Japan, India, and Russia) is certainly not an imminent danger, but neither is it an inconceivable prospect. In this subsystem, just as happened in nineteenth century Europe and different from the cold war experience, the ideology seems to cover a very marginal role in determining the status of relationships between the four main regional powers. It could rather be said that nationalism, hegemonic aspirations and economic interests are the strongest motives to drive the players' behavior. In some cases, for example, for China, they are heavily influenced by the worry of political and military leadership, to conserve power which is no longer justifiable on the basis of the old communist ideological orthodoxy.

A third subsystem is to be found in the Middle East; this coincides problematically with the "Greater Middle East" conceived in

Washington, and representing a pre-Westphalia system in many aspects. Here war is still characterized and justified for religious reasons. The use of religion as a tool and pretext for foreign policy and security has not yet been deactivated and, more importantly, we are dealing most often with extremely fragile states: that is, the two processes, necessarily linked, of secularization and state-building were not established without faults, and they may never be able to be faultless. This explains effectively why it is totally inconceivable for the State of Israel, the only Middle-Eastern democracy, to abandon their policy of resorting to violence, without jeopardizing its own survival. But this highlights the difficulties for any leadership in the Jewish state to believe completely the promises made by its regional counterpart, apart from the fact that it is impossible to sign peace treaties that are not guaranteed (also in military terms) by the United States. In this system there are also emerging powers like Iran and states with delicate, complex internal problems like Pakistan and Egypt. For theocratic Iran, religion is also the "raison d'etre" for internal political order. For Pakistan and Egypt, even if in very different ways, radical Islam is a threat or an ambiguous partner compared to the political elite in power. It is not necessary to remember that the area is strategic for its oil resources and that the two countries in possession of most of the crude oil (moreover with more moderate extraction costs, i.e., Saudi Arabia and Iraq) have enormous problems of stability. The particular relationship that has tied the United States and Israel since the war in 1967, and that has become more important than the relationship between the United States and the oil monarchies in the Gulf, dating back to the 1940s, makes the picture even more complex.[2]

The last subsystem is in Africa; as a matter of fact it is a scenario of gradual deterioration and is unlikely to be reversed. There has been a worsening in the general conditions that coincided with decolonization and with the disastrous failure of that process.

The idea of the decline of a real world political system outlined by Henry Kissinger was already contemplated indirectly by Samuel Huntington in his famous work on the *Clash of Civilizations*. Huntington sketches a world divided into fields of action and influence of the main civilizations (Chinese, Japanese, Hindu, Islamic, Western, Latin-American, and African); they are divided along fault lines,[3] and he associates each one of these to a conception and a certain direction of foreign policy that make conflict more probable than cooperation—*rebus sic stantibus*—(or harmony, to retrieve an old liberal concept).

Indeed, the situation suggested earlier, as well as this latter one are complicated by the fact that some actors are part of different subsystems. Russia, obviously, is included partially in the Western subsystem, but it is also part of Asia and it is involved with phenomena that share characteristics with the Middle-Eastern subsystem. One only need think of the Islamic infiltration of Chechen warfare.[4] The ex-Soviet states in central Asia (Uzbekistan, Kazakhstan, Tajikistan, and Kyrgyzstan) straddle the Asian and Middle-Eastern subsystems. Even India, because of the Kashmir problem and its disputes with Pakistan is forced to face the fact that Islamic fundamentalism tries to be the unifying factor for the Greater Middle East, managing, in fact to enlist recruits right down to Southeast Asia (Malaysia, Indonesia, the Philippines). The actors that participate in the different subsystems, intermittently or continuously, consequently change their own "political behaviour," suiting themselves as much as possible to the methods of the subsystem in which they find themselves operating. So, for example, when France decides to intervene in some conflict with its own African client-states, it does not behave the same way it would within the Western system, but rather adapts its behavior to the stage in question. For that reason, just to be clear, it will resort to military force far more easily *there* than it would be willing to do in the West or even in Asia.[5] Similarly, when the Western powers decide to work toward peace in the Middle East, they have to take into consideration that they are in a situation in which to forego an armed fight and to renounce the formalization of international political procedures, has very different consequences than the reaction that might be had by the peaceful West. There is also a sort of hierarchy between the different subsystems, so that the state of relationships within the West and the role of the only remaining superpower is of significant importance. As Angelo Panebianco observes, by and large the international political system is still characterized by three elements: (1) the fact that "the engine and the core of the whole international system today, the area where there are the greatest amounts of wealth and power, is the Euro-Atlantic area"; (2) the role carried out (within and outside the Euro-Atlantic community) by the only surviving superpower since the end of the cold war; (3) the "developments within the Euro-Atlantic community provoked by the process of European integration."[6]

It is the participation of the United States in the different subsystems that makes the situation particularly complicated. This happens because of the type of relationship that the United States has with the other actors—basically of hegemonic nature—both because of the way America participates—often with military intervention—and second because of the fact that the "one-track" mindedness of these interventions reinforces the idea that only the hegemonic power, and in its exclusive interest, is permitted to establish temporary connections between the different subsystems. It is permitted to do so as long as it is not possible to force America to face the bloody unity of the complex system through international terrorism. Starting from this fragmentation of the international political system into many systems, three other characteristics of the "international order" become more obvious; they are materializing under our very eyes and we had previously introduced them.

The first is the prevalence of threats and challenges to global security coming from areas and regions outside the Western subsystem. As we have seen in the relationships between the Americas, Europe, and Japan (and also in increasing measure, Russia) the prospect of violence is basically absent. To this must be added that this area is the most densely populated of institutions and that in it the hegemony of the United States is carried out in a highly institutionalized form. Vice versa, in the other subsystems, a far less peaceful nature corresponds to an institutional fabric which is not so rich and a management of American hegemony which is at the same time decidedly more disputed and very much "more crudely exerted." It is not unjustified to claim that outside the West, and in particular in those areas that present greater endemic tension or for which a feeble indirect control is normally believed to be sufficient, American hegemony emerges as a veritable empire, perhaps wielded intermittently, every time indirect rule entrusted to some local client-state or to allied states proves unsatisfactory. When America "reconnects" these peripheral regions to the Western system, all too often it ends up doing so by means of force, assuming the role of "policeman of the world." All the American administrations programmatically like to disclaim this title. Furthermore, since the United States intervenes in areas where the situation has already precipitated or is on the point of precipitating, after the local players have started a spiraling of increasing violence, one cannot be surprised if the perception that America is an arrogant power is strengthened, when it only intervenes with Marines, aircraft carriers, and intelligent missiles. This sensation is obviously particularly strong with all those who refuse to submit to American hegemony and who see the system of international rules mocked by precisely the one who should have it at heart. In this light one can read the September 11 attack as a deliberate attempt to reconnect in a violent way the center of the system and its most problematic periphery; the latter, however, is a new type of player coming from the Middle East.

Different from what had usually happened, means and timing for reconnection were not chosen by the superpower, America. They were imposed and nullifying at the same time the most important of the differences between "zones of peace" and "zones of turmoil": that is, the daily experimentation of insecurity in its most extreme form.

The second characteristic (already dealt with partially) is that of the proliferation of "failed States" precisely in those subsystems which are different from the Western one, above all in Africa. This phenomenon is linked to the loss of unity of the international political system. It fuels violence at local level and makes the difference between a rich, peaceful West and the rest of the world (given up as a bad job) even sharper. The latter is perhaps even exploited economically but left at the edges of the "showcase," in which peace is founded *also* on the rule of law and not only or not prevalently on the rule of force. The proliferation of failed States has frequently induced the United States to guide or support intervention of a military nature, maybe even under the reassuring label of "humanitarian intervention," thus contributing to the lengthening of an already long list of states that see America as the cause of all evils and the enemy to be defeated. As was commented, as brilliantly as it was polemic: "The legitimacy of the imperial ordering supports the exercise of police power, while at the same time the activity of global force demonstrates the real effectiveness of the imperial ordering. The juridical power to rule over the exception and the capacity to deploy police force are those two initial coordinates that define the imperial model of authority."[7]

The third characteristic that must be dealt with, even if briefly, is that of the noncoinciding between security threat, political challenger and economic rival, so that there are noncoinciding subjects (like China, the EU, and Islamic fundamentalist terrorism), and of different nature (states, territorial public subjects, and "private" terrorist groups) that find themselves challenging the hegemonic power in the various arenas (politics, economics, and security). In a similar context it is highly likely that the hegemon tends to privilege adopting a variety of tools according to the multiplicity of sides to the situations that it ends up having to face. So, it is not the "economic" nature of things to make it unthinkable that even the harshest commercial dispute between the United States and Europe might end in military conflict. History is indeed rich with examples that certify how economic causes can be seen to be responsible for many bloodthirsty conflicts. Impeding such a consequence is the common affiliation of the two rivals in the West that was controlled by the United States, but which is also the one that has the richest institutional infrastructure. In the case of fundamentalist terrorism, that is, the new kind of threat brought to the military security of the hegemonic power, it cannot surprise that the latter reacts in a revolutionary way compared to the rules of the system, revolutionary as the means of the attack were, just as was the nature of the attacker itself. It remains to be seen whether the choice of reaction adopted was appropriate and effective.

The problem is that as the political-military threats gradually take on forms different from the classical ones of the confrontation between territorial states, and as security is challenged by nonstate players, there is the risk that the effectiveness of international law ends up both being reduced to the size of private or commercial law, and with the vision limited to the particular area of concrete enforceability to the "internal relations" of the Western subsystem. With the loss of prominence of the state and its sovereignty, with the reduction of its real monopoly of politically legitimate holder of force (including aggressive force), the whole formal-legal structure begins to disintegrate. This structure, based on state sovereignty, permitted an enormous work of systemization, equalization, and universalization of relationships between states. In short: it was the assumption that sovereignty was equal for all states and the idea of a world made of power ascribable to the form of state, that allowed us to imagine that the relationships of power and wealth between the most diverse subjects could be reduced to a more reassuring legal form. If the "state" is no longer the only or the main actor able to threaten the security of citizens in another country, the whole structure aimed at guaranteeing both individual sovereignties and the principle of collective security creaks ominously.[8]

IRAQI FREEDOM OR THE LONELINESS OF THE HEGEMON

After a period of preparation which basically took the whole winter, the Anglo-American offensive against Iraq got underway on March 20, 2003. While the U.S. Marines concentrated on the oilfields in Rumalia in the south of the country, to prevent them being destroyed by Saddam Hussein's Republican Guard, the 3rd Infantry Division headed north toward Nassyria and the British forces began the battle to conquer Bassora. The war was to last longer than the seventy-two hours unwisely predicted by some, but it would be over in a mere forty-three days, overthrowing Saddam Hussein's regime. It was also to be the beginning of the indefinite military occupation of Iraq of about 160,000 American soldiers. The exiguity of military forces involved is to be one of the severest criticisms raised against the Defense Secretary

Rumsfeld. The Anglo-American expeditionary force was integrated with several thousand troops from other countries (Italians, Poles, Spaniards, and Dutch among others) immediately after the official conclusion of hostilities. But even like this, the occupational forces are not enough to keep order and encourage the return to a minimum of civil organization, and the chaos that follows supplies at first an alibi and then real fuel for terrorists and insurgents. Between March 2001 and June 2004, thirty-one of the thirty-three Army brigades went on the firing-line, reducing permits and rest to a minimum and exasperating the reserves and members of the National Guard, massively employed on the front lines, insufficiently equipped and even badly nourished, thanks to the wild privatization imposed by Donald Rumsfeld.[9] From June 2004 to date, the number of reservists and National Guard members employed in Iraq has fluctuated from 50 55,000, compared to the roughly 80,000 soldiers in active service.[10] Rumsfeld was severely criticized for this in the fall of 2004, right in the middle of the election campaign. He got out of it with statements which were contradictory and embarrassing for the administration trying for a second term. First he declared that the American troops might be withdrawn just after the elections, even if the country is not at peace. Then he admitted, along with Paul Bremen, the person responsible at that time for the Coalition Provisional Authority (CPA), that the plans predicted an insufficient number of troops and that there was no proof of a link between Saddam and Al Qaeda.[11] Above all, in January 2005, the Whitehouse spokesman Bianca Scott McClellan announced the end of the hunt for weapons of mass destruction because "the weapons that we all believed were there, based on the intelligence, were not there," adding also that from the report by the person in charge of the Iraq Survey Group, Charles Duelfer, it clearly emerged "that the regime retained the intent and capability, that Saddam Hussein was pursuing an aggressive strategy to undermine the UN oil-for-food program and bring down the UN sanctions through illicit finance and procurement schemes, and that he intended to resume his pursuit of weapons of mass destruction once those sanctions were eliminated. It also made clear that he was in material breech of Security Council resolutions, including Resolution 1441, which gave him one final opportunity to comply."[12]

The Third Gulf War belied all the predictions, not only those imprudently optimistic, but also those apocalyptic ones on the two million refugees (there were only 100,000), the hundreds of thousands of civilian deaths (these vary from between 3,000 and 7,000), environmental catastrophes, and much more. But the postwar period has been a real disaster. Even following the crazy privatization of supply services and the logistics of the American Armed Forces, the first fifteen to twenty days following the fall of the tyrant were thrown to the winds; it was essential, and would have been a winning card, to have shown a concrete difference between the regime time—terror, death, destruction, penury, and a total absence of rules—and the occupation—made of security, peace, law, and order, but also of food and powdered milk for the children, drinking water, and fuel. It has been commented that it was not possible to improvise all this in such a short time. This is precisely the point. The aid and assistance for the freed Iraqi people should have been planned alongside the military preparations. This would have won the war against Saddam and the terrorists and, first and foremost, the hearts and minds of the Iraqi and Arab people. Germans, Italians, and Japanese have experienced losing a war to the United States. It seems as if there is no trace of the plans elaborated by the Pentagon for the liberation of Iraq. Whatever certain populist and nationalist "revanchism" may deny, where mood and "being intellectual" are united, those defeats were a blessing for those countries.[13] If we consider what might have been their destiny, if the Axis powers had won the war, we should say that it was lucky for Italy, Germany, and Japan that they lost the war to America. In winning over enemy populations to the cause of liberty and an alliance with the United States, who until the day before had paid a high price in terms of human lives, material destruction, and political identity, a decisive contribution was supplied by the obvious link between coming out of the nightmare of the war and hunger and American occupation. The first thing that propelled the revival of the economy, even if it was only in the shape of the black market, came by means of American logistics, the real keystone of the American victory in two world wars. How is it possible that this lesson was ignored? How is it possible that no one posed the question as to whether democracy could be exported *before* security? How could it be taken for granted that political freedom would take root even before the freedom from need (or at least from survival)? Reflecting on Bush Jr's war against Iraq, there has been much talk about the excessive influence of the neo-conservatives on the administration; the right-wing Wilsonism that inspires these ex-liberal intellectuals, when not ex-Trotskyites. In truth, their influence was not sufficient to give the conflict the semblance of a "consistently neo-con conflict." "Rumsfeld's longing to shelve the case as quickly as possible had made him lose sight of the biggest objective: to try to transform Iraq into a new country, to an oasis of democracy at the heart of the Gulf. It was not the reason for the war, but now it had become the most ambitious objective."[14] This lack of consistency between means and objectives, tied to the fact that the same objectives had been insufficiently explained and documented and, above all, rearranged in the course of action, supplied an easy target for polemics in both good and bad faith. Moreover, Rumsfeld's error is much more serious if one thinks that "the urgency to win did not justify a strategy that renounced a priori discarding the basis for the construction of the country and the Iraqi society freed from the rais."[15] So, paradoxically, the initial decision to limit the ground troops to prevent the Americans being perceived as occupying forces, threw out the premise for an indefinite occupation, branded the war against Saddam even more as "American" and undermined the possibility of any temporary government asserting itself as legitimately decent. Was the war against Iraq, all in all, a neo-con war or a war of the "neo-liberalist conservative" kind? Sometimes we need to be reminded that George W. Bush's America is quite simply not the same as Franklin Delano Roosevelt's. What I mean to say is that probably the grandness of Roosevelt's project of world order needs to be understood, beginning with the choice of the New Deal as a political response to the enormous economic and social crises of 1929. Roosevelt responded to this great crisis of the national system with the New Deal. Similarly, following the enormous crises in the international economic and political systems leading up to the Second World War, Roosevelt and his successor responded with the Atlantic Charter and the Marshall Plan. To conceive and execute out a similar response, it was not only necessary to have great faith in politics itself (this also characterises the neo-cons), but also an optimistic vision of the role of the state as a "resolving power," irreplaceable in times of crisis aiming to pursue a common good achievable by means of public intervention and not thanks to the forces of the market (here the neo-cons pay for their excessive liberalism).

The lack of troops was from the beginning the real problem in the eyes of the neo-conservatives.

If the war against Saddam from the strictly military point of view was a success, the task to transplant democracy started off on the wrong foot. Many claim that the responsibility lies in the excessively ambitious plans drawn up by the White House. Indeed, among the "maxims" in the Bush Doctrine and Rumsfeld's light war, there is a hiatus. The Defence Secretary fought a light war different from the one that was prescribed, only in part because of intelligence information which completely misunderstood the public feeling towards the *Yankees*. They were not going to be welcomed with open arms in Iraq. There was no space for nation building on Rumsfeld or Cheney's horizon. For them the hostilities were only useful in annihilating Saddam and in averting the threat of weapons of mass destruction. They were the "be all and end all" of the mission.[16]

And as time passes the suspicion grows that the information was deliberately doctored. For the neo-cons, however, the weapons of mass destruction "were only the reason for the war, but the main objective was to give a kick to the past, to the balance of power, to the old ways of treating the Middle East and to mould the region on new democratic foundations."[17]

At the end of 2004, the situation was still very complicated even though some "recent trends are somewhat more encouraging: foreign aid is beginning to be spent more quickly, even if much of it is being directed toward security rather than rebuilding cities and towns; Iraqi security forces are now being trained more rigorously—and they are beginning to perform better on the battlefield; the overall quality of public services may finally be inching ahead of late-Saddam Hussein levels; the transfer of sovereignty to the interim Iraqi government has continued to deflect some of the anti-American anger on the street; and Iraqis are for the most part bullish on their future."[18] But there again, these positive signs are not enough to define a situation "rosy" that is still characterized by many worrying elements: "Prime Minister Ayad Allawi's popularity has fallen in recent months, unemployment rates remain far too high, insurgents continue to attack oil pipelines and police stations, and Iraqi security forces still cannot begin to take the major responsibility for combating the insurgents."[19] Thus emerges a balance of ups and downs, certainly not particularly promising since political trends are hopeful but fragile, even though the success of the two elections held in 2005 is worth special emphasis, in particular the latest of December 15, with a turnout of 70%.

So, all did not run smoothly, right from the very first excited days of war when Saddam Hussein's army was not dissolved as had happened in 1991, when tens of thousands of Iraqi soldiers surrendered almost without fighting. The units of the Republican Guard and above all Saddam's *mujahideen* very often fought in civilian clothes in order to hide among the population, which had been taken hostage for the umpteenth time by the regime. This made the conquest of some important strategic objectives extremely difficult, objectives near the Kuwait border from where the offensive had started, such as Bassora or Unn Qasr. The Shia population did not rise up against the dictator either in Bassora or in the ghetto areas of Baghdad. Probably it no longer trusted the "Westerners." The last time it had done so, in the final part of the previous Gulf War, it had paid a high price for its good faith. Then the Shias had rebelled with weapons against Saddam's praetorians, but the armistice agreed by the latter with the UN forces had taken them by surprise. The ceasefire had permitted the regime to organize an extremely tough repression, carried out with every type of weapon available, and it had massacred Shias in the marshlands around Shat-el-Arab, giving rise to thousands of men escaping for their lives to neighboring Iran. The allied losses in this campaign were perhaps less important than in 1990/1991, but the concentration of accidental deaths because of friendly fire in the very early days of the conflict and the capture of some American soldiers on March 23, with the ritual televising, had heralded possible coups de théatre right up to the last minute. The uninterrupted sequence of mortal attacks in this "post-war period" reinforces these fears.

Only in the north, in Iraqi Kurdistan, by now semi-autonomous for years thanks to the protection given by the *no fly zone*, did things proceed without a hitch, despite the Turkish last-minute refusal to give assistance and permit transit to an allied expeditionary force, which would have screwed the clamp tightly around Iraq. Paradoxically, despite the initial difficulties, the campaign proceeded so swiftly that from March 24–26, helped by a long sand-storm, the American command was just about to take the decision to stop the march of the armored columns, fearing that the speed of the advance might expose the unrealistic supply lines to the danger of breaking up. Even the conquest of Baghdad was quite unexpected and almost "too easy," yet again, so much so that it was feared for several days that some diabolic trap had been set. It was in some ways true, even if in different ways than those foreseen. In any case, on May 1, forty-three days after the beginning of hostilities, President George W. Bush, on board an American aircraft carrier, officially declared the war in Iraq "over."

The "post-war period" has proven to be decidedly worse than the "official" conflict. It has been studded with attacks, massacres, and kidnappings. From May 1, 2003 to October 26, 2005 the Americans lost 1,861 soldiers (2,000 from the beginning of the war), 1,511 of them being killed by terrorists and guerrillas. The peak was reached on the year anniversary of the "victory," when 131 fell.[20] Baghdad itself has proven paradoxically to be the most dangerous outpost for the GIs, followed by the province of al-Anbar and Falluja, the theater of a bloody battle at the beginning of November, strongly and noisily opposed by the UN General Secretary, Kofi Annan.[21] In the same period of time, America counted 15,444 injured (15,999 from the beginning of the war). The British victims (97) need to be added to the American losses as well as those of the other coalition countries (102, 27 of which were Italians, the third largest contingent to suffer losses after the United States and the United Kingdom). What was supposed to be the first, paradigmatic example of the "coalition of the willing" has gradually disintegrated as the Iraqi situation has worsened under the pressure of kidnappings and attacks (Honduras, Philippines, Spain), showing that the coalition *à la carte* risked staying . . . *on paper*. The security forces and Iraqi police have been most brutally hit by the terrorists. In the first nine months of 2004, a monthly average of 160 policemen and Iraqi security forces were killed, while from June 2003 to October 2005, 3,475 recruits and policemen lost their lives, mostly by suicide bombers: there were 49 in one single massacre on October 25, 2004.

It has not only been the troops and police forces to have been the object of terrorist and rebel action. There have been 278 attacks against pipelines, extraction equipment, and personnel employed in the energy sector, well known as being the country's main resource, and decisive in getting the reconstruction off the ground. Over 322 non-Iraqi civilians have been killed and 235 kidnapped; in one fell swoop 12 Nepalese were slaughtered. From between 10,000 and 18,000 Iraqi civilians have lost their lives postwar in suicide attacks and acts of war. The macabre see-sawing results go from around 10,000 reported by Amnesty International (September 8, 2004), from the British Foreign Minister Jack Straw (September 8, 2004), and from those responsible for the Shaik Omar Clinic in Baghdad (here the figure only refers to the Baghdad region) right up to the 30,000 reported by the Iraq Body Count and by the Iraqi Human Rights Organization.[22] On September 12 there were 60 deaths in a veritable street battle in the center of Baghdad; shots from an American helicopter killed Mazen-al-Tomaizi, a twenty-five year old Palestinian journalist who worked for Al Arabiya, worsening even more the already abysmal relationship between the Arab mass media and the Coalition Forces. In the meantime, it is estimated that the rebels have quadrupled in number over the last year from 5,000 to over 20,000, foreign terrorists being 700 to 2,000.

The war in Iraq also marks a turning point in the relationship between information and war or, if preferred, between the power of the media and military power. Despite the countermelody continuously favored by "Al Jazeera," the Arab Emirates private TV company, in this war the allied military command clearly overrides the media, settling a score from the time of the Vietnam War when they ended up being at the mercy of the means of communication. It was highly predictable that the Baghdad regime would systematically turn to propaganda and misinformation. The Iraqi Information Minister Al Sahaf became an involuntary "star" of this effort, appearing in ever more surreal press conferences, where he supplied news which was in blatant contrast with the reality of the situation. His last appearance, the day of the fall of Baghdad at the Hotel Palestine, the general headquarters of the Western reporters, was worthy of a Woody Allen film or the best Peter Sellers.

Having to admit that the allies have nonchalantly resorted to the *fog of war* was not quite so expected. The amount of news that has been given and then denied or adjusted by Anglo-American spokespeople is, to say the least, embarrassing. For example, on March 20, the first day of the war, it was announced that Iraq had launched some Scud missiles (the UN had forbidden Iraq to own these). Three days later the American General Stanley McCrystal admitted: "No Scud missile was launched." The capture of the port Unn Qasr, near Bassora, was announced several times both on the March 20 and 21; the truth is that violent battles continued until the March 23. On the evening of March 25, Commander Peter Wall announced that a popular revolt was underway against Saddam in Bassora. Denied by Arab TV, the news was repeated the following day by the British spokesperson, who diminished the importance of the revolt and did not acknowledge its "size or aim." On March 26, there was an announcement of an explosion in the market in the Shaab area. It killed at least fourteen civilians and initially the Pentagon claimed that Saddam had concealed nine missiles a hundred or so meters from there. Subsequently the hypothesis is put forward that an Iraqi antiaircraft missile which went out of control may have caused the massacre. On March 20, a new explosion, this time at the market in the Shula area, killed over fifty civilians. American sources, published in the *New York Times*, British sources, from the mouth of the Minister of Defence, Geoff Hoon, and the Foreign Minister, Jack Straw, supported the hypothesis of "friendly fire," so that the massacres were carried out by mistake or out of Iraqi self-interest. On April 2, however, in the square where the second explosion took place, Robert Fisk, correspondent for the daily newspaper the *Independent*, found a piece of shrapnel 30 centimeters long with the series number of a bomb corresponding to an antiradar missile produced in Texas by Raytheon and sold to the U.S. Marines. On March 27, in a dramatic press conference, Tony Blair announced that Iraq had executed two British prisoners.

"If anyone needs further proof of the depravity of Saddam's regime, this atrocity certainly provides it," the British Prime Minister declared. Some days later, the Downing Street spokesperson admitted that there was no "definite proof" that British soldiers had been executed after being captured. The list of "blunders" could go on ad infinitum.

Perhaps the greatest scandal of all as regards transparency of information is the basic lack of discovery of weapons of mass destruction. This dispute involved above all Great Britain and Tony Blair and was fueled by a real settlement of accounts within the British *establishment*. The British secret service leaked the news to the BBC that from the outset, the Communications and Strategy Office in Downing Street had "sexed up" their reports on Saddam Hussein's chemical and bacteriological programs. The problem that is raised is particularly serious, because the question is no longer whether the war was or was not a suitable strategy, but what is left of a democracy when both the Parliament and public opinion have to take a decision, without being certain that the information supplied by the government has not been manipulated. But then again, it should be noted that the "results of the independent enquiry led by Lord Hutton have shown that it was rather the BBC's accusations against Blair's staff that were sexed up and that the government intervention on the secret service's dossier was minimal."[23]

At the beginning of summer 2003 the dispute reached the United States, where it was seized upon by one of the nine claimants to the office of democratic candidate for the Presidential elections of 2004, Senator John Kerry, Vietnam War veteran and George W. Bush's future challenger. For months the predominant opinion was that even if it did emerge that "Bush the younger" had lied on the question of Iraqi arms, the consequences would have been limited by the fact that that question fell in the "realm of foreign policy," where more often as not there were two sides to the truth. In effect, the suspicion that the truth had been manipulated remains serious and this allusion to the *arcana imperii* and to the harsh need for double standards in foreign policy, never explicitly admitted in the United States, does not seem able to be summoned, since with September 11, the same American citizens experimented in first person as to how difficult it is to make a clear distinction between foreign policy and domestic affairs. An attack by international terrorists led to a massacre in New York, the creation of the Department for Internal Security, two international wars, the isolation of the United States in the UN Security council and an unfinished postwar period at a cost of over 2,000 deaths of American troops. If the boundary between outside and inside is indistinct, also the possibility of different evaluations on the sincerity of behavior becomes senseless, even more so in those democratic systems that can only be founded on truth and trust. It is obvious that lying can only be destructive in any relationship of trust, at least for the one that is at the receiving end of the lie. The point probably lies here: in representative political systems, founded on popular sovereignty and legitimized mainly by universal suffrage, the politician who lies *in public* lies also *to the public*.

It must be said that the disclosure of the scandal in Abu Ghraib prison, where violence, humiliation, and torture seem to have been systematically inflicted on the prisoners by American prison officers, sheds a different light, far less sinister, on the relationship between the mass media and military high command. The scandal supplies a sort of alibi for the beginning of kidnappings and the slitting of hostages' throats (mainly civilians, but not only Westerners) which are to pepper postwar Iraq, and the Coalition forces' task is made even more difficult as it almost completely alienates the support of the Iraqi population from the CPA and the interim Iraqi governments which have followed. Testimonies and photos were published by the big American newspapers and they do not make any excuses for those responsible for that veritable "suicide of image" carried out by America. The press requests (without success) the resignation of Donald Rumsfeld. The Arab press have come out of these long months of conflict particularly badly, as might have been imagined: Al Jazeera, whose behavior regarding the continual kidnappings and throat-slitting of foreigners by terrorists and rebels, not only goes so far as to side with these acts, but it is also suspected of lending itself to being an accommodating resonance box, when not a veritable "letterbox" for the murderers' bloody messages. Particularly barbarous was the case involving the British citizen Ken Bigley, beheaded on October 8 after a long humiliating captivity; but all the countries present in Iraq have been hit hard by kidnappings and executions (in Italy Fabrizio Quattrocchi and Enzo Baldoni). Even when faced with episodes that take place far from Iraq, like the attack on the Hilton Hotel in Taba (Egypt) where 35 people died and 120 were injured (for the most part Israeli citizens), Al Arabiya and Al Jazeera spread "without filtering, declarations by spectators that explicitly accuse Israel";[24] they were, moreover, accompanied by Saudi and Egyptian press and television companies, all controlled by their respective governments.

Military victory in Iraq can certainly be considered a turning point for America's role in the world. In order to eliminate Saddam's regime it seems, in fact, that America has decided that military power is worth more than the undisputed hegemony on the West's conscience. The Iraqi campaign shows that American military power is overwhelming, but the legitimacy of the United States' leadership is decidedly in crisis. Which of these two elements will outweigh the other when taking stock of this war, remains to be seen and will depend greatly on the success or failure of the peace process in the Middle East. This was laboriously set up in June 2003 with the famous *road map* which, thanks to the assistance of the "quartet" of the United States, Russia, the UN, and the EU, it was hoped would set out a path toward peace. That path of negotiations becomes even more bogged down in the increasingly violent eruption of the second *intifada*. Yasser Arafat's exit opened a new ray of hope, at least on the Palestinian front, and again the result was tied to an electoral process, as in Afghanistan and Iraq. Abu Mazen's success in the first free presidential elections held in the Palestinian National Authority reinforces the hope for a future resumption of negotiations. On the Israeli front, unfortunately, things seem to move more slowly, in an evolution which is certainly not helped either by the traditional double standards applied by Washington as regards Israel, or by the Bush administration's excessively conciliatory behavior toward the Prime Minister Sharon; the Israeli premier must be acknowledged for his ability and courage to have the occupational troops withdrawn from the Gaza Strip.

So, was the war against Iraq simply a stupid war, dictated by personal grievances, political short-sightedness, and hysterical ideology? Or was it, rather, a war which was badly thought out politically and badly carried out strategically? The Washington strategists' intentions for the Third Gulf War should have been to produce a radical change in the Middle-Eastern scenario. Up until Saddam's regime was eliminated, the Americans could count on a faithful but not easily conditioned ally (Israel) and on a series of client-states which were not particularly reliable but quite easily influenced (Saudi Arabia, Jordan, the Gulf Emirates, and Egypt). Since the end of the war, America has been directly present in the region with an expeditionary force of 160,000 men, which should have permitted them to exercise considerably more significant pressure on the clients, just as on the states under target by the Bush administration (from Syria to Iran). The transfer of American bases outside Saudi Arabia, first to Qatar and then Iraq, would have given the United States an extraordinary strategic platform to exert their influence in an area ranging from Turkey to Egypt, from Lebanon to Iran, from the Arab peninsula to the Republics of ex-Soviet Central Asia. That is, on the whole of the Greater Middle East which, as we have already mentioned, remains the main hotbed of tension and the most unstable quadrant in the whole international political system. Moreover, if the withdrawal of military bases in Arabia, on the one hand permitted the removal of one of the main objects of disputes with the Muslim world, on the other it announced to the governors in Riyadh, that they would no longer be able to count on the unconditioned support of the United States for their fragile throne. And not only that. The presence of a high number of American soldiers in Iraq would even force Israel to pay more attention to the American encouragement toward moderation, both because one of the main threats to the Jewish State had been removed, and because a worsening in the Israeli-Palestinian conflict would risk turning the U.S. military into appetizing targets for pro-Palestinian kamikaze. This is exactly what happened in Iraq.

It is sad to have to say that what actually happened is the exact opposite to what has just been described. Postwar Iraq has proven to be a never-ending nightmare; the coalition troops have seen the basic loss of control of considerable portions of the country, despite having been reinforced by Italian, Polish, Spanish, Danish, Dutch, and other military contingents. The disaster was symbolically announced by the sacking of the archaeological museum in Baghdad, carried out in full view of completely indifferent American troops. Of course, such troops were not sufficient to guarantee any more than their own security and the security of strategic objectives. But the fact remains that that act of vandalism made the future terrorists understand that once the American's war on Saddam's regime was over, a new deadly war could begin for the control of the inheritance. It was precisely the paltriness of the contingents sent, a fact criticized by many commentators during the preparatory phase of the conflict, that made it impossible to mark symbolically and for the best, the transition between before and after the fall of the regime. It is significant that in the days preceding and following the fall of Baghdad, the Iraqi population basically stood by and watched. Then, the situation gradually but inexorably slipped out of control of the coalition troops; they appeared increasingly incapable of guaranteeing law and order and they became more and more often the object of terrorist attacks and popular hostility.

The Iraqi population, already exhausted from years of absurd wars (first with Iran and then Kuwait) from years of economic sanctions and decades of Saddam's reign of terror, diverted all the ill-will it had shown toward Saddam's regime the moment it fell, to the coalition. Above all, for the Sunni population in Baghdad, Saddam Hussein's fall also meant the end to a series of privileges that the regime had assured it, in order to obtain a minimum consensus: from public offices to the tolerably regular supply of light, water, and gas. In the memory nurtured and handed down by generations of Europeans in the post–Second World War period, Paul Bremen's administration could not have been further from the model of the "Allied Military Administration." Even as regards ex-enemies like Germany and Italy, the American military occupation of 1944 and 1945 resulted in a considerable improvement the living conditions. After the bombardments, the invasion troops had brought order to the German cities, but also food and medicine and they had restored a minimum of organized life. None of this happened in Baghdad or in the rest of Iraq for months. On the contrary, the humiliation of military occupation was added to by further degradation in the living conditions and a decline in safety; kamikaze attacks, car bombs, and American retaliatory bomb attacks became the norm. Bremen is not without responsibility for the occupational failure in Iraq: first of all he dissolved the army and the Iraqi security forces; then he tried laboriously to rebuild them; he managed to lose the support of the Shias without knowing how to gain the support of the Sunnis he lured contractors and suppliers prematurely into a trap for security, to then witness their murder or hasty escape.

Is it nevertheless possible to imagine that America wants and can pursue a sort of "domino strategy" in the Middle East? Can we believe that the Bush administration intends to take on the responsibility of the destruction *manu militari* of every threat in that region and intends to democratize with force the Arab world? The question is controversial. To give credit to Condoleeza Rice's explicit statements, we should opt for a negative response. In all her statements and in every public meeting during and after the war, the Advisor for National Security (now Secretary of State) categorically denied that the American strategy is aimed at the search for a "domino effect." On the contrary, Rice and the other members of the administration, including the president himself, talk repeatedly of the "demonstration effect," implying the demonstration that an Arab population "can build democracy." In this light, an outbreak of military action against Syria would only by counterproductive. The Americans, however "expect the countries in the region to play a positive role," so that it is possible to build a new Middle East around an independent, democratic Iraq.[25]

In truth, a hypothesis mooted from many parts is that there is an American strategy, whose aim is to force Syria to withdraw from Lebanon, occupied over twenty years ago and reduced to a real protectorate and that this could lead to a series of important results. On one hand it would limit Syria's importance in the region and it could even cause indirectly the fall of the Syrian dictator Bashar el Assad. A Lebanon outside the sphere of Syrian influence would conquer again the valley of Bekaa (virtually annexed by Damascus) and it would put an end to that veritable "Hezbollah Republic," which rose under Syrian protection. Without the Syrian hinterland, Hezbollah (the warriors of "God's Party," also supported by Iran) would have difficulty being able to continue their control of the Southern highlands on the border of the Jewish State. In this way not only would a further threat against Israel's security be removed (and so an obstacle to any peace process), but Lebanon itself would revert to being a fundamental buffer state between Israel and Syria. Significantly, similar prospects have also been outlined by Joseph Bahout, a Lebanese professor in the prestigious Saint Joseph University in Beirut founded and supervised by Jesuit priests: "The rapid success of the military operation in Iraq put the USA in a position that would be difficult for anyone to oppose; today the disarmament of the Hezbollah in Lebanon depends on the degree of pragmatism of the Syrian leadership. If the Syrians adopt a policy of exchange with Washington, they will find an elegant way of dismantling Hezbollah."[26] In 2005, the mass rallies and the international pressure that followed the assassination of the former Lebanese Prime Minister Rafik Hariri forced Syria to withdraw from Lebanon, even though Hezbollah remains a major actor in Lebanon political life. According to Stephen Zunes, from the University of San Francisco, the United States is deliberately pursuing a strategy of "militarization" in the Middle East, insensitive to the fact that for years it has been "backfiring."[27] The fact is that today, with six of the eighteen Iraqi provinces outside the Coalition's government control, it seems unlikely that the initiative for the Greater Middle East can have a easy future, as still seemed possible in May 2003.

Richard Perle, ex-President for the Defense Council in the Pentagon, considered to be one of the ideologists most heeded by the hawks in the administration, has never hidden his opinion: "I hope that Congress will examine the possibility of examining how many want to free the Syrians from Baathist tyranny," he stated at a conference held mid-April at the *American Enterprise Institute*, one of the most influential neo-conservative think tanks in Washington.[28] A leading exponent during Ronald Reagan's administration, Perle not only had no intention of giving Arab public opinion the impression that they would behave in a more conciliatory manner toward the Palestinians, in order to compensate for what had been done in Iraq, but he also believed that there should be no involvement on the part of the United Nations in Iraq. In his opinion, the new postwar Iraq needed no legitimisation by the United Nations "In any case," continued Perle, "the UN did not free Iraq and many of its members are despotic regimes. Today our European friends, and particularly those who were opposed to our attacking Iraq, insist on a UN role in Iraq because they know that they themselves would not be welcome in Baghdad. I think that we can pardon the future Iraqi government if it does not want to receive Chirac or French companies that will be anxious to be involved in its reconstruction. The same goes for Germany and Russia. They have deeply disappointed us."

The reconstruction of Iraq and the substantial piling up of public commissions guaranteed by the sizeable oil reserves in the country has presented fertile terrain for media and political *complaints* between America and those European countries that were so fervently opposed to the war. They also fueled a moderate amount of polemics within the United States itself, when it was realized that the reconstruction risked taking on rather too much the appearance of a "family affair." The company "Bechtel" is known to be one of the biggest construction companies in the world and already in April 2003, it had won its first tender of 680 million dollars for the reconstruction of schools, hospitals, and other public structures in Iraq, apart from a "minor" contract of 34.6 million dollars for the reconstruction of the drainage, water, and energy networks. On the board of governors of this company sits George Schultz (Secretary of State in Ronald Reagan's day) and also until very recently Caspar Weinberger (Secretary for Defense under the same president). Still in April 2003, Halliburton, a Texan company specializing in drilling, had in its turn won an enormous contract of 7,000 million dollars to get the Iraqi oil wells back into shape again, while its subsidiary, Kellog, Brown & Root had won a tender of 600 million dollars for the renewal of Iraqi wells burned under Saddam Hussein's orders. Even in this case there was perplexity in the fact that Dick Cheney was one of its board members before becoming George Bush's vicepresident.

It is estimated that the reconstruction of Iraq will cost several billion dollars, even if worsened by a sort of "mortgage" of 117 billion dollars for the Iraqui foreign debt. But how much did the Iraq war really cost the United States? In April 2003, reliable assessments by the Organisation for Economic Cooperation and Development (OECD) established a direct cost of about fifty to sixty billion dollars for the United States. This shows that the Third Gulf War has been the least expensive war of all the wars fought by the United States since the rebellion against the British Crown in 1776. The calculation is made compared to GDP in invariable dollars in 2002. However, in

March 2004, an assessment by the weekly newspaper *The Nation* calculated that the cost of the war for the American taxpayers up to that moment had been 155 billion dollars.[29] This figure seems realistic, at least for the expenses sustained until the end of 2004, while it is estimated that the cost for each extra year of occupation in Iraq from 2005 will be 50 billion dollars.[30]

If we set out the cost of the war at the official end of the war on May 1, 2003 in a comparative table produced by the weekly journal *The Economist*[31] we have the statistics as represented in table 2.1.

The war against Saddam cost less that the one in 1990–1991, 80 percent of which was indeed financed by the allied coalition; this time each American taxpayer is to be lumbered with a cost of 220 dollars each. The 60 billion dollars (approximately) that the Iraq conflict cost the United States is a considerable increase in the American Defense budget, rising in 2003 from the 380 billion dollars forecast to over 408 billion. The figure may seem enormous if we consider that it is more or less the same as the GDP of an OCSE country of average size like Australia, but it takes on an entirely different significance if one calculates that it corresponds to 3.9 percent of American GDP.[32] Despite the fact that funds for defense have increased considerably since September 11, and continuing to spend on average far more than most NATO countries (even if not so much more in terms of percentage than France and Great Britain or even Germany) the United States sustains a military expense/GDP ratio among the

Table 2.1   War costs for America

Wars	Direct costs of conflict in billion $ (prices of 2002)	Percentage of GDP at time of war
War of Independence (1775–1783)	2.2	63
Anglo-American War (1812–1815)	1.1	13
Mexican War (1846–1848)	1.6	3
Civil War (1861–1865)	62	104
Hispanic-American War (1898)	9.6	3
First World War (1917–1918)	190.6	24
Second World War (1941–1945)	2,896.3	130
Korean War (1950–1953)	335.9	15
Vietnam War (1964–1972)	494.3	12
Gulf War (1990–1991)	76.1	1
Iraq War (2003)	60	0.5

lowest in its history, much lower than the levels reached during the Korean War, the Vietnam War, or the entire cold war period. The creation of the new Department of Homeland Security up until the spring of 2003 had cost about 36 billion dollars.[33]

The cost of reconstruction in Iraq is a much more uncertain and changeable calculation. According to the World Bank, in an assessment made in April 2004, the bill amounts to at least 9,301 million dollars for 2004 and will amount to 26,518 million dollars for the three-year period 2005–2007: a total of 35,819 million dollars, that will certainly be reviewed and increased. At the *International Donor's Conference for Iraq*, held in Madrid, on October 23–24, 2003, the donor countries had pledged to give a figure oscillating from between 22,782 and 23,232 million dollars in grants and 9,450–12,700 million dollars in loans.[34]

CAN DEMOCRACY BE EXPORTED?

The most delicate question regarding the whole business of the Iraq war, is perhaps the question as to whether it is possible to export democracy with arms and acknowledging this, if such an operation is also legitimate. This delicate point inspired considerable debate in the last weeks of the war involving (also in Italy) some extremely authoritative commentators and intellectuals. Angelo Panebianco has meditated on various occasions on this point, commenting in particular that much depends on the "conditions of the country and the way the occupiers behave."[35] In Panebianco's opinion, the success of different cases such as Germany and Japan, tells us that the "de-Nazification," that is, the dismantling of the regime's hold of the bureaucratic apparatus and the structure of society, is the necessary step so that democratization can have some chance and so, in the case of Iraq a similar process must take place. Panebianco reminded us that the necessity for the occupiers to "force reciprocally hostile groups to make compromises (Kurds, Shias, and Sunnis) and to gain the consensus of the heads of the clans that control the different social segments into which Iraqi society is divided," would make an immediate transition to democracy difficult, because the prerequisites did not yet exist in Iraq. In any case, the author concluded, the imposition of "rules that define—at least on paper—juridical equality between citizens (including women)" and the progressive transition toward a market economy could, in time, ferry Iraq over to democracy. Democracy is difficult to export but "it is a good in itself": born in the West, it is also appreciated by non-Westerners when put in the condition of being able to experiment with it and enjoy the moral and material fruits that are derived from it, as the "democratic reforms that Mac Arthur imposed on Japan prove."

Significantly, Ralph Dahrendorf[36] expanded on similar observations warning, however, of the risks of a radical "clean-up." Starting from the analogy of the German case after the Second World War and East Europe after 1989, Dahrendorf remembered that the "process of de-Nazification" was certainly important, but this case has to reckon with a dimension "that closely regards the memory and the relationship with the past with a particularly practical problem: who will be able to rebuild a country on the ruins of the old regime?" Because it is extremely unusual "for a counter-elite to emerge in a short time, it is even more unlikely that there actually is an elite waiting to substitute the government." Dahrendorf underlined how in the case of post-Nazi Germany and post-Communist Europe, many of the supporters of democracy and opponents of the previous totalitarian regimes feared that the reappearance of ex-Nazis and ex-Communists in democratic clothing holding positions of importance, implied a sort of "restoration" of the old regime. But Dahrendorf then explained how in fact these *aparatchik* "were no longer the same: the people had changed along with their change of circumstance." Indeed, from a certain point of view, "countries like Germany post Second World War or post '89 Poland had gone ahead without paying-undue attention to the past"; they had made the right choice. More than a general radical clean-up of the Iraqi public administration, and even more than a speedy enaction of free elections, the possibility of implanting democracy in Iraq moved toward the "establishment of a rule of law." It is true that "lawfulness, which has a different importance according to culture, presents particular problems in Islamic countries." It is also crucial to make every effort to establish an impartial, incorruptible judicial apparatus. Even though the process of the establishment of a legal state has created great difficulties and has still not been accomplished in most of the countries that have emerged from dictatorial regimes, "even in Iraq this is the key to revival."

The comparison with Japan has been referred to most often in the debate on the democratization of Iraq because of the fact that it was one of the few cases in which an effective democracy was exported by the West through war. Commenting on the concurrent anti-Saddam and anti-American demonstrations that took place in free (or occupied) Iraq, it has been mentioned that "the exportation of democracy is already at work with the Marines who, armed but discrete, assure the crowds that they are free to rail against Saddam and Bush at one and the same time," while "during times of tyranny, dissension was suppressed with the prospect of the gallows and poison gas."[37] On the American strategy for the democratization of Iraq, however, the Shia sheik in Najaf, Mohammad Fartusi argued: "We will have a formal democracy that will permit Iraqis to say whatever they think, without having the right to decide their own destiny." For the moment things have been like that, following the "Japanese model" applied by General Douglas MacArthur after the unconditional surrender of the Empire: basic freedom of speech and minimum freedom of decision-making.

In fact, other Western intellectuals have been far more critical, starting with many Americans like Benjamin Barber who insists that "Democracy can't be exported because rights can't be imported . . . Democracy cannot be gifted to an unwilling people or imported into a culture not ready for it. Democracy's most important virtue is, in fact, patience. Indeed, it is a necessary condition for its development,"[38] adding that forgetting "their own gradualist democratic history, Americans too often not only urge others to do it quick and do it easy. They also urge others to do it à l'Americaine, as if Americanization and democratization were the same thing, as if the United States has proprietary rights in and a political patent on the quintessential democratic process."[39] Instead, the author of *Jihad vs. Mc World* continues: "there are, to be sure, universal ideas that undergird the human struggles for freedom everywhere, but democracy's forms are as various as the struggle through which it is won and as distinctive as the myriad cultures that win it."[40] It seems to be that, at least in the case of Afghanistan, things would seem to say the opposite: that is, that even in a Muslim country, backward and lacking in previous experience, democracy may have a chance even if it arrives on the bayonet of a foreign army. The Afghan elections on October 9, 2004 were a great success: certainly the freest that have ever been held in the country, they recorded a high turnout, noticeable the female participation and despite the reciprocal accusations of election rigging, even the defeated opponents acknowledged Karzai's victory, the ad interim president. As Angelo Panebianco commented, it is true that "to bet on the possibility that democracy will be consolidated in Afghanistan seems highly risky." But without this beginning, which may even seem to be a parody of democracy, we will never give the representative institutions the possibility to last "long enough to instil the idea into the minds of the Afghans that it is good for everyone that the legitimization of power takes place by means of the electoral ballot, rather than by arms and armed militia."[41] Evidently the security situation in

Afghanistan is much better than in Iraq, even if during 2004 over 1,000 people lost their lives in clashes between government forces and rebels. And it is precisely this question of Damocles' sword that encumbered the Iraqi elections, with vast areas of the country, in which it could be impossible for people to exert their voting right; the risk of mass desertion of the ballot box on the part of the Sunni population was overcome just in December elections.

Before facing the question of future scenarios of democracy in Iraq, this premise is necessary: nothing prevents the exportation of democracy *manu militari*.[42] If we were not so often afflicted by timely bouts of amnesia, we should remember that the exact same thing happened to Italy; Italy found the motivation and the determination to move into the realm of democracy only under the pressure of the Anglo-American bombardments and the defeat of war. As long as the Fascist regime did not face defeat, Italians fought like good Fascists for the aims laid down by Mussolini, without being too scandalized either by the racial laws which all of a sudden had transformed the "Jews" into noncitizens in their own country, or by the fact that up to that moment they had fought as allies for Hitler's Germany. Frankly speaking, they were on the wrong side and against democracy. Until the allied bombing on Italian cities, the disastrous campaigns in Africa and Russia and the invasion of the motherland led to the fall of the regime, anti-Fascism was a limited phenomenon of the elite with marginal political publicity. As stated by Ernesto Galli della Loggia,[43] it is the development of the fortunes of war, "the death of the Homeland," after September 8, 1943 that transforms that movement into a political-military phenomenon and that makes the "Resistance" assume almost epic importance, resulting in Italians losing the awareness that their democratization took place on the strength of a war that was disastrously lost.

Going further back in time, it can be argued that even when "imported democracies" have a hard and short life, at times the values brought about by democratization survive and are even subsequently transformed into values which are more authentically "national." Even if the Jacobin Republics and the Napoleon kingdoms (exported with French bayonets after 1789) did not go further than the Congress of Vienna, the values of liberty, secularization of the state, and the people's sovereignty became fact in the liberal and national changes of the seventeenth century. The positive effects of living under a democratic regime are so obvious and deep as to permit the claim that cultural relativism must succumb to the universal value of human dignity. Even without going so far as to say that the mere fact of exporting democracy legitimizes a war, it must be acknowledged that the prospect and will to democratize ones ex-enemy, makes the difference between war and war, since in this way the conquered enemy (by definition "different from us") is made "one of us."

One can certainly sympathize with the criticisms aired by more than one analyst on the objective difficulty in winning the formidable challenge of democratizing Iraq. The task is extremely ambitious, because it deals with bringing democracy, human rights, modernization, secularization, and general equality all at once: the Arab world and more generally the Islamic world seems to be rather late in acquiring all this. "Western civilization has left behind its religious belief and its sacred text, to place its trust not in religious certainties but in open discussion, trial and error, and the ubiquitousness of doubt. But the odd thing is that, while Islamic civilization is riven by conflict, Western civilization seems to have a built-in tendency to equilibrium. Freedoms that Western citizens take for granted are all but unheard of in Islamic countries, and while no Western citizens are fleeing from the West, 70 percent of the world's refugees are Muslims fleeing from places where their religion is the official doctrine."[44]

There is another crucial point that is so relevant as to transcend the current Iraqi crisis. It seems to me that it could add something to the large mass of ideas on the topic of the exportability of democracy. It is this. If we take as a starting point the German and Japanese experiences and we ask what they have in common, what the key to success was in the process of democratization, I think we can more or less say this: the annihilation of ideological sources of the overthrown regime and the contemporary nonexistence of previous alternative ideological sources. In Germany, the fall of the regime's institutions was inextricably linked with Nazi ideology. In Japan, the surrender to MacArthur also marked the end of the divine cult of the emperor. Precisely the totalitarian nature of the two ideologies—Nazism and the divine nature of the Mikado—different from many points of view but exactly the same as regards the effects they had on their respective societies, had created the prerequisites so that once they had fallen, nothing else could hinder the work of the democratizing forces that had come from outside. Added to the destruction of the bombs and physical landscape was the destruction of the moral and political panorama. It was this latter desolation that defeated the population, made them ready to acknowledge their own failure, without being under the illusion that they would find opportunities in the dregs of other ideologies to get revenge. In short, it would seem that we can claim that the destruction of the ideological sources of anti-democracy was so important as to permit the democratic regime to take root well and swiftly, despite the fact that because of the prevailing of different logic tied to the beginning of the cold war, the process of de-Nazification was incomplete and superficial.

It seems that at times the true characteristics of Baathism have been overestimated and its capacity to shape Iraqi society right to its last breath, when it is presumed that the nearly thirty-year-old regime created a sort of ideological desert. First and foremost, Baathism is nothing but a historical variety of that Arab nationalism that was for so long the regime's flag: so the death of Baathism does not mark the death of nationalistic Arab ideology. Second, in the long decades in which Saddam Hussein lorded it in Iraq, he progressively turned the regime into a terrible personal dictatorship: illegal, barbarous and as arbitrary as you like, but for all of this it was unable to become the real "political religion" of Iraq (as happened in Nazi Germany and Japan in the 1930s). In this climate, a new reserve ideology—even more hostile to the West and its values than Baathism—already existed. It is of transnational nature, has prosperous bases of external financing and created more followers within the country, as the increasingly struggling regime was forced to be a makeshift interpreter. It is Islamic fundamentalism. This war has obtained vital sap from it; it makes followers at every burnt oil pipeline, every allied soldier killed, and every suicide attack, reminding us implicitly, as happened in the attacks in Casablanca in May 2003, that in fact what is really unleashed by fundamentalism is firstly an internal civil war on the Islamic world in which we find ourselves embroiled despite ourselves.[45] As Ian Buruma and Avishai Margalit conclude in their fine book: "Although Christian fundamentalists speak of a crusade, the West is not at war against Islam," which must be won first of all by Muslims themselves. It is true that there is "a worldwide clash going on, but the fault lines do not coincide with national, ethnic, or religious borders. The war of ideas is in some respect the same as the one that was fought several generations ago against various forms of fascism and state socialism."[46]

The specific case of Iraq must then be set in the wider picture of the relationship between democracy and the Islamic world. Ali Ahmad Said Esber expresses touchingly the uneasiness felt by some, above all among Arabs, who could not accept that the liberation from their domestic tyranny had been by the hands of a Western invasion: "We should be ashamed to see smiling Anglo-American soldiers wandering around the roads in Baghdad and Bassora claiming to be liberators. We should be ashamed to see Iraqis begging for a piece of bread and some water, as if they had never before seen them—they who were born in the country of bread and water. We should be ashamed of the sacking and robberies carried out by some Iraqis driven by need and greed. All of us Arabs should be ashamed of what has happened and what is happening in Iraq. We should apologize to the great Arab language from which we are called: Arabs. But is not Saddam Hussein the first one responsible for what happened and is happening in Iraq? Instead of dedicating his life to the people, he stripped life from the people and purloined all the wealth of the country, as if it was his own and his family's property."[47]

But what is the weight of moderate Muslim reform in the Arab world? Is there hope that Islamic renewal can mean a critical rereading of the Koran, so as to permit the stimulus of modernity to influence both popular culture and also the culture of the political and social elite? It is clear that as long as democracy does not take off within Iraq and in the countries in the region, the spread of Islamic democracy would seem problematic, to say the least. Paolo Branca reflects on the fact that the return to a mythical Muslim society, where the Koran is presented as a kind of panacea for the ills of society and the individual, is a recurring and illusory temptation. It is a real myth, according to which from the sacred texts it should be possible to infer a *corpus* of rules which are always valid and suitable for every situation, a kind of panacea for any illness.[48] On the contrary, the illness is precisely not wishing to compete with the present in all its complexity, thinking that if things are not going well it is always the enemy's fault: the West, the Americans or the "Zionists."

Modernization seems to be the sorest point for the Islamic world; up until now it is only in Muslim not Arab realities that modernization has taken root, like Kemal Ataturk's Turkey or the city-state of Singapore or the distant, exotic Sultanate of Brunei. They have taken different paths, sharing both a certain degree of authoritarianism and a more or less radical disassociation from excessive encroachment of religion in politics and institutions. Transformation to these states was certainly not easy; its success in these countries seems tied to the limited size, great wealth or strong national personality. They have, nevertheless, taken root outside the Arab world, that is, the cradle of Islamism. Then again, it must be acknowledged that breakthroughs toward democracy have been made in Morocco and Jordan and that civil rights are essentially protected in Bahrein and Dubai; even Iran—where the clash between civil society and theocratic power is becoming increasingly acrimonious—knows something of basically clean competitive elections, to the extent that all the conservatives can do is to thwart the effect a posteriori, because they cannot infect the process.

The personal question of those responsible for Al Qaeda (Osama bin Laden and his mentor and right-hand man Ayman al-Zawahiri) allows us to highlight two fundamental reasons for the development of modern international Islamic terrorism: the importance of the unresolved Palestinian question and the experience of the Afghan civil war in the Nineties. "The Afghan Jihad against Soviet occupation marked a turning point as Muslims in record numbers travelled to Afghanistan to join in the jihad against the oppression of Muslims. The experience and success of that jihad created a new, more global jihad sentiment and culture embodied in Arab Afghans—Arabs and other Muslims who had fought in Afghanistan—and in a sense of solidarity, which subsequently brought Muslims from various parts of the world to participate in jihads in Bosnia, Kosovo, Kashmir, Central Asia and Chechnya."[49] In discussing the reasons for the difficult relationship between Islam and democracy, John Esposito starts by recognizing the basic failure of the process of de-colonization in the Muslim world, where almost all the countries are fragile, recently independent, and with borders marked arbitrarily by ex-colonial Western powers (in some cases following long Ottoman domination). In particular Esposito presents three types: the declared Islamic state, like Saudi Arabia, the secularized state, like Turkey and the Muslim state, that is, the majority, created on the model of the modern Western state and superficially grafted with Islamic requisites in the Constitution, like the requirement for the head of state to be Muslim or acknowledging the *Sahara* as "a" source of law. All these forms have proven incapable of managing politics satisfactorily and have ended up favoring the spread of Islamic radicalism, which has virulently taken root where it was repressed most forcibly. In Egypt, Algeria, Saudi Arabia, and Palestine strong movements like the Islamic Jihad, the AIG (Armed Islamic Groups), the Salafihites (or Wahhabites) particularly active in central Asia and the Caucasus, and the Hamas have been greatly strengthened. Esposito pointed out how the road to secularization, undertaken with great enthusiasm by the elite Arab reformists and revolutionaries in the 1950s and 1960s, has proven to be an almost complete failure, precisely because it coincided with a modernization of Western nature incapable of taking deep root in Muslim societies. "Few questioned the accepted wisdom that modernization meant the progressive westernization and secularization of society . . . It seemed reasonable to expect that every day in every way westernization and secularization were making things better and better."[50] In reality, secularization managed simply to divest the masses and the middle classes in Muslim countries of a "traditional" identity without being able to replace it with anything else. Probably, it is the "identity" nature of these crises generated also by the terrible political and economic performances following independence or the socialist revolution that makes it so difficult to deal with the Islamic problem. And the fact that "religions go to war when they become the sacred language of collective identity, of a people or a human group that feels its own physical and moral survival is threatened," makes it even more essential to find an effective path to secularization so as to avoid a repetition on an even greater scale of the vicious circle already at work at the end of the twentieth century in the Balkans, in "civilised" Europe, in which "religions disguise the conflict, even if perhaps they embrace the reasons later, when the spirit of war blows."[51]

Today, the Iraqi campaign, with the inglorious fall of the *rais'* regime and his even more inglorious capture (hidden in a hole dug in the ground), seems to have produced a sense of frustration in the Muslim world similar to that caused by the humiliating devastation suffered by the Arab armies in the Six-Day War in 1967. The widespread support for guerrilla warfare and terrorism that has been causing bloodshed in Iraq since July 2003, seems to be the best the way to reconquer; it is very similar to what happened in 1973 with the Yom Kippur War. The net result is that society has increased its own paranoia of hostile encircling, and in increasing sections of its "bourgeois" stratifications, it proclaims itself open to the enchantment of who wants to carry out a "defensive" *jihad* for the Muslim world in its entirety, attacking opposing societies and terrorizing the enemy. Almost all the hijackers on September 11 came from the bourgeois elite in Egypt and Saudi Arabia, anxious to avenge with violence two humiliating conditions: that of Muslims ostracized by "crusades and Zionists" and that of the emerging Arab bourgeois class, frustrated by their own political rights in corrupt authoritarian systems. Contrary to what many believed in the 1990s that the *jihad* would die out,[52] the "powerful symbolism and revolutionary meaning of jihad dominates modern Muslim politics to an extent unparalleled in history. Islamic movements and organizations have become primary vehicles for its spread and implementation. If many thought that Iran's revolution was a single event, successive decades have demonstrated the force and pervasiveness of an Islamic activism that has moved from the periphery to the center of Muslim societies."[53]

The dilemma of modernization and democratization can certainly not be reduced to the mere acceptance or the simple spurning of models outside the Arab-Muslim culture. It should be resolved through critical and creative reinterpretation of the tradition, on the one hand, and with the capacity to make the values of liberty their own on the other. The problem is intensified and dramatic choices are made, when, in order to create the prerequisites for liberty, it is necessary to experience a lost war. Said Esber made this observation: "Bloodstained Iraq can only be understood if we consider both its 'internal' and its 'external' wounds. Liberty is the necessary requirement for the fight against external aggression. Saddam Hussein eliminated liberty. And along with that he eliminated the nation itself, substituting it with the regime. Iraqi culture was nullified and the culture of the 'enlightened leader' was erected. A country that receives the 'gift' of dictatorship and single party policy is nothing less than a prison."[54]

Perhaps it is a lost cause democratizing the Arab-Islamic world; and yet it is precisely the lack of liberty—"Freedom of the mind from constraint and indoctrination, to question and inquire and speak; freedom of the economy from corrupt and pervasive mismanagement; freedom of women from male oppression; freedom of citizens from tyranny"[55]—that is the most obvious cause of the backwardness that this world is atoning for today in all fields. The first step necessary for Muslims themselves to manage to "escape from a downward spiral of hate and spite, rage and self-pity, poverty and oppression" is to put an end to falsely superior attitudes toward "Western responsibility" for the current pitiful state in which the Arab world wallows. As Bernard Lewis concludes, only if "they can abandon grievance and victimhood, settle their differences, and join their talents, energies, and resources in a common creative endeavor, then they can once again make the Middle East, in modern times as it was in antiquity and in the Middle Ages, a major center of civilization. For the time being, the choice is their own."[56]

In political terms the Jury is still out on the question as to whether it is possible and proper to export democracy with arms, and whether it might take root in the Middle East. What is certain is that the "aggressive democracy promotion in the Arab world is a new article of faith among neo-conservatives inside and outside the (Bush) administration."[57] And there again there can be no doubt, as Robert Kagan commented uniting for once the two sides of the Atlantic, that "one of America's and Europe's most serious mistakes in the Middle East has been to favour realism over the promotion of democratic values, when in fact, the socially retrograde, politically repressive, and economically regressive post-Ottoman order is a major cause of international insecurity."[58]

But what does it mean exactly to encourage a transition to democracy in the Islamic world? Can the requirements for the development of democracy in Islamic society and culture be the same as those that characterized democracy in the West, starting from secularization? Within the history of the West secularization was undoubtedly the central junction, through which the internal pacification of political systems passed, along with the reduction in levels of violence in the European political system. Significantly, the origin of the international political system is traced back to the Peace of Westphalia in 1648, which put an end to the Thirty Years' War. This peace ends the last bloody conflict for power carried out in the name (or by the tool) of religious agreement. Since then, the process of secularization, the progressive segregation of religion and its hierarchies in the world of politics has reached a point of no return. Just as unity can no longer be threatened in the name of religious diversity within the political community, so between different political communities religious *cleavage* can no longer be held fast as a "legitimate reason" for reciprocal hostility. The assertion of the state had to pass through secularization. Full state sovereignty could not tolerate others demanding to limit its legitimacy, not even in the name of transcendent forms of authority. Metaphorically, for a new God to live, another had to die. I believe there cannot be much doubt about the fact that the seventeenth century state is the closest one can imagine, in terms of claims much more than performance of course, to an absolute and almost "secularly religious" form of power.

This is the historical experience of the West that links inextricably secularization, modernization, and state. Having had the capacity to build this incredible artifice of the modern sovereign state has given the West the extraordinary advantage, which is the root of its success, being rowdy and even violent in its contact with the other forms of political organization. Since the seventeenth century the West has been on an expansionist march through the world, literally annihilating the other political forms it has come across. This date marks an inverse trend in the relationship with the Muslim world. If, up until then, the Turkish Empire, that is, the most successful political reality, is still continuing its territorial expansion and still represents an incredible threat, from the end of the seventeenth century onward, it begins its progressive retreat from the heart of Europe. The defeat of the Turkish armies that attacked Vienna on September 11, 1697 marked a turning point that only ended with the destruction of the Ottoman Empire over 200 years later.

In the Western experience, secularization is not only a phenomenon that permits the assertion of the state and modernization. It is also the obvious requirement for the development of two other formidable political categories, which first of all challenged the state until it was thoroughly transformed, making it even more solid in the long term: the nation and democracy. Even though all three of these concepts—state, nation, and democracy—have fascinated, in different eras, practically all the elite Muslim reformers, it is difficult not to agree on the failure of reception in the Islamic world. If the main justification for secularization lies in considering it the obligatory tool (and the passage) for the development of the democratic state, in the eyes of the Muslim world the sacrifice may not be worth the objective. Unfortunately, secular states, nations, and democracies have been experimented with in various ways, albeit unsuccessfully, by those societies, and they have proven such a failure as to appear extremely unattractive, if the price demanded is the clear division between politics and religion. Even more so if religion remains (or returns to being) the main tool with which to help the Muslims come out of their identity crisis, it is unrealistic to imagine that secularization may have a *chance* for success, or indeed that it may even be proposable, perhaps without going so far as to believe that the only way to defeat armed fundamentalism is to "restore the normal conditions of the religious market," allowing the "fundamentalism but non-violent and the conservative traditions to enter into competition with ultra-fundamentalism."[59] In truth, looking at the relationship between secularization and democracy with greater relativism allows us to search for a kind of "Islamic" route toward democracy; it seems that finding this is more crucial than ever before. Finding the "South-East passage" of democracy is a task for which we must be equipped without haughtiness and we must be convinced that we are acting for the common good. The only alternative to exporting democracy, even more so if achieved through war, is to elaborate new forms of democratic experience that know how to take advantage of the characteristics of Muslim societies, rather that try to contrast or negate them through "Westernization."

It is certainly true that the global resurrection of religion has been particularly obvious in international politics. Religion, nationalism, and ethnic differences have proven to be long-lasting sources of identity and conflict from Somalia and Rwanda to Lebanon, Bosnia, Kosovo, Kashmir, India, and Sri Lanka. But the events of recent decades should lead us to consider that perhaps in the West we have left "for dead" rather too soon and too definitively the importance of the political struggle. If we want to continue to be able to confront and shape a political stance that is not simply numbed by Western historical experience, we should have the courage to consider that the "post-modernity" of politics is perhaps more an intellectual temptation than a universal reality. Today, an Islamic world that fears it cannot preserve its own identity because it lacks the resources of power on a global scale, wonders, distressed, whether "being modern means that our only option is to talk, dress and think like them?" By recognizing the legitimacy of these worries, we Westerners should perhaps stop questioning ourselves as to whether Islam is compatible with Western civilization, ignoring past and present exchange and continual inter-cultural fertilization. Whether we are aware or not, posing such a question implies having already chosen not a mere Western civilization *for us* (by means of a perfectly legitimate operation), but having arbitrarily an abstract idea of Western civilization as a universal norm. And not only that. A similar claim is based above all on the false idea that civilizations are mutually exclusive and opposed, while in reality civilizations and cultures overlap; they have similarities and differences. Whoever excludes the compatibility between democracy and Islam, even if the form has yet to be discovered, commits first and foremost an error of historic perspective. It is an error that I believe would not be so very different from the one that might have been made by someone observing the map of Europe in 1815, who came to the conclusion, maybe even with ill-concealed satisfaction, that liberty could not take root in continental Europe. What came to pass in Europe was seen in the incredible years following 1989. No matter how much more difficult the conditions or no matter how much longer it may take, there is nothing in Islam to hinder the development of democracy.

As regards Bush's America and its international position, there is no doubt that particularly within the left wing, there is a feeling of veritable "horror" at the prospect that a "new Black Era is descending on the human race," or rather the era of "Armed democracy."[60] It seems to be taboo to even consider the exportability of democracy in left-wing culture. This is particularly surprising for those who remember the traditional internationalism of the left: from the Jacobins to Mazzini, from the socialists to the anarchic-revolutionaries, from Rosa Luxemburg to the international brigades during the Spanish Civil War. "Once upon a time, the more radical was the left, the more internationalist it was, too. Today it wants everyone to stay at home. And the reason is that democracy, the rule of law, individual liberty and the market are all things that are 'made in America'. Exportation. Enculturation. Oppression. The Americans are the Jesuits of the Third Millennium. Culture and local traditions need to be protected from change. Often it is violent, it provokes wars, anarchy and perhaps terrorism." Among many left-wing commentators in Europe, a completely opposing attitude seems to prevail compared to the old socialist internationalism. It seems that they have wanted to favor an obsession for order, a typically conservative prerogative, so in tune with a Europe that becomes "older" (but really, not just like Rumsfeld's polemics). This makes Antonio Polito's reprimand even more caustic, when picking up on an article in the *Financial Times*, he ends his comments on the end of liberal-democratic internationalism, like this: " 'there is a dangerously thin line between realpolitik and the horrible cynicism of those that say that the oppressed world must stay oppressed to safeguard something that is called strategic stability'. The day after September 11, Tony Blair elicited loud applause at a congress of militant labour members when he claimed: 'the kaleidoscope of the world has been hit; let's make sure we rectify some injustice before the pieces move back into place'. In this sense we cannot say we are not Blairistes."[61]

"No Ifs and Buts: The Return to Pacifism"

Less than two years after the attacks on September 11, the enormous amount of sympathy and the extraordinary solidarity that they had aroused for the United States seemed to disappear completely; perhaps this happened because, as many believe throughout the period of time since September 11, "Bush has not fully articulated a vision of post-war international order, aside from defining the struggle as one between freedom and evil [. . .] This failure explains why the sympathy and goodwill generated around the world for the United States after September 11th quickly disappeared."[62] Denying what many had predicted that September 11 would mark the decline of the long "unipolar moment" and the return of America toward a more collegial role as regards its leadership,[63] Washington decided to force the pace in the direction of an ever more assertive and unilateral leadership as regards its own international politics. The war in Iraq, that led to the swift fall of Saddam Hussein and his regime made the world a decidedly better place. But it also made the whole construction of international institutions creak and parted the doors to an infinite front for Islamic terrorism.

The military success that ended the war against Saddam Hussein's regime cannot stop us from considering the conditions in which it started—disastrous—nor can we hide the recurring problem of our incapacity to deal with non-Western worlds. The Third Gulf War started under the worst auspices. It was the most "announced" of all the wars, because the Americans did not make any mystery of the fact that it was only a question of "when" and not "if" before the offensive against the raìs in Baghdad would start. In a book at one and the same time the "manifesto" for the reasons for the war and its legitimate preventive nature, Kenneth Pollack wrote: "We are at an important moment in the history of the United States. We know that we face a grave problem with Saddam Hussein, and we have good evidence that it is going to be a much bigger problem in the future than it is today. We can ignore the problem and hope it will just go away, or we can take the steps needed to solve it."[64] In the long preparatory phase, the war attracted the opposition of an increasing proportion of public opinion (above all in Europe) that did not believe it justifiable that the United States decided for a unilateral war against Iraq. Pacifistic demonstrations followed one after the other all over the place taking on increasingly anti-American tones, outside the United States. Popularity for the United States reached extremely low levels, struggling to rise even after the war was over when, on the wings of a swift victory and at relatively little expense, support for the United States remained low. The worsening of the situation in the long "post-war" period only re-launched the hostile movement against "Bush's America." It was a somewhat widespread situation that involved French and German public opinion (the two countries that challenged Washington in the Security Council), but even Italian, Spanish, and British public opinion were also involved (that is, countries which do eventually side with America). In the House of Commons, 122 Labour members, 30 percent of the parliamentary group, abstained from voting for the motion presented by the Prime Minister, which committed Great Britain to standing alongside the United States in the war against Saddam Hussein. The *speaker* in the House of Commons (a government nomination) and ex–Foreign minister Robin Cook resigned from office to stress their disagreement with Tony Blair and gave harsh interviews at the end of the war.

Tony Blair's solitude was particularly important because it exemplified how difficult it is to make it understood how a choice can be arrived at which is ethically aware and responsible but favors a fight to capitulation. In an interview given to the *Guardian*, and published on March 2 also in the *Corriere della Sera* the British Prime Minister repeated what was to become the *refrain* for all his declarations during the months of the Iraqi crisis: "in a situation such as this, you have to do what you believe to be right because that is the price of having responsibility."[65] Tony Blair's position was particularly important just because it was laden with a strong moral sense, that idea of the spirit of service that brought him to make precise declarations without frills, and yet decisive "I've never claimed to have a monopoly of wisdom, but one thing I've learned in this job is you should always try to do the right thing, not the easy thing. Let the day-to-day judgments come and go—be prepared to be judged by history." And again: "A majority of decent and well-meaning people said there was no need to confront Hitler and that those who did were war-mongers. When people decided not to confront fascism, they were doing the popular thing, they were doing it for good reasons, and they were good people . . . but they made the wrong decision." It is no surprise that because of the strong ethical tension that emerges from declarations like these, the British Prime Minister became the object of severe criticism particularly from the pacifist left on the Continent; it seemed to them that the right moment had at last arrived to settle old scores with that "strange labour," to be able to avenge the Jospins and Lafontaines and finally dissociate themselves from a "too highly" reformed socialism.

The question of the judgment of history continually gave rise to heated debate (before during and after the conflict) between the two fronts; "no to the war with no ifs and buts" (generally the majority) and "war as a last resort" (decisively in the minority). Debate has often been acrimonious in which some—be they "pacifists" or "warmongers"—have distinguished themselves through their desire to brandish their arguments as if they were blunt weapons to fling at their opponents' reasoning. As usual the privates have been angrier and more vehement than their generals. It is another war, involving the media and verbal aggression, but nonetheless a war with no holds barred, in which not even the Pope's sorrowful words of worry and pain are heeded. Instead they are used carelessly by one choir or the other. Meanwhile, other prelates, finding themselves under the spell of the marching crowds, throw out improbable anathemas, risking in this way confusing the lucid nature of the Papal position. The editor of *Avvenire*, the authoritative daily newspaper of the Italian Bishop's Conference, commented on Easter Day 2003: "Shouts of indignation have gone up in recent weeks in the squares and in newspaper columns. Many are genuine, others perhaps less so. Populism and coquettishness hidden behind moving spontaneity. Clever old foxes and quibbling shrinking violets. Untiring people who imagine ulterior motives behind events and serial idealists."[66] And yet, the Vatican's position, whether we like it or not, is lucid. It is founded on the idea that if a "new world order" is to last, it cannot be accomplished with war as a starting point and by resorting to the use of force. It is exactly the same point of view expressed on the occasion of a "legal and legitimate" war in juridical and political terms like that in 1990–1991. Then the Polish Pope warned that the epoch-making success of the defeat of Communism (and the end of the last great ideological division within Christianity) deserved more than the new order being constructed with recourse to arms (even if at that time they were used impeccably). Added to the desolation at a weakening in the international institutions, apart from the defense of the value of life, was the worry that the clash of religions (the Vatican's fear of all fears) might emerge. And we must acknowledge this: the fact that the Pope pronounced himself so desperately against the war has made it much more difficult for those who wanted to present the war as a Western conflict against the Islamic world. And not only this. With the worsening of the situation in Iraq, the warning from the Catholic church—forcefully emphasized by cardinal Camillo Ruini, the Pope's substitute and president of the Italian Bishop's Conference—rises up against any hypothesis of a withdrawal of the allied troops, because it would mean abandoning the Iraqi people to the hands of the terrorists and fundamentalists. It would result in an isolated Iraq, cut off from the international community for the third time in a row: first the sanctions from the UN, then the Anglo-American war and finally because of the terrorists. Even in this case the Vatican's position is tough but consistent: any form of isolation of Iraq would be a tragic error. But there again, on the occasion of the first anniversary of the war on March 19, 2004, in an article that the *Osservatore Romano* (the Holy See's daily newspaper) dedicated to the project for the "Greater Middle East," one reads that a "long term project and of such enormous bearing regarding such a vast area, thick with internal conflicts and full of resentment of all kinds towards the Western world, needs to be assessed extremely carefully . . . At the same time, the real and serious Israeli-Palestinian conflict must not be allowed to be used as an alibi to hinder any progress towards personal liberty, recognition of political rights, female emancipation and universal suffrage."[67] These are words that certainly cannot please the absolute one-way pacifists of left-wing Europe; but one year after the beginning of the war, the Holy Father was no longer their favorite icon.

Millions of people, men and women of all ages and mainly European, marched up and down the streets and squares of the main European capitals against "Bush's infinite war." At their side, ideally but sometimes even physically, they had marching companions who were by and large predictable, from the Pope to Anglican bishops and from trade union leaders to aspiring anti-globalization leaders. Alongside these first almost paradigmatic supporters of "no to the war," others found themselves in the most unlikely guise of pacifist. Our first thought is for Schroeder, chancellor of the new *Berlin Republik*, who had sent German soldiers to fight alongside the Americans in Afghanistan against bin Laden and his followers. What can be said of Putin, and the war in Chechnya, of the thousands and thousands of dead, killed to bring order to Grozny, which was reduced to a heap of smoking rubble and the dozens of civilians gassed in a theater in Moscow, collateral victims of the fight against terror in true Muscovite fashion. And lastly, there is Chirac, who, while he sends thousands of legionnaires to fight in Chad, the Ivory Coast, and Central Africa to support a tyrant friend against an enemy tyrant, he discovers he is a pacifist and the standard-bearer for international legality. The incredible thing is that this is the same Chirac of the French nuclear experiments in Mururoa, carried out in contempt of all the international treaties, world public opinion and even common sense (quite apart from being ridiculous), to verify and update the efficiency of a *force de frappe*, that seemed able to caress the *grandeur* of the Elysée Palace rather than frighten potential enemies of France.

In Italy intellectuals, cinema *starlettes*, and directors, celebrated comedians, *maitre à penser* of television talk shows and anchormen and women from junk programs on a Sunday afternoon, aspiring and outgoing mayors, "no-global activists" and "spokespeople of the Movement" constantly on the job, were united against "Bush's War," forgetting their own pasts which were not perhaps so impeccable. All of them, without exception, followed and fueled the shared popular movement of horror toward the war, without in the slightest wondering (or asking) "if not war, how?" How can we put an end to a dictatorship that in thirty years caused a million deaths only among Iraqi citizens, resorting to systematic extermination of its opponents, minority ethnic groups and whoever was even slightly suspected of not being a loyal servant of the regime? How could a dictator be removed from power that provoked an aggressive war against his neighboring Iran for almost ten years, who invaded peaceful Kuwait provoking a reaction from the world, in the form of a coalition that included over 50 countries headed by George Bush's United States? How can a man be trusted, who while claiming not to have weapons of mass destruction, had shown evidence of having no scruples about using them against external enemies (during the war with Iran) and internal (the Kurds in the North)? In Italy, the slogan "no to the war, with no ifs and buts," was also the unseemly weapon used for the umpteenth feud within the Ulivo[68] and around it, with which left-wing political factions and fractions, minorities in the party congress and programmed assemblies, continued their private little war to over-turn unwelcome results, trying to fuel their own ideological maximal-ism (and sometimes their own personal power) with the intoxication of immense rallies, of the marching people. Newscasts always on the point of describing the end of the world for the umpteenth time, the next clash of civilizations, and the "hapless destiny" of the Berlusconi government, invariably painted as an "unpresentable government" on an international level, witnessed, astonished, the fall of Baghdad, as they had already done with the fall of Kabul, the conquest of Pristine, the capitulation of Belgrade, and the liberation of Sarajevo. Just before the outbreak of war, but when it is sure to happen, a sophisti-cated intellectual like Alberto Asor Rosa, goes so far as to write: "To put it briefly, I believe that whoever among Westerners did not feel 'ashamed' at least once by the Gulf War, might steal from his neigh-bour, or most probably has already done so." (It should be noted that Asor Rosa is referring to the 1990–1991 war.) In a devastating article, considering his own past as a militant communist and editor of *Rinascita*, the historical Italian Communist Party's cultural magazine, he railed against "the damned idea of 'progress' that produces this mental deformation of the masses, so that what goes 'forward', is better than what 'remains behind'."[69]

In an excellent but bitter article published in the *Corriere* in Spring 2003, Francesco Merlo observed that from February 25 to April 25 there were no less than 24 "important" marches in Italy: "one every three days, as in Arab countries and Latin America, far more than in France, which is also a country where the people congregate in the squares in demonstration, and without parallel to the other advanced countries, civilizations of individuals and thought. To demonstrate once every three days is a job, albeit exerted for noble reasons from peace to justice to health. They are the themes that cap-tivate the soul, but where the misery of real politics is to be seen."[70] Merlo went on to say how "the greater the number of demonstrations the longer the holiday of thought," and he wondered why in Italy "instead of producing thoughts we produce demonstrations, which are not even a shortcut to thought," and if perhaps this happened because people wish to escape from the "usual struggles" of "think-ing," that is, "we run to the squares to avoid thinking." And yet, the question of how to do it if not with war should have been approached by a movement that knew how to give concrete, realistic answers and point out an alternative solution to the conflict. But to do that it would be necessary to have at least one prerequisite: the renunciation of an anarchist and irrational support of grass roots initiatives that regards "pragmatism" as a sin of lese politics.

"Yesterday's summit confirmed the negative drifting of the Union, a 'pragmatic calling' . . . After the war against Iraq, in the middle of a permanent war, the objective to collocate the simple principle of the 'rejection of war' within this Constitution, just as it is incorporated in the Italian Constitution, is indeed not only the way to give continuity to the organisation, but, in the attempt to draw a profile of another Europe and therefore another politics, it is also the occasion to achieve a result."[71] Reading this article in *Liberazione* on the European summit in Athens in April 2003, we can only be perplexed about the fact that a similar result might even be on the horizon. But then again, the day before had been defined in another leading article in the same newspaper as "a rotten day," "a black day" . . . for the left and peace. That day had produced a hard-won "yes" from the Ulivo in the parliamentary vote on the sending of Italian troops to Iraq to help keep peace (a real, possible, and concrete peace "after Saddam"). It was a black day barely made brighter by the "resistance of the only possible nucleus of an alternative left-wing, acting as the representative of that vast mass of 'peace people' who, despite everything, are not yet surrendering."[72] It is not surprising that *Il Manifesto* has the same tone on that vote; it scornfully dismisses the troubled internal debate between the Democratici di Sinistra (DS) and the Ulivo: "In order to jump on the winners' bandwagon, the majority of the Ulivo did not limit itself to descending quickly from the wagon of social opposition to the war by throwing down the rainbow flag to raise the tricolor, only three days after shouting with the peace movement that no help, no soldier would leave Italy with the consensus of the opposition, unless endorsed by the UN, or at least the EU. The majority of the Ulivo did not limit itself to descending from the movement's wagon—which had gained the consensus and the sympathy of the majority of public opinion—it risks making it derail by putting a spoke in its wheels."[73] Frankly, it seems difficult to imagine that a culture that is authentically and responsibly reformist, can easily exist in the Italian left-wing, especially if clever, experienced public figures, like the ex-secretary of the CGIL,[74] Sergio Cofferati (now mayor of Bononia) condemned that vote as an "incomprehensible error," which produced "the scattering of a value that the Ulivo, even if with some difficulty, had managed to gather up and strengthen by building a positive relationship with a widespread, composite movement on the difficult terrain of war and peace."[75]

A typical expression of this attitude is the popularity that smiles upon Luis Rodriguez Zapatero, the leader of the Spanish Socialist party (PSOE) who succeeded José Maria Aznar after the elections on the March 14, 2004. Only three days after the Madrid massacre, at a cost of 191 lives, Zapatero won the elections against all the odds and announced the withdrawal of the Spanish troops from Iraq "by the June 30," unless the UN took the place of the United States. In the meantime, on June 8, 2004, a resolution 1546 proposed by the United States and Great Britain was approved. This resolution fore-saw elections on the January 31, 2005 and the withdrawal of allied troops no later than the December 31, 2005. Despite this, the Spanish troops were withdrawn hastily several weeks before the ultimatum deadline. The Spanish contingent was not numerous and it did not distinguish itself particularly during its stay in Iraq. But the political uproar caused by the gesture was extraordinary, because Aznar's Spain, a temporary member of the UN Security Council when the war against Saddam was decided, had openly supported Washington and London. The PSOE's electoral program foresaw the withdrawal of the troops, but many commentators observe that after the attack, the withdrawal of the troops would obviously look like a capitulation. Immediately after the elections there was enormous publicity for a strategic resolution drawn up by Al Qaeda of 42 pages, published at the end of 2003, in which Spain is named as being "the first pawn to take in order to provoke a domino effect, forcing the other occupying forces to leave Iraq . . . To oblige the Spanish government to withdraw from Iraq, the resistance will have to inflict serious attacks on its forces . . . We have to exploit to our best advantage the election deadline. We believe that the Spanish government would not be able to stand more than two or three attacks, before being forced to give way under pressure from the people. If it should not do so, a Socialist Party victory would be well-nigh certain and a withdrawal from Iraq would be one of its priorities."[76] Zapatero's decision gives rise to predictable irritation among the leaders of the other countries that have troops in Iraq, and who see the risk that the success obtained in Spain might cause the terrorists to repeat the terror campaign in the streets of New York, London, and Milan.[77] Even the democratic can-didate for the United States' presidency, on whose victory most of the European center-left leaders were counting, criticizes the Spanish leader's choice. Michael Walzer, despite being close to the Spanish socialists, deems "their victory contaminated, because it was favoured by Al Qaeda. Zapatero had been saying for some time that if he were elected he would withdraw the troops from Iraq. But after the Madrid massacre he should have changed his mind." In fact the whole of the European left-wing should "break out of its usual mould" and "side in favor of the Iraq war . . . If not only Spain but also Italy and other countries were to withdraw from Baghdad the world would consider it a triumph for al Qaeda, who would carry out more and more attacks. Europe has to work seriously with the UN towards a peace plan and Iraqi reconstruction. Unfortunately I doubt whether France, Germany, and socialist Spain are ready to pay the price."[78] Zapatero's position sent the European left into raptures, both governments and oppositions, as well as Chirac's France; and the then president of the European Commission Romano Prodi assumes the same stance, mindless of the fact that the "winds of Munich" might blow again on the old continent and that "democratic Europe, as it did in '38 in relation to Hitler, and Europe makes the mistake of sending erroneous messages of appeasement to the enemies of our civilisation."[79]

Arab governments, more or less respectable as regards internal democracy, respect for human rights, and basic freedom, made a stand against the war and permitted their own masses to unleash their feelings freely about the widespread anti-Western sentiment that this war may well have strengthened but certainly did not create. This sentiment would not have disappeared nor would it have lessened if the Americans had renounced putting an end, once and for all, to Saddam Hussein's regime (an unlikely scenario). The very same Arab masses, who showed how much the values of peace, tolerance, and respect for others' right to existence meant to them, with the macabre dances they performed on seeing pictures of the fall of the Twin Towers, demonstrated in favor of Saddam and against "Bush's War," with threats of holy wars, oceans of blood and seas of fire. But none of all this, from the Pope's sorrowful entreaties and worries to the restless scenarios conjured up by those more or less self-interested harbingers of catastrophe, was enough to dissuade President George W. Bush from employing the enormous military might that America possesses from carrying out the second phase of the "War on Terror," announced and defined in the first "State" of the Union Speech after September 11:

> What we have found in Afghanistan confirms that, far from ending there, our war against terror is only beginning . . . Our second goal is to prevent regimes that sponsor terror from threatening America or our friends and allies with weapons of mass destruction. . . . Iraq continues to flaunt its hostility toward America and to support terror. The Iraqi regime has plotted to develop anthrax, and nerve gas, and nuclear

weapons for over a decade. This is a regime that has already used poison gas to murder thousands of its own citizens—leaving the bodies of mothers huddled over their dead children. This is a regime that agreed to international inspections—then kicked out the inspectors. This is a regime that has something to hide from the civilized world. States like these, and their terrorist allies, constitute an axis of evil, arming to threaten the peace of the world.[80]

While the postwar period in Iraq seems "never-ending," we cannot restrict ourselves to lamenting the fact that the Americans have remained bogged down between Falluja and Baghdad or, on the contrary, count on yet another triumph of the United States' technology and worth. No matter how much the peace movement was exploited to improper political ends (above all in Italy, as often happens), and no matter how simplistic we may consider the proposals made to avoid war, we cannot ignore the size of the phenomenon and its transnational scope. Perhaps a "victorious peace" may happen one day in Iraq and for the whole of the Middle East. This may well contribute to reducing the size of the phenomenon, but it is certain that this pacifism has borne witness to a split in how international politics is perceived.

The war in Iraq forces us to question the deep reasons for this split which would seem to revive what in the years between the two world wars contrasted a legalistic conception of international politics with more or less liberal realism. Even then it was a transition phase between an old order (the one destroyed in the fields of the Battle of Verdun, the Marne, and the Isonzo) and a new one, which in fact was only to be confirmed by means of another horrific conflict and the substitution of France, Germany, and Great Britain with the Soviet Union and the United States. Even then, the supporters of the "force of law" and those for the "right of force" seemed to speak deliberately autistic language, oriented toward the pure act of witnessing their own absolute reasoning as opposed to any reasonableness.[81]

We should try to understand the difficulties that many "well-intentioned people" have, as Blair would say, in tackling the problem of war, placing themselves deliberately outside the choir of the self-satisfied interpreters of pure logic of power like those sad supporters of a simplistic pacifistic vision of international politics. In the words of Michael Walzer, a *liberal* American philosopher who was against this war, even though he is a "non-pacifist," who observed clearly ten days before the outbreak of hostilities that "a movement against war must be able to explain convincingly why this war is wrong: Pacifism, which is an important component of the left-wing cannot be the predominant or exclusive voice . . . The real question that the leaders of the movement against the war must pose is 'are we sure that the victory of our movement will not reinforce Saddam Hussein's regime?' I realise that it is easier to shout 'no to war' or 'discharge Bush not bombs' than 'let's strengthen the embargo' or 'let's make the sanctions more effective'. But it is not possible to build a new movement that supports more mature positions than the simple 'no to war'."[82] Perhaps it would be enough to start from a simple and, we believe, shared affirmation that international politics remains a basically "anarchical" arena, a place where no international organism is legitimately authorized or concretely capable of rising as a guarantor for international security. At the same time, however, it is not only necessary but also positive to acknowledge that this anarchical arena will suffer continual tension as regards its own self-regulation. The use of force, that is, war, remains a possibility to guarantee security and sovereignty, but at the same time, it is a fact (and a mark of civilization) that war "as a final resort" has been progressively limited by law, by custom and the evolution itself of the feelings of public opinion and the democratic political classes.

In 1914 the governments of France and Great Britain did not hesitate to choose war, so as not to have to renounce what were considered legitimate national interests. Only until the beginning of the last century was war considered a painful necessity and a tragic constant factor in human history, even in the "civilized" West, which had indeed invented international law. To understand how the spirit of the times had changed, suffice to reread the first lines with which Marc Bloch, one of the greatest historians in the twentieth century and founder of the celebrated "Annales d'histoire économique et sociale" described his state of mind and the state of Paris in August 1914:

> The atmosphere in Paris during the first days of the mobilization remains one of my most beautiful memories of the war. The city was peaceful, even solemn. The slowed-down traffic, the absence of buses, the rarity of taxis made the streets almost silent. The sadness at the bottom of everyone's heart did not spread outward; still, many of the women had red, swollen eyes. National armies have turned war into a democratic ferment. There were but two social classes in Paris: one, made up of "those who were leaving," was the nobility; the other was made up of those who were staying, and whose only concern for the moment was to coddle the soldiers of tomorrow. On the street, in stores, on tramways, people chatted familiarly, and the unanimous

benevolence was evident in words and gestures, often awkward and puerile, but touching nonetheless. For the most part, men were not merry; they were resolute, which is preferable.[83]

Today no Western government is willing to treat war with the same fatalism. The precise fact that the democratic political classes are less and less inclined to resort to the use of force is, as we will see, the delicate and painful point in the whole question, because it cannot be denied that in assuming this position, they decide to avoid hiding behind *new age* millennarianism and politically correct hypocrisy. This is true. Democracies do not wage war against each other, they tend to limit resorting to force and they "seem more inclined to explore ways of negotiation and resort to forms of arbitration for the peaceful resolution of controversies[84] because there is an innate respect for human life and tolerance. But it is also true that the same thing does not hold true for nondemocratic countries, who are ready to resort to external war in almost equal measure as they would do internally, violently repressing their own people. Regrettably, democracies are widespread only in the West. The threats to our security arrive from countries that are both non-Western and nondemocratic. So, the risk that every conflict caused by a nondemocracy may be deliberately presented as an episode of the many (and rightly so) feared clashes of civilizations remains extremely high. In short, if law in the international field is far from being effective in offering concrete guarantees of security of democracies, the malfunctioning of theory and practice reaches maximum levels when the tension is between Western democracies and states which are nondemocratic and non-Western. What no-one says is that international law and the institutional fabric that represents and implements it were conceived when the world states basically corresponded to the Western countries (the first) and when the democracies were the large majority of independent states (the second). Both were born when the universal and monopolistic value of democracy and liberty as sources of the legitimization of political power was certainly not as widespread and as theoretically unchallenged as it is today.

THE DECLINE OF SOVEREIGNTY

The Third Gulf War was not fought mainly for oil and in Washington there is not a group of crazy unilateralists, desperate to destroy all those international institutions that different generations of American administrations contributed to creating. It did, however, make it obvious that there are different positions as regards the characteristics that the new order should have in replacing the old dying order. Unfortunately, in many ways the United Nations is the institution which is most typical of the old order. "The founding principle of the United Nations is that of the inviolable sovereignty of the nation states. But in today's globalized world this concept of sovereignty cannot guarantee the sovereignty of any country. The same forces that make globalisation possible have also produced transnational terrorism, climactic catastrophes and global miscry. These are all aspects that involve the whole world and cross borders as if they did not exist."[85] Ulrich Beck expresses the whole complexity and inevitability of the phase of uncertainty and transition that characterizes the international political and economic system. But, then again, the awareness of the stateless and transnational nature of the phenomena that we are experiencing today leads us to believe that what that sacrosanct sovereignty implied is morally unacceptable: "the absolute right of each sovereign government to violate the rights of its own citizens."

It is true that the absolute sovereignty referred to by Ulrich Beck ceased to exist a long time ago in the West, and in other areas in the world it was the domestic curtain with which intolerable dictators hid their "non-sovereignty" in the international arena. And yet, precisely that "watered-down sovereignty" was already the keystone that had permitted the construction of hegemonic peace in the West. In the transition toward the really global nature of American hegemony, the reduction of sovereignty is at one and the same time too much and too little. It is *too much*, on a consensual basis, because those states, which up until now have remained outside the Western arena, are not offered the same important political and economic advantages by "globalisation" (intended as an ideological proposal) as postwar Europe had been offered by NATO and the Marshall Plan. It is *too little*, on the basis of pure imposition, because only a more noticeable relativization can offer the hegemon a real and substantial increase of its own security. It is significant that already at the time of the Clinton administration, America had introduced and widened the meaning and use of the category "rogue states," which implies not so much the limitation of sovereignty of this or that state, as the placing in default of the category of sovereignty as an absolute value. The concept of "rogue state," albeit still rather undefined (when is a state a rogue? when it *behaves badly*, violating international law, or when it is *formed badly* because it is void of any internal democratic legitimacy? And to what extent are the two characteristics reciprocally related?) is so ambiguous that there are those who polemically believe that the United States is indeed the most dangerous *rogue state*[86] on the planet, and affirm that there are principles the violation of which no border is sufficient refuge.

Since the end of the cold war, operations of a humanitarian nature have been enacted on several occasions. The so-called *right to intervene* "is commonly conceived as the right or duty of the dominant subjects of the world order to intervene in the territories of other subjects in the interest of preventing or resolving humanitarian problems, guaranteeing accords, and imposing peace . . . Now supranational subjects that are legitimated not by right but by consensus intervene in the name of any type of emergency and superior ethical principles. What stands behind this intervention is not just a permanent state of emergency and exception, but a permanent state of emergency and exception justified by *the appeal to essential values of justice*. In other words, the right of the police is legitimated by universal values."[87] Even though the term "humanitarian" has often been used with the meaning of "survival" (as in Somalia, Rwanda, Burundi, and Kosovo) and at other times it has been interpreted less literally (Haiti, Bosnia, and East Timor), the operations have had two main characteristics in common. In the first place, all the cases have been operations aimed against governments (at least when government institutions were identifiable) which had begun to face more or less widespread and well-grounded ostracism from the international community. Second, operations of a military nature were resorted to only when determined by the United States. As a result "long before George W. Bush arrived on the scene, great resentment was felt against the power of the super-power or, as defined by Hubert Vedrine, of the hyper-power."[88] Inter alia, the case of the American intervention in Haiti, following the violation of the democratic electoral results in 1991, is a perfect example of how the "right to intervene" has progressively widened far beyond the urgency of humanitarian aid, since "the large majority of the international community in 1994 supported the American government's decision, insofar as it believed that the citizens in Haiti had the right to have their political decision respected."[89] On the other hand "until Kosovo, in Kurdistan, Bosnia, Somalia, Rwanda, Haiti and Albania, the ratio of operations was based on the canon of the restoration of 'peace and international security', rather that on a full-blown right to humanitarian intrusion."[90] The Security Council preferred to authorize the military intervention of the international community within the confines of a member state in the traditional meaning that the fear of the situation of internal disorder might cross the borders and involve the neighboring countries. It was not by chance that in the case of Belgrade, where there was a government at the height of its state activities, and the fact that it was a "legitimate" government that was persecuting its own citizens, that the West was forced to remove its veil of hypocrisy and act for reasons that were not easily ascribable to the restoration of peace and international security. Consequently, this action did not receive endorsement from the United Nations, creating a precedent for subsequent similar operations.

After September 11, George W. Bush and Donald Rumsfeld pushed further. On one hand they redefined American power as a "power of last resort," echoing, who knows how consciously, Carl Schmitt's idea of sovereignty as the power to decide in an exceptional case. Basically, "the United States currently claims to make sovereign judgements on what is right and what is wrong, particularly in respect of the use of force, and to exempt itself with an absolutely clear conscience from all the rules that it proclaims and applies to others."[91] On the other hand, it has announced a new principle: as regards non-Western states, the concrete participation in the fight against terrorism (or at least the possibility to exhibit a spotless record) takes the place of sovereignty as a cardinal point of that new world order that has been announced so many times. According to America, sovereignty is no longer the pillar of international order (as seen in Kosovo), because it is no longer the time to renounce explicitly the importance of the concept of justice. In a word, for the Americans, Westphalia is over.

Whoever rejects, legitimately, the scenario of American hegemony substantially limited by *check and balances* within that constitutional system, knows that the contestation of U.S. unilateral strategy cannot be founded either on regrets for the sovereignty of times past, or on a "manualistic" idea of international law. If it is in fact true that even today "the only peaceful world is one governed by the law," it is also true that "there is always force behind the law,"[92] so that the question we have to ask is how to reduce the wide distance between force and law in international politics.

There is one point that I would like to highlight, and it regards the different conceptions of Europeans and Americans toward international order and the role that the institutions have within it. It may seem to be an absurdity that the United States—perhaps among the greatest driving forces of international law, certainly among the greatest contributors of international institutions—with its behavior and because of the kind of thought that lies at its roots, may today place in default those laws and institutions that they worked so hard to create. As John Ikenberry commented, "The lesson of American order building in this century is that international institutions have played a pervasive and ultimately constructive role in the exercise of American power." Despite the "conventional view" he tends to collocate them in an antithetical way; the "power and institutions are related to each other in a more complex way. Institutions can both project and restrain state power."[93] The governors of the United States who complain about the limitations to freedom for action that often come from the international institutions, should bear in mind the lessons of the past, remembering that this capacity to connect power and institutions is "what has made American power durable and acceptable."[94] Even in this new century, after September 11 and in the era of the war on terror, the possibility that American power can be perceived again as legitimate "will be due in no small measure to the way power and institutions operate together to create stable and legitimate relations among the industrial democracies."[95]

The paradox of an America that undermines the institutions that it helped to create is in fact only superficial, for it is explained by means of the presumption that laws and international institutions cannot enter into contrast with the will of the United States, unless they have been deliberately diverted from their usual objectives. The implicit assumption is that there should be a sort of "natural harmony" between American interests and aspirations for a just, peaceful law founded on the "rule of law" and the spreading of democracy on the part of the international community. This is not any less true in the current unipolar order of the world. On the contrary, this need is even stronger precisely because of the status of solitary superpower at present occupied by the United States. "The single superpower status of the United States poses a paradox: the international community cannot do without the United States in most areas of international community activity and in most areas of international lawmaking. At the same time, the United States needs the international community in order to promote its own national interests and foreign policy goals."[96] This was Woodrow Wilson and Franklin Delano Roosevelt's intuition and intention. The latter was the creator and promoter of the highly institutionalized international order built up by the United States in the "American century." According to Robert Kagan only in this way can the Americans be defined legalistic, since every time the principles of *political legitimacy* (democratic) have collided with those of *juridical legality*, the United States has opposed the latter:

> By nature, tradition, and ideology, the United States has generally favored the promotion of liberal principles over the niceties of Westphalia diplomacy. Despite its role in helping to create the UN and draft the UN Charter, the United States has never fully accepted the organization's legitimacy or the charter's doctrine of sovereign equality. Although fiercely protective of its own autonomy, the United States has reserved for itself the right to intervene anywhere and everywhere, generally in the name of defending the cause of liberalism.[97]

Right since the generations of the founding fathers, the Americans have considered foreign tyrannies as transitory, destined to fall at the feet of republican forces freed by the same American Revolution:

> In this sense, the United States is and always has been a revolutionary power, a sometimes unwitting—but nevertheless persistent—disturber of the status quo, wherever its influence grows. For Europeans, who are consumed with radical changes on their own continent and seek a predictable future in the world beyond, the United States has once again become a dangerous member of the society of nations.[98]

There remains no doubt that there is nothing further from reality than the concept of "international community" to describe the world of states and their rivalry. And yet, precisely the United States has made a particular effort, from Wilson to Roosevelt, to make a similar expression have a concrete meaning, starting by conferring on it suitable institutional "clothing."[99] After all, as has been underlined, in the period after the Second World War, "power and law have been entangled in much more complex relationships than the conventional imagery would allow: if collective security in the League failed because it lacked the support of power, the United Nations seems to have suffered from its becoming indistinguishable from power."[100]

The ways in which it is carrying out this transition beyond sovereignty—which from being a not limited or moderate category becomes less absolute and more relative—perhaps makes it difficult to seize the movement in course, at least for us Europeans, who on the strength of that idea have built the last 400 years of history and a large part of modernity. For us, sovereignty remains a concept with certain connotations of sacredness, given that its origin is tied to the end of religious civil wars. In the memory of European culture there is this two-fold link between sovereignty and the construction of the State (on the internal front) and sovereignty and neutralization of religious wars (on the external front). However, it is precisely the strength that the creation of the State acquires from sovereignty (dating from the seventeenth century), that hides the fact that as regards systems, the invention of sovereignty was an extraordinary tool. It contributed to the realization of collective security and was the first principle of self-limitation of arbitrary power, accepted by each state in the name of "correctly interpreted self-interest."[101] The *success* of sovereignty comes not only from having been able to chain the demon of religious wars, putting the state in the position of a merciless guard, but also from having shaped, through reciprocal recognition of plural sovereignties in place of a single and *christiana respublica*, the idea that peace can reign among the like-minded. The *decline* of sovereignty today, derives from the fact that it no longer seems to be of great use. It is not among the like-minded that there is war (states against terrorists), there is no *christiana respublica*, and we are not facing religious (civil) wars but, if anything, the risk of wars between religions.

When the recognition of the equal sovereignty of each state no longer contributes to guaranteeing the security of the hegemon, or rather when it even seems to make it more vulnerable, why are we surprised when it searches for new rules for a new system?[102] The critical point of the current American dominance is that "because of the norm of sovereignty, the international system is *de jure* anarchical, but because of vast inequalities of material power, it is *de facto* hierarchical. The problem for any hegemon is how to reconcile the reality of its dominance with the useful fiction of state equality."[103] This concretizes the transition from an idea of order founded on the acceptance of plurality and on the principle of anarchy of the international political system, to that of an order based on the reduction of plurality and on the principle of hierarchy—from an anarchicae-plurae vision to an imperial hierarchical vision. This is what is implied, according to Negri and Hardt, in the reduction of war to international police operations, every time it is possible, that is, when it is possible to create a minimum of political agreement around the decisions of the hegemon: "There is certainly something troubling in this renewed focus on the concept of *bellum justum*, which modernity, or rather modern secularism, had worked so hard to expunge from the medieval tradition. The traditional concept of just war involves the banalization of war and the celebration of it as an ethical instrument, both of which were ideas that modern political thought and the international community of nation-states had resolutely refused. These two traditional characteristics have reappeared in our post-modern world: on the one hand, war is reduced to the status of police action, and on the other, the new power that can legitimately exercise ethical functions through war is sacralized . . . [Just war] has become rather an activity that is justified in itself. Two distinct elements are combined in this concept of just war: first, the legitimacy of the military apparatus, insofar as it is ethically grounded, and second, the effectiveness of military action to achieve the desired order and peace . . . Today the enemy, just like the war itself, comes to be at once banalized (reduced to an object of routine police repression) and absolutized (as the Enemy, an absolute threat to the ethical order)."[104]

Whether it is called *Pax Americana*, hegemonic peace, neo-empire, or new world order, we face considerable discontinuity compared to Westphalia, the corollary of which is that sovereignty (as happened historically) paradoxically only works among the like-minded, where it is willingly and multilaterally approved (on principle) and relativized (in concrete results) as happens in the West. The idea of sovereignty and a good part of its practice have in fact continued to survive more than half a century into American hegemony over the West, and they have produced that new "constitutionalised" form of dominion, that has made the reduction of sovereignty (both in different areas and with different intensity) a reciprocal phenomenon and with effects which are not so limiting a effective liberty. But outside the West?

As a consequence of their own historical fortunes, the U.S. relationship with the world had always been determined by the unresolved question as to whether their own foreign policy should move in a revolutionary way with respect to sovereignty or whether it should rather accept it as an ineliminable tie. In other words, the question which always lies behind American foreign policy is this: Should the United States limit itself to the "force of example" or should it "actively support the cause of freedom" wherever it may be threatened? There is no doubt that the Bush administration on more than one occasion seems to be under the spell of this second prospect. It is President Bush's same religious fervor that pushes him to take an "ethical" approach toward foreign policy, as was common of all the recent presidents of the United States, starting with Jimmy Carter. Indicative of George W. Bush's religiousness is the text of his message broadcast on the radio throughout the nation at Easter: "This holy season reminds us of the value of freedom, and the power of a love stronger than death. This year, Easter and Passover have special meaning for the families of our men and women in uniform who feel so intensely the absence of their loved ones during these days . . . This season brings a promise: that good can come out of evil, that hope can arise from despair."[105]

According to various commentators, U.S. foreign policy is dominated by a limited group of neo-conservatives, that is, of those in the left-wing who escaped (the Democratic Party) to the right (the Republican Party). One of their intellectual cornerstones is that the end of the cold war gives the United States not so much the possibility as the duty to export democracy, market economy, and freedom throughout the world, using, if necessary, military power. "One of their most important think tanks was the 'Project for a New American Century', founded in 1997 by William Kristol and Robert Kagan; among its original members were Richard Perle, Paul Wolfowitz, Lewis Libby, Donald Rumsfeld, Elliot Abrams and Zalmay Khalilzad."[106] This group was inspired by the Wilson tradition but, different from Woodrow Wilson, it had no faith in international institutions. Contrary to "classical" conservatives like Henry Kissinger, they were not in favor of politics founded on balance, they did not fear challenging the status quo, and they were not tied to stability. For them, the debate that has held the stage in the years subsequent to the cold war between "interventionists" and "sovereignists" is easily resolved by what their critics like to define as "double standards." American neo-conservatives, who excel in cultural terms within this administration, incarnate a sort of syncretism between the different traditions of American foreign policy: "The Americans are absolutely against any encroachment on their own sovereignty but absolutely in favor of intervention against others."[107] They mistrust permanent alliances and believe that it is legitimate to pursue a strategy that aims to found a *Pax Americana*, paradoxically also pursuing an aggressive policy toward authoritarian regimes, at times adopting "a crusading spirit towards authoritarian regimes" which democracies "from a neo-Kantian perspective" should consider "void of moral legitimacy."[108]

CHANGING THE UN TO SAVE THE UN

A radical reform of the United Nations could be the supreme attempt to revitalize it. Complaints of the inefficiency and ineffectiveness of the United Nations are as old as the institution itself, and the uproar they cause is often similar to clamour provoked by those who declaim the thaumaturgic virtues of the organization on the banks of the Hudson. But it is paradoxically since the end of the cold war that there has been pressure for a restructuring of the United Nations, rightly held to be the greatest institutional expression of an order which has now disappeared. As is well known, within the United Nations two basic principles coexist. The first is that of the formal equality of the sovereignty of all states. It is in the General Assembly that this finds its full expression, where every member state is equal, irrespective of whether it is the tiny island of Tonga, highly populated India or the American superpower. The second principle is the "opposite" one of the "strategic importance" of states. This is applied within the Security Council, where only the "Big Five" sit permanently (the other members being selected on a rota basis), and they have the right of veto, able to block any decision that they deem contrary to their own interest. The "Great" states are nothing other than the effective winners of the Second World War (the United States, USSR, Great Britain) with a couple of "formal" winners (France and China: for a long time Taiwan and from the 1970s, Beijing). They were included in the group to make it slightly less obvious that the winners had the honor and the responsibility of supervising the new order that had emerged from the conflict.

Postwar affairs made sure that the permanent members of the council ended up siding with the USSR or the United States, within a bipolar logic where only the two superpowers were able to make their veto of any value in questions regarding the whole order of the system. With the decline of the cold war, and even more after the last Iraqi war, the debate on the necessity to reform the United Nations has been revived but in specular directions: a basic democratization and a greater adherance to a new international distribution of power. On one hand there are those who,[109] like the ex-deputy secretary Pino Arlacchi, hope for a change of the same kind in the United Nations, pushed to the extent that it is transformed into an "Organisation of citizens," with elective offices, greater autonomy for the Secretary General and with an Assembly which is more like the European Parliament and a Security Council (also elective) and without permanent members. On the same line, the political scientist Luigi Bonanate hopes for a reform in three stages: the abolition of the power of veto, open representation for civil society and not only for governments and the capacity to exert autonomous military pressure. Antonio Cassese, for a long time president of the International Criminal Court for the ex-Yugoslavia, underlines that the United Nations "remains an essential, indispensable organism in the life of international relations," but he seems sceptical about the fact that it should be equipped with autonomous military capacity and about the possibility that the Big Five would accept renouncing their power of veto. The United

Nations could, however, modernize in the sense that it could create real "political diplomatic strategic structures able to act as sensitive 'antennae' to verify whether a crisis might degenerate into an armed confrontation, and act as an 'alarm bell' to alert the Security Council in order to avoid the outbreak of war, international or internal." For Giandomenico Picco, former deputy secretary of the United Nations, it is better to concentrate on the "reconstruction of the unity of the five permanent members of the Security Council" rather than imagine difficult paths of reform.

As can be easily gathered in this foretaste of debate, the positions are very different and alongside those who hope for an effort toward "institutional creativity and political ideology," there are those who call for harsher realism, highlighting a fact in itself indisputable: no institutional reform is able to substitute the lack of political agreement that reigns today among the principal powers in the system. We find ourselves in a considerably paradoxical situation. The United States wishes for radical reform of the United Nations that takes into consideration the new unipolar order of the world; the European countries plus Japan ask to count more; China and Russia, even if in different proportions, are basically for keeping the status quo, while the countries in the southern hemisphere would like a reform that give them some *chance* of reducing the "white" domination of the international community. What is certain is that if it does not intervene quickly, it risks aggravating the phenomenon described well by Michael Glennon, in whose opinion "the international system has moved rapidly to a parallel universe of two systems, one *de facto*, the other *de jure*."[110] In the latter the formal rules of the United Nations Charter would continue to hold importance, while in the former geopolitical considerations would predominate. This dichotomy would thus mark the decline of the particular and virtuous relationship between power and institutions in the international system which, as we have seen with John Ikenberry, was the golden rule in the American century and the hegemony of the United States.

It is clear that to consider a reform of the United Nations that could reduce the power of the United States is pure fantasy. Looking at it from Washington, the UN headquarters at times seems empty, a house inhabited by a ghost that history has left behind or at the most it is a "foggy port," where any coherent politics gets stranded or risks going astray. As Richard Perle commented, we must not exaggerate with fears. The United Nations is certainly not dead because of the Iraq war, since "part of the good actions will survive, the bureaucracy of low risk *peace keeping* will remain. Even the chit-chat will remain.

What has died with the Iraq War is the fantasy of the United Nations as the basis for a new world order."[111] Then again, the United Nations never was this, nor is it written anywhere that a similar evolution would progress. In the spring of 2002 the fact that Libya was elected (with French, British, and Italian votes) to the presidency of the UN Commission of Human Rights caused a sensation. This commission is the only organism in the organization with the task to survey the application of the declarations and conventions on the subject. As could reasonably be expected, less than a month after his instalment in office, the Libyan neo-president, the ambassador Najat Al-Hajjaji, brought the commission to declare that no violation of human rights was underway in Zimbabwe (where a government campaign of terror has been prospering for years in the country) or in Cuba (where Fidel Castro has imprisoned seventy dissidents sentenced for extremely long terms only for "crimes of opinion", or in Sudan (where the black minority, mostly Christian or animist was reduced to slavery or else exterminated) or in Chechnya, Laos, Syria, Pakistan, Vietnam, and so on.

Incidents like these are unfortunately not isolated cases in the history of the United Nations and they prove quite clearly how the way toward a "democratization" of the United Nations might coincide with "less liberty for the world." Joseph Nye may be right when he goes hammer and tongs at those at the heart of the Bush administration who "talk of creating a new organization of democracies," given that after the Iraq War the "deepest division over U.S. legitimacy are precisely among the democracies." Undoubtedly, a successful and benevolent hegemony must try to make the *soft and hard powers* coexist, the reason why the United Nations is so important particularly for America, because they "are a way to legitimize America's disproportionate military power and enhance its soft or attractive power."[112] But what happens when what is desirable is unrealizable? The real weakness in Nye's reasoning is revealed by Michael Glennon, a jurist certainly no neo-conservative, who in *Foreign Affairs* commented, "Although the effort to subject the use of force to the rule of law was the monumental internationalist experiment of the twentieth century, the fact is that that experiment has failed" and the UN crisis is simply a child of the changing times, of the new international situation: "It was the rise in American unipolarity—not the Iraq crisis—that, along with cultural clashes and different attitudes toward the use of force, gradually eroded the Council's credibility," which anyway "reflected the real world's power structure with the accuracy of a fun-house mirror—and performed accordingly."[113]

After much discussion, reform of the Security Council can begin, also because the United Nations would not survive without radical reform after the failures suffered over recent years: included are the shameful cases of corruption tied to the scandal "Oil-for-food" in Iraq. During the period of sanctions, many officials were involved in the disgraceful plundering, to the detriment of the Iraqi people. Whoever hopes to be able to reduce by legal-formal means the power of the United States is under an illusion. Moreover, if an endeavor of this kind were to be stubbornly brought forward, the United States could only put two and two together and either "get out" of the New York organization or paralyze the Security Council with a volley of vetoes. Whoever has the survival of the United Nations at heart would be best to leave both mannerist rhetoric and noble but abstract idealism aside. The norms and international institutions are of delicate construction; they cannot be overwhelmed with excessive weight, take on decisions on crucial questions when there is no agreement at the political level. There is no doubt that rules and institutions go hand in hand with the life source of the international political system. It is just as indisputable that they have progressively modified the international political panorama making it less barbaric, particularly over the last 100 years. We must not forget, however, that the rules, just as much as institutions can take on "bare power," and in so doing make life more civilized and make people's lives more pleasant, but they cannot substitute it. Bold legal and institutional skyscrapers can be built, but only if they are dug into the hard foundations of concrete power and political agreement. So, as regards the United Nations, "it would be a mistake to lay the responsibilities at the door of the institution, rather than at the difficulty encountered by states in communicating with each other, and in particular between the major powers that are part of the institution. Such responsibilities are incumbent on the states because of the way they use the tool they themselves created, without respecting roles and principles. The importance of the Security Council as a forum for discussion and where interests differ widely seems however to be irreplaceable."[114]

The United Nations was relieved of this function of "forum" for over forty years of the cold war. Since 1946, the Resolutions in the Security Council were blocked more than 252 times by a veto from one or more of its permanent members (mainly the USSR and the United States). It is needless to recall that these vetoes were concentrated in the years of the cold war. And yet, no one had really ever radically contested the usefulness of the United Nations Organisation, as happened after '89, when it was more able to act even on a military level: from the 1990 to 1991 Gulf War, to the presence in Bosnia, from Cambodia to Somalia to East Timor. Paradoxically, it was the "success" that smiled upon the United Nations in the 1990s, united in the hopes that the end of Communism fueled, that created the illusion that finally the United Nations could succeed where it had always failed: to propose itself as a tool for collective security. It is this illusion that shoulders the most incredible demands: to transform the United Nations into a sort of "World Constitutional Court" able to decree the legitimacy or not of any military action or to sanction the juridical relativization of the principle or sovereignty in the name of the right to humanitarian intervention; to imagine that the United Nations can become something like what the EU represents for its member states, that is, a partner in their own sovereignty. Seized with a sort of delusion of omnipotence, assisted in this by an excessively "optimistic" reading of globalization and the policies of the Clinton administration which rode the rhetorical tiger of "global governance," many scholars and players in international politics end up overloading the United Nations with unsustainable tasks and lose sight of the only consideration that explains the increased success of the United Nations after the cold war. In a unipolar world, where there is only one power, the United Nations has worked any time it held the same point of view as the United States; it did not work at all any time it tried to oppose Washington.

The novelty in the Iraqi crisis is not that America decided to act without the formal approval of the United Nations. The same thing had happened with Kosovo. Long before the formulation of the "Bush Doctrine," "the Reagan, Bush Sr., Powell and Clinton doctrines were advanced" and, "from a legal perspective . . . apart from the Reagan doctrine on 'collective defence', they do not deal with international law at all . . . the Bush, Powell, and Clinton doctrines were comprehensive explanations of overall United States policy regarding the use of force, irrespective of the matter of legality."[115] The novelty lay in the fact that this time a large number of its allies had decided not to follow it. And so America decided to act alone. It acted anyway, but alone. And it is this break in political solidarity between the member states of the "international community" that puts the institution that this community represents at the highest level into crisis. This is why the crisis, different from the others, may decree a long slow process of euthanasia for the United Nations. Whatever serious attempt to keep the United Nations alive and even relaunch it in a different role, must start from this realization. And we need to ask at least which international community Americans have in mind when they use this concept referring to the search for a new political legitimacy for their actions.

The feeling is that the criteria for the "coalition of the willing" (baptized in the fire of Iraq) is not so much the idea of an "*à la carte* alliance*" which risks transforming NATO into an old iron, but also the "international community." Richard Perle comments quite simply on these new coalitions: "Instead of criticising them as a threat to the new world order, we should recognise that they are the greatest hope for this order and the real alternative to the anarchy of the shameful failure of the United Nations."[116]

So, to prevent the most extreme positions from prevailing—those that would like to declare the United Nations bankrupt—it is necessary for the Security Council to be reformed, maybe by trying to introduce mechanisms that recognize a hierarchy of power and responsibility, but also allowing other factors to have their due weight, such as the importance of GDP or the demographic structure or the participation in peacekeeping operations or humanitarian aid. At the moment there are two different proposals on the table; they are the fruit of the "Committee of the Wise" nominated by the secretary general, Kofi Annan. The first foresees the change in the security council from fifteen to twenty-four members, with the entrance of three nonpermanent members on a rota system and six new permanent members, without the right to veto, and representing large regional areas. In such a solution, Japan, Germany, Brazil, India, South Africa, and Egypt should obtain long coveted status. The second proposal, supported also by Italy, speculates on the introduction of eight semi-permanent members elected for four years on a regional basis, and of one extra member on rotation. This second proposal seems far more preferable than the first, which would seem to be an inadequate answer to the challenges of the new millennium, apart from being dangerously unbalanced. While exhuming tools which are now anachronistic, like the eighteenth century "concert of powers," it would be unable to make the council more representative of the membership of United Nations, and it would give life to an oligarchic structure that would not justify the increase of the responsibility of the council itself.

Perhaps it is true that the entrance of Germany among the permanent members would mark the end of the division between winners and losers of the Second World War, but certainly it would move the clock back to mid-twentieth-century history. It would not help the European countries to reach greater integration, nor would the EU be encouraged to assume greater international responsibility, so as to force the reluctant United States to recognize the desirable existence of a new European subjectivity. It would on the contrary amplify the differences in the political assessments between the governments of the Union and the destructive potential of the tension between Berlin and Paris, on the one hand, and London and Washington, on the other: it would have the two-fold result of driving the latter to increasingly assertive unilateralism, also jeopardizing European unity. In the context of a more complex reform of the United Nations, there could be a reassessment of the possibility of offering a permanent seat without the power of veto to the European Union, which would not substitute France and Britain's seat, but would be additional. No matter how "UN-orthodox" such an option may seem, it would avoid irritating Paris and London's sensitivity and would also push the Europeans to formulate common positions on the most delicate questions, before being submitted to the Security Council. Perhaps then we would not have to witness the sad spectacle of two member states of the Union and the Security Council totally divided and ready to show an *escalation* of such a break leading to reciprocal vetoing. The United Nations itself, could only benefit from an adjustment of its representation of reality to effective reality.

Whatever the solution that is adopted, it is essential that everything must be done to prevent the United Nations from dying. It would be most uncharitable to forget that if it has failed in its "mission impossible" to guarantee peace for the world, the United Nations has collected a series of unexpected and extremely important successes in less ambitious activities, but which are in fact of crucial importance. The specialized agencies in the United Nations daily carry out incredible work in the field, often at high personal risk, assisting orphaned and malnourished children, refugees, and desperate and sick people. Tens of thousands of employees in the twelve specialized agencies and other tens of thousands of volunteers work in very difficult conditions, often "guaranteed" only by the blue insignia and the prestige that the organization still emanates in the world. This work makes the difference between life and death, in what are for us "times of peace", for millions of people every day. It seems a good enough reason to insist that everything possible is done to make the United Nations survive and it does not seem to me that these aims are any less noble than the grandiose process of peacekeeping.

CHAPTER 3

The Remains of the West

PRO-ATLANTIC OR PRO-EUROPE?

Not only in Italy, but in practically every country in Europe, in the months leading up to the Iraqi conflict and the weeks during which it was fought, the doubt was voiced as to whether Atlantic loyalty was not in total contradiction to European interest. The mass media emphasized and exaggerated the opposition of an "American party," favorable to a military solution for the Iraq situation, and a "European party" that, in order to show Europe's different point of view regarding the best way to face Saddam Hussein's regime, was prepared to decrease its solidarity toward its American ally just when it was crucial to show it.

It is not only true for Italy, of course, but above all for our country; this latent conflict between the two historical postwar allegiances was a complete novelty and was obviously far from welcoming. It seemed that for the first time fundamental choices, which had been made not without a certain degree of trauma by the Republic in 1949 and 1957, would have to be in some way reformulated, and that the promises would have to be reaffirmed. It was also true that there had been some tension on other occasions in the past, as regards allegiance and loyalty. However, it could not be forgotten that having established those two original choices as the pillars for Italy's international political position, had not only contributed to building up security, but had also ensured that the republican political class was safe from the wounds and trauma that the unresolved question of the presence of a strong communist party (long aligned to the USSR) might risk opening during the cold war.

The transition from Fascism to the Republic, made by means of a wretched, lost war, marking the end of the monarchy, had also signaled a discontinuity in the determination of national interest. The newborn Republic had renounced the pursuit of the foolish aim to make Italy one of the great European powers, an objective pursued by Fascism, and by liberal Italy during the years of the First World War. The continual "chase" by the great powers had ended, and it had resulted in making it impossible to achieve even the most modest goal of carving out an autonomous role, and to achieve effective integration into a system of European states on an equal footing. The Republic of Italy even renounced trying to play a powerful regional role, and categorized its own national interest within a collective scenario. This is outlined by the double allegiance to NATO and the European institutions, which in any case complement each other throughout the duration of the cold war years.

Political and military security of the country is left to the affiliation of the Atlantic Alliance and its democratic system: guaranteed by the stable relationship with the United States, this works both as regards the external threat posed by the USSR and regarding the internal threat represented by the risk of a bloody seizure of power at the hands of the communists. An even more complex, detailed objective is left to the affiliation with the European institutions, possible only on condition that military security was guaranteed: in the first place, Italy's strong anchorage to Europe put an end to the risk that the country would flirt with a Latin-Mediterranean identity which was completely inconsistent in political terms. Staying in Europe, much more than being part of NATO, was Italy's way of consolidating its "Western identity"; this was anything but a forgone conclusion, given the past record of the country's united history. Of course, the idea of a particular "Mediterranean vocation" will always be a recurring temptation for a substantial part of the political class of the "First Republic". But such a vocation will never become the objective alternative that it might have risked becoming without the institutionalization of the choice for Europe and the West.

Moreover, Italy seeks further consolidation of its own democratic institutions through Europe; these institutions are quite new and can only in part be associated with the roots of liberal institutions. The split effected by Fascism, in the first place, and the hegemony of new political cultures different from those in pre-Fascist Italy, make the link too insubstantial to be able to make continuity the principal foundation of new democratic Italy. Second, the European situation supplies a stable, institutionalized link between the young Italian democracy and some of the oldest and most stable democratic systems in the continent. And finally, belonging to Europe means that Italy has the chance to take part in the formation of the new continental market, which will offer the country important commercial opportunities for its own products, contributing significantly to its swift economic development.

NATO and Europe are the choices at the base of Italian foreign politics for the whole period after the Second World War. The veritable freezing of the international political system created by the cold war was to result in these choices, made amidst extremely strong adversity from the left-wing opposition, being interpreted as definitive and irreversible. The synergetic effect of a "joint international condition," that seemed would never have to undergo modifications, and the acrimony of the internal political clash that those choices caused, resulted in it being removed from daily political debate (with the silent consensus of the Communist Party itself).

The end of the cold war and the transition from the old to the new party system restored mobility to that rather stale setup. On the one hand, it forced Italy to take a stand on questions for which it was not possible to rely on decisional mechanisms under the cover of the Atlantic or European institutional situation. The crises that followed 1990 (the Gulf War, Balkan wars, the Somalia emergency and the war against terror in Afghanistan) were all characterized by taking place outside the realm of the traditional range of action of NATO and also by the failure of Europe to move as a single political unit. On the other hand, confirming itself with new parties and the radical transformation of the few survivors of the "clean hands revolution"[1] objectively supplied a voice and for the first time gave decisional power to politicae subcultures which were different from those that had dominated the clash of the "big choices" between the end of the 1940s and the mid- 1950s.[2]

But it is the outbreak of the last Iraq war that forces unprecedented mediation, since the pro-Atlantic and pro-European choices seem to risk collision. The mediation is made even more complex by the instability of international sympathies as regards that conflict (with EU countries both for and against the war). It is also made more complex by the obvious fact that a hierarchy between Atlantic allegiance and European allegiance is senseless and indeed dangerous. This is true in particular for Italy; the political design that from its unity had tried to anchor the uncertain political and cultural identity of the country to the side of Europe and the West would be thwarted.

Whether or not the tension between Atlantic loyalty and European allegiance has been more or less exaggerated by the media, the fact remains that over recent years the feeling has been growing that Europe and the United States view the world with different eyes and do not share the same position on the main issues regarding international politics. The state of the Euro-American relationship is, in short, not at its best. The transatlantic community of security still exists, undoubtedly, but only, and above all, in the sense that to hypothesize tension between the two sides of the ocean that may reach a veiled threat of the use of force or even simple military pressure by America on a Europe unwilling to follow, is without rhyme or reason. This was seen during the self-same war against Iraq when, despite the fact that the safety itself of the Anglo-American troops in the Gulf was at risk, and although some European capitals had reached unprecedented levels of acrimony (at least not since the Suez Crisis in 1956), in Washington it was never considered an option to defend its position, alluding even indirectly at forms of military pressure or reprisals. Only the satirical French newspaper *The Monde* at the end of April 2003 conceived of the operation *Opération Grande Fesse*, "Big spanking," an Anglo-American invasion of France, with Chirac disappearing after pushing to resist the invader, Tony Blair having been killed in friendly fire on returning from the bombings in Normandy, the Marines taking control of the Louvre mistaking it for the Hotel de Ville and the Kurds proclaiming an autonomous state in the Eastern suburbs of Paris.

A war of jeers and sneers and of trade retaliation (declared rather than actually waged) was what took place between Washington and Paris; symbolic pin pricks like the mini-summit for European defense, called at the end of April 2003 by the Belgian government, with the participation of France, Germany, and Luxembourg and which received a hasty and shortsighted "blessing" from the then president of the European Commission, Romano Prodi, but nothing more. It may seem a predictable comment and not worth mentioning. But it is certainly not the case, if we only consider how alliances are by nature and historical experience reversible every time the conflict that has created them disappears. If the transatlantic security community continues to exist, in terms of the area in which even the remote prospect of an armed conflict is excluded, we must however ask ourselves to what extent the permanent alliance between Europe and the United States, which emerged victorious from the exhausting conflict of the cold war, still enjoys good health. To answer this question it is worth looking in the following pages at what explains the expectations of reciprocal peace between members of a security community: shared collective identity, institutions able to govern the relationship and economic interdependence.[3]

In terms of shared identity, the peak recorded after September 11, 2001 when most European public opinion was united behind the

United States is now a distant memory. As was authoritatively commented, "Within six months of 9/11, the nearly unanimous global support for America gave way to increasing scepticism regarding the official U.S. formulation of the shared threat. That poses the risk that America could find itself increasingly isolated in coping with the political dimension of the dangers it faces."[4] We can debate all we like as to whether the dissipation of such a high degree of solidarity and authentic sympathy was due to its volatile and ephemeral nature, lack of expertise, and the choices made by the Bush administration, or to the necessary evolution of history. It is certain that America has committed some errors of judgment in these years, as regards the use of its own power. It assumed simplistically that a more powerful America would see the rest of the world falling in with its positions. It underestimated the importance of the international institutions, taking account only of the function of containment of American power and not that of support for international stability. It overestimated the autonomy (above all as regards its allies) that military supremacy is able to offer. Even in its principal strategy "the war on terror," President Bush did not specify what role the allies should play in the fight against the common enemy, and so it is not understood either "who is on the American side" or "why so many of those who are included in what Bush calls 'this mighty coalition of civilized nations,' such as countries in Europe and Asia, are still griping that they do not feel a part of any larger cause."[5]

Europeans and Americans certainly continue to share the same sense of belonging to the West even if this common affiliation seems increasingly hazy. We both identify with a common Jewish-Christian tradition and with the values of illuminist modernity, but the way in which these traditions and values are experienced and interpreted changes radically from one side of the Atlantic to the other. We both have solid democratic institutions, but we reciprocally grimace at other models of society, in economy and politics. We are divided on capital punishment and on the role of force in internal and international politics; we have different views of the world around us and different recipes, at times totally opposite, for resolving its problems. According to one of the most critical scholars on transatlantic relations, Charles Kupchan, a young, authoritative counsellor in the Clinton administration, the situation has reached a critical situation, a stone's throw from collapse: "The two sides of the Atlantic follow different social models. Despite recent deregulation across Europe, America's laissez-faire capitalism still contrasts sharply with Europe's more centralized approach ... Americans still live by the rules of realpolitik, viewing military threat, coercion, and war as essential tools of diplomacy. In contrast, Europeans by and large have spent the past fifty years trying to tame international politics, setting aside guns in favor of the rule of law. On July 1, while the EU was celebrating the launch of the International Criminal Court, the Bush administration was announcing its intention to withdraw U.S. forces from Bosnia, unless they were granted immunity from the court's jurisdiction. Europeans see America's reliance on the use of force as simplistic, self-serving, and a product of its excessive power; Americans see the EU's firm commitment to multilateral institutions as naïve, self-righteous, and a product of its military weakness."[6] If Kupchan may have exaggerated slightly in his catastrophic vision, a decidedly less pessimistic observer on Euro-American relations like Henry Kissinger warns: "What the current generation of Americans knows about Europe grows far more out of business deals than political or cultural ties. On the other hand, the United States, about which most Europeans learn through their mass media, is defined by the death penalty, the allegedly inadequate system of medical insurance, the vast American prison population, and other comparable stereotypes."[7]

A WIDENING OCEAN

The perception of the widening of the ocean that separates Europe from America is a phenomenon that does not only regard the large, forgetful public or the left-wing. It is an idea shared also by careful, disillusioned, and decidedly conservative scholars. Such was a comment by Sergio Romano in December 2002: "There are an infinite number of reasons for Europeans and Americans to get on and they are better than those not to get on, but we have reached a historical point in which without a scuffle there will be harmony no longer. Europe cannot exist without measuring itself against the champion, without saying 'no,' " and he concluded by adding: "America has built a wise, moderate empire, but with 725 military installations. What would happen if an ideologized, feverished empire were to mobilize this apparatus? It is the fever that worries me."[8] It is clear that for a conservative like Sergio Romano, follower of Kissinger and of the most forthright and traditional Realpolitik, the problem takes its origin from the return of assertive idealism at the head of American foreign policy; this was also defined by Pierre Hassner[9] as a sort of "Wilsonism in boots" ("idealism with boots," paraphrasing the image that was supplied by Napoleon: "the Revolution that put on boots"). For others, however, it is precisely the return of a politics which seems to be pure power politics, Machtpolitik, which is to represent the problem of future years and to mark America's gradual detachment from Europe. In this sense, American unilateralism, be it motivated by idealism or by mere power politics, disconcerts the principle of the institutions of security community, that is, NATO.

The story of NATO at the end of the cold war really is quite unusual. Given up for dead toward the beginning of the 1990s by those who saw its fate tied indissolubly to that of the enemy against whom it had been created, it did indeed survive thanks to the redefinition of its own strategy. Assisted by a long series of crises and conflicts that peppered the whole of the 1990s (from the Iraqi invasion of Kuwait to the wars in ex-Yugoslavia), the Atlantic Alliance found itself being considered an irreplaceable integrated political-military structure, the only one capable of permitting an international community led by the United States to carry out effective military intervention for the purpose of peacekeeping or peace enforcement. In Bosnia and Kosovo particularly, NATO proved itself effective in managing out of area interventions, that is, those that are outside NATO's traditional operational areas. Paradoxically, the days following September 11, 2001 mark at one time the maximum demonstration of institutional solidarity within the Alliance, but also its objective decline, highlighted by the concrete decision on the part of America to belittle it. Although the Atlantic Council for the first time in its history managed to invoke Article 5 of the North Atlantic treaty (i.e. the key article for the Alliance itself, the basis of which every military attack led against one of its members will be considered an attack against all the other allies), Washington shows its clear disapproval of a formal "multilateralization of the crisis," be it even within an environment decidedly favorable to the United States, as NATO had logically been for over forty years.

The moment America experienced the most serious act of war that had ever happened in its territory since the time of the Civil War (the last one fought on American soil and the bloodiest in the whole history of the United States), the Bush administration rejects the future possible offers of help by its historical allies. There is no doubt about the fact that Washington considered the attacks on September 11 a veritable act of war, and not a terrorist attack, which would have been no less serious. Their refusal to act within the ambit of the Alliance is not explained by an (inexistent) American will not to confer a military profile to the crisis. Rather it highlights their determination to be able to choose freely the type of response, by exercising first and foremost its sovereign right to self-defense. No snare or impediment was to be allowed to thwart the United States' desire to plan the structure and dictate the timing for the war on terror; the proposals are announced immediately after September 11. Long before this fatal day, American libertarian circles, reflecting on the Clinton interventionism in the Balkans, had noted how the "transformation of NATO from an alliance to defend the territory of its members to an ambitious crisis-management organization has profound and disturbing implications for the United States." Although America has indeed some important strategic and economic interests in Europe, it should not let itself become involved in "parochial quarrels and conflicts that should be left to the leading European states to resolve as they choose," without embroiling the United States in an infinite series of irrelevant, dangerous disputes.[10]

America's decision had immediate serious repercussions on the Alliance, because it underlined the political (and in part also strategic) irrelevance, just when the moment to release the *foedus* seemed to have arrived unexpectedly. But there is more. The option adopted by the Bush administration, with the speed and unanimity of vision between the State Department and the Pentagon, which will subsequently be a mere memory, marks the start of the concept of "à la carte alliance"; this is probably the most significant change in the post cold war scene. The transition from a concept in which "The coalition determines the mission" to the contrary—"The mission determines the coalition"[11] is perhaps the clearest signal that Washington considers the present concept a phase of noticeable discontinuity compared to cold war times.

This conviction was so deeply rooted as to push the United States to have no hesitation not even when risking throwing the key institution during the cold war into disarray, the Atlantic Alliance which only a few years previously had been considered so important as to challenge the hostility of the new Russia (apart from the fears and frostiness of some European allies) to accelerate the entrance of the ex-Soviet satellite states into its own military structure, from Poland to Hungary and Bulgaria to Czech Republic. Possibly some people still remember the air of ill-concealed irritation that was breathed in the 1990s in Brussels and in other capitals in the old continent, when NATO's race toward the East was considered to have been almost "imposed by Washington" and was experienced as an implicit challenge launched during the most difficult process of widening and deepening of the Union. Long gone are the days when NATO seemed destined to be a sort of "UN for Democracies." In a speech made to the cadets at the Military Academy at West Point in May 1997, Bill Clinton supplied four reasons to justify the need to expand NATO: "it will strengthen our alliance in meeting the security challenges of the 21st century . . . will help to secure the historic gains of democracy in Europe . . . will encourage prospective members to resolve their differences peacefully . . . will erase the artificial line in Europe that Stalin drew and bring Europe together in security, not keep it apart in instability."[12] More than ever before NATO stimulates queries in the United States, which until very recently would have been quite inconceivable. Even among those who believe that to "extend the reach of American or Atlantic influence into other regions of the world may be desirable"[13] the question "But is NATO the right instrument for that mission?"[14] elbows its way into the discussion. Henry Kissinger comments on the specifically internal terms of the transatlantic relationship: "Is the Atlantic Alliance still at the heart of transatlantic relations? If so, how does it define its purposes in the post–Cold War world? How will a unified Europe affect the concept of an Atlantic partnership? Is the Alliance a set of common purposes or a safety net?"[15]

It is prevalently in terms of economic interests that the transatlantic relationship seems basically sound and not so easily assailable. During the weeks of the war against Iraq and in the subsequent months, above all in relations with France, a real desire on the part of the Americans to "punish" the French for their "betrayal" by hitting them on the economic front seemed to loom large. Extremely tough declarations were made both by the hawks in the Bush administration, like the National Security Advisor Condoleezza Rice—to whom, in the aftermath of Operation Iraqi Freedom, was attributed the advice to "punish France, ignore Germany, forgive Russia"—and the Defense Secretary Donald Rumsfeld, and by the "doves" like the Secretary of State Colin Powell. Such declarations were in tune with a widespread anti-French attitude in the American middle and working classes, also fueled by the popular press that had led to the renaming of french fries to freedom fries. The French, meantime, did not miss any opportunity to denounce melodramatically the arrogance of American hyperpower.[16] In fact, as had been immediately clear to the analysts, the network of European and American economy is so close that boycotting one without damaging the other is an illusion.[17] Certainly, in the sectors in which there is less economic penetration, and where there is more rivalry than cooperation (where it makes sense to depict "national winners," albeit limited to a few countries) things were different. In the aerospace industry, for example, strategy is highly developed both in the United States and in France, and Paris claimed they paid a high price for its open opposition to Washington during the war. Some international purchasing contracts regarding the new Airbus aircraft were not respected or clinched by third parties who were convinced by the American administration to change to Boeing.

In the most troubled weeks of opposition between Bush and Chirac, the Polish decision to abandon the idea to renew the aircraft fleet of dozens of fighter bombers Mirage, and to decide for 48 American F-16s, caused quite a sensation. In truth, the superior avionic and technological quality, along with considerations of cost and methods of payment, seem to have been the decisive factor for the Warsaw government. It is, however, impossible not to notice that during the Iraqi crisis Poland did manage to bring upon itself French anger and excite American applause at one and the same time. France accused Poland of having failed to show solidarity for Europe, even before becoming a full member of the European Union. The accusation was decidedly arrogant, even more so if we consider that it was accompanied by undisguised threats of retaliation on France's part; their farmers, generously subsidized by the Union, see themselves threatened by Polish competition. Incidentally, and having witnessed the state of anxiety that the structure of the Union was subjected to due to the wounds inflicted by some of its most important members, not even the president of the European Commission Romano Prodi seems to dissociate himself from them with the necessary promptness. The irate reaction to what Paris insisted on treating as a mixture between "betrayal" and "lese-majesty," was tied to the so-called *Document of the 8*, a declaration of solidarity toward the United States promoted by those circles that both in Europe and in America were worried about the state of the transatlantic relationship. It is signed by a group of countries (Great Britain, Italy, Spain, Czech Republic, Hungary, Portugal, Denmark, and indeed Poland) and was published in the Wall Street Journal at the end of January 2003.[18]

The document came out shortly before the outbreak of hostilities and some weeks before the Athens summit, which was supposed to sanction officially the change in Europe from 15 countries to 25, or else proclaim the birth of a renewed and different European Union, made up of the reunification of the "old" and the "new" Europe. Significantly, once Saddam Hussein's regime had fallen, when in May and June 2003 George W. Bush began his long journey that would take him first to St. Petersburg, for the 300th anniversary of the city, and then Evian, for the G8 summit, and finally to the Middle East where he hoped to boost the beginning of the so-called road map, the U.S. president first of all called in at Krakov, to pay homage to his new Polish ally. Poland, there again, had taken part in the Iraqi campaign, albeit with a basically symbolic military contingent. This gesture was particularly appreciated by Washington. Not only because it contributed to attenuating, as much as possible, the purely Anglo-Saxon nature of the expeditionary corps, but also because everyone was aware how much it must have cost the Warsaw government to take that step precisely at a time when the Polish Pope was taking a firm stance against the war. In short, when confronted with possible tension between the Franco-German or American pressure and with the dilemma of who to displease between the Vatican and the United States (the two powers to whom they most owed their new-found liberty), Poland twice chose America.

As we will see shortly, it would be unfair to consider the position expressed in the Franco-German declaration "more European" than that expressed in the *Document of the 8*. In the former there was an emphasis on the "rift" as regards the Bush administration's decisions to go to war. And yet, at the same time, it cannot remain unsaid that on the whole, the differences in evaluation on the state of the world between the United States and Europe continue to increase, to the extent that some have commented that "there are no signs of community between the two entities that the world insists on labelling 'The West'."[19] This is quite an obvious fact at the level of public opinion. The extraordinary cross-spreading (beyond national boundaries and ideological-cultural allegiances) of the peace movement during this last war bears witness to this. Perhaps less obviously, but in many ways far more importantly as regards its consequences, is that the Euro-American differences of opinion on how the world is perceived increase also at the level of political and economic elite and between the governments themselves. Many of these same European governments that supported the United States during the war against Iraq, did so not out of a deep conviction of the objective incontestability of "evidence" advanced by the United States about the organic link between Al Qaeda and Saddam Hussein or the regime's possession of weapons of mass destruction. They decided to do so to prevent a severe rupture in transatlantic solidarity, that is, worried that America and Europe would end up isolated and isolationist one against the other. The praiseworthy intent of this initiative and its political intelligence cannot hide the fact that Europeans are increasingly divided not so much as to how to do things but what exactly to do. To be even more explicit, America and Europe seem to be less in agreement not only on the solutions to problems, but even on the identification of problems and the order of priorities. In the current phase of Euro-American difficulties there is, to say it in Henry Kissinger's words, "an important qualitative difference. The early crises within the Alliance were generally in the nature of family disputes, having to do with differing interpretations of the requirements of an agreed common security and, indeed, of common purpose being questioned."[20]

Paradoxically, Islamic international terrorism, which seems to have been one of the main causes for triggering Euro-American tension and for the crisis of the international institutions, is in fact one of the few areas in which the differences of opinion between the two sides of the Atlantic are "limited" to the identification of the most suitable responses. Americans and Europeans, particularly after the wave of attacks that hit North Africa and the Middle East and with yet stronger reason after the massacres in Madrid on March 11, 2004 and in London on July 7, 2005 believe that Islamic international terrorism is objectively an extremely serious problem, and that the fight against it is a priority. Of course, while America tends to favor a reaction of a military nature, and at the level of intelligence aims to eliminate physically the terrorist organizations' structures and their logistic bases, Europe seems to promote a more extensive politics that aims at fighting the economic and cultural reasons for fundamentalist terrorism. On other questions, however, the differences regard the identification of the urgency of the problems. An example of this is the question of the proliferation of the weapons of mass destruction. Europe and America agree on the principle that an indiscriminate diffusion of these weapons systems must be avoided. But on the question of means and the price we are willing to pay to reach the goal, the differences are enormous. The fight against this phenomenon is of strategic priority for the United States, while it is far less so for Europe. Europe does not feel immediately threatened by the fact that one of the so-called rogue states might come into possession of weapons of extermination. America is obsessed with this danger. Europe is not even particularly convinced by the category rogue state, or by the notion that states like Iran or Syria represent the "axis of evil." America seems willing to build around this category its own idea regarding international relations in the twenty-first century, and believes that countries like Iran and Syria must be treated accordingly. For Europe, the United Nations is a precious asset to be conserved even to the detriment of possible greater efficiency in the decision-making process on the most difficult questions in international politics. America thinks that the United Nations is a cumbersome relic left over from the cold war, more of a hindrance than of any use.

"More and more over the past decade, the United States and its European allies have had rather substantial disagreements over what constitute intolerable threats to international security and the world order, as the case of Iraq has abundantly shown. And these disagreements reflect, above all, the disparity of power."[21] This is the well-known thesis of Robert Kagan, who sees the Europeans dictated by Venus and the Americans as followers of Mars, the former under the illusion that they can live in a Kantian world, where violence is basically outlawed and the latter are wrestling with a tough Hobbesian arena, in which force is the only currency that pays. As for the Europeans, the "incapacity to respond to threats leads not only to tolerance—it can also lead to denial" and even to remove the existence of the threats to security, to worry above all about those problems that are more likely to be resolved or at least faced, with political effort and large amounts of money.[22] "The different psychologies of power and weakness" push the Europeans to concentrate on questions— "the challenges"—in which their strengths are called upon and not the "threats," in which their weakness makes the solutions uncertain.[23] And yet, it is peculiar that a military man, General Hugh Shelton, the former chairman of the Joint Chiefs of Staff, reminds us—paraphrasing the English saying "for whoever has a hammer, every problem is a nail"—that "the American military is a terrific hammer. But not every problem is a nail."[24] The idea of a confrontation between a more muscular and political America and a Europe almost "intimidated" by exercising political sovereignty also finds intelligent mentors on this side of the ocean. It has also been mentioned that "while in the United States a strong idea of state sovereignty persists," and although there "war and democracy, far from being opposites, are considered not only perfectly compatible but in a certain sense even complementary," we West Europeans "who have fled, disgusted, from sovereignty and war, manage to think of politics only with a weak meaning, where it is basically reduced on one side to procedures and on the other to the sphere of rights."[25]

It is often reiterated, by way of a reassuring and at the same time supercilious refrain, that the trans-Atlantic institutions just as much as the Euro-American relationship have known other moments of crisis, and even of extremely dramatic nature. From the Suez Crisis in 1956, when the Anglo-French occupation of the Canal was thwarted by President Eisenhower's peremptory "clear-out diktat," to the Vietnam War, when more than one ally maintained cordial relations with the Hanoi regime against which the Americans were fighting. Looking carefully, it would seem that the question of the Iraq war should not be over-dramatized. If such a recommendation cannot be accepted, we must add that this new crisis has come to the fore in a global context that has changed radically. This happens when, to contain the possible destructive effects in the institutional fabric and on the structure of the Atlantic relationship, there is no longer the imminent threat of a "third party" (the USSR) which constituted just as much an objective common threat to the survival of Western democracies, as a formidable challenger to the United States in the fight for world hegemony. And there is more: it happens in a world which is no longer bipolar, which is far from being able to return to being multipolar, and rather which is characterized by being unipolar. It is the very first time in modern history that such a situation exists. There is one case in the very distant past retraceable to almost two thousand years ago, to the times of the Roman Empire.

In such a changed context, the destructive potential for transatlantic relationships in a crisis which is not managed properly could be irreversible. It would be extremely difficult to rebuild relationships and the institutional fabric.[26] But then again, the bitter tones used by Donald Rumsfeld when referring to "old Europe" as opposed to "new Europe" addressing France and Germany after the publication of their document openly dissociating themselves from the American politics of challenge regarding the United Nations, is more than just a verbal excess. It is taken from a consolidated tradition of the vision of international politics on the part of America, a vision, it must be quickly added, that basically precedes the political invention of the concept of the West. To understand completely how the notion of the West risks being subjected to an extremely tough test, we must look back into the past.

Old Europe, New Europe

Between the end of the seventeenth century and the beginning of the eighteenth, several thousand Europeans decided that to "put an ocean" between their own past and future was the only way in which they would be able to live by their own values, free from war and from political and religious persecution carried out in the name of power, justice, or the "real" faith. Who knows how many of those future "Americans" thought of those lands that they left behind as an "old Europe," compared to which even the uncertain fate that awaited them in the new world seemed better. The Secretary of State, Donald Rumsfeld, in order to whip up action in the allies who were reluctant to take action against Saddam Hussein's regime, made a less "intimist" use of the same expression—the "same old Europe." Who knows how many of the current Europeans grieved for the times when it was still possible to put an ocean between one's own life and political power. Who knows if any one of these new inhabitants of old Europe realized that by entertaining that bizarre thought that almost four centuries after the crossing of the Mayflower they were trying to flee from power and politics, from the tireless attempt of politics to "put order" into space, by deluding themselves that a Utopian Island might exist. Lastly, who knows how many of these Europeans asked themselves (as had happened to the Pilgrim Fathers) whether this escape would not end with the only effectively secure result: giving life to a dream through a Declaration of Independence, which was so bold as to sanction the revolutionary idea that another kind of politics could really be possible.

Perhaps we should keep these thoughts in mind in order to approach the subject calmly, the subject of the future of Euro-American relations which are simple and at the same time vital for the fate of world order. Remembering the historical reality of a relationship does not in any way mean lessening its importance; if anything, the opposite is the case: only through being aware of the long road that lies behind us, and of the even longer one that preceded it, can we fully comprehend the extraordinary importance of the friendship between the United States and Europe, and avoid flirting fancifully, maybe even "indulging in virtuosity," with the prospect of a progressive divergence of the destinies and interests between the two main bastions of democracy that ever existed. It may seem rhetorical to wish to start from this shared element, the faith in democracy, now that it seems to have become a hazy concept, laid aside by recent events that tell of reciprocal incomprehension and intolerance. And yet, neither the nature of the past relationship between Europe and America, nor the objective inevitability of its future can be understood if we neglect to see that they are intertwined because of the fight for the defense and success of democracy. Even when it appears to us that the disagreements make us "unbearably different," suffice to look around and remember that there are internal seas that are far wider than the oceans.

About a hundred and fifty years after the landing of the Mayflower, in the name of liberty and the faith in democracy, the Founding Fathers took the serious decision to renounce their British citizenship and become American citizens. The second secession from Europe also marked the beginning of that American idealistic isolation; the best outline of this can be found in George Washington's famous political testament, in which he warns his successors to steer clear of Europe and its power politics: he claimed that they were obsessed with the fight for power and the domination of the world. "Since George Washington's Farewell Address, Americans have been wary of military alliances with other nations. For much of the twentieth century, their concerns were directed at the possibility that an international organization of which the United States was a member could oblige it to use armed force without its consent. Thus, the United States declined to join the League of Nations and joined the UN, NATO, and other alliances, only after making clear that it reserved the right to decide for itself when to use armed forces, and that in no circumstances would it automatically be required to do so."[27] Washington's ideas were believed for a long time to be the origin of American "isolationist" thinking. And to a certain extent it is. Basically, at the end of 1700, Europe was the international political system, so that to seek one's own separate path, was tantamount to "isolating" oneself from world politics. Looking at things from a less "Eurocentric" perspective, however, we need to consider that from George Washington onward, a tradition is started which might be more usefully defined as "exceptionalism," rather than isolationism. This term "exceptionalism" conveys the idea that the United States is the bearer of a message and a destiny different from all the other political communities (better and indeed outstanding). If we apply the concept of isolationism, it may appear that the United States alternates between seasons of openness toward the outside world and seasons of uncooperativeness. In the whole of its long history, from George Washington to George W. Bush, the United States has never ceased to consider itself the bearer of a message and an outstanding condition.

Faith in the exceptional nature of America is the truly constant factor in American foreign policy throughout the ages. The Monroe doctrine of 1825, the one summarized in the slogan "America for the Americans," not only tended to close the doors of the new continent to possible European ambitions to portion out the ex-Spanish colonies, which had just declared themselves independent. Neither can this be liquidated as a merely inept ideological cover for imperialistic ambitions on the part of the United States on the Western hemisphere. It also reflected the idea that the North-American example could be paradigmatic for the whole continent. About 70 years later, Theodore Roosevelt brought the United States back to the context of great international politics, bringing it a role of great power. After the Hispanic-American War of 1898, the United States had in fact consolidated its position of an emerging power in Asia and the Pacific along with Japan, whose powerful status was recognized in 1905, after a victorious war against another European power, Russia, which was far more formidable than Spain.

We have to await the beginning of the twentieth century and the "call" from European democracies in danger (Great Britain, of course, and also France) for the two sides of the Atlantic to reestablish political ties which had been broken more than a century before. Since then, the two worlds become one again only when there is the loud cry in defense of democracy. Each time this idem sentire relaxes, as in the two decades between the two world wars, it inevitably weakens the awareness of their common identity and this is always a sign of a general weakness of democracy. But even when America and Europe realize that they have the huge patrimony of democratic institutions in common, so rare in the world, the Americans never stop considering themselves different and better. The American idea of the "shining town on the hill" (Ronald Reagan's favorite image), of a new Jerusalem, of a place where politics is reestablished, has never faded. If we think of the Founding Fathers, after all, how can we prove them wrong, if we consider that when they gave life to a republic legitimized by popular sovereignty and almost universal suffrage of citizens engaged in the "pursuit of Happiness," the rest of the world, the whole of the rest of the world, knew no institutional system that was remotely comparable. It is no accident that quite apart from any other consideration, the unconditional support which America has given Israel since its birth (and to an exceptional degree since 1967) is facilitated by the natural sympathy that is evoked in American political culture by an experiment like the Jewish State, which closely echoes the origins of the United States. It is not only the Messianic nature of the American conception of foreign policy, so that for "many generations most Americans seem to have believed that American society was the best possible society and that the rest of the world would be better off if they became more like us."[28] But rather it was obvious to the eyes of American leadership that the United States "could not be just another great power playing the old games of dominance with rivals and allies," because by virtue of an interpretation of history in no way naive or idealistic, it was obvious that such "competition led to war, and war between great powers was no longer an acceptable part of the international system. The Americans were replacing Great Britain at a moment when the rules of the game were changing forever."[29]

If we choose the concept of "exceptionalism" to categorize American politics, it permits us to understand yet another element, which is decisive today for our understanding of why the United States, starting from the end of the cold war and more drastically with the advent of George W. Bush's administration, decided to pursue a policy of increasingly assertive unilateralism. If we reflect on the history of the United States, we have to remember one fact first and foremost. For America it is normal that its own power has encountered limitations deriving from its own capacity and its own will. From the end of the war fought against England between 1812 and 1815, and up until the second half of the twentieth century, America never had to pit itself against any external challenger that was able to "contain" its power. Each time it was unsuccessful, faced a threat or a serious problem, the American response has always been the same: "We will call upon more resources, time and determination and this way we will solve the problem, eliminate the threat or rectify the failure." The Americans upheld this idea throughout the two world wars, even in dramatic moments like Pearl Harbor and during the long years of the fight against Nazism. They never considered that an external power might be able to obstruct their intentions to solve problems, eliminate threats, and make the world a better place.

With the cold war, for the first time in its history the United States had to experience that sense of limitation imposed from outside which is, indeed, normal for us Europeans. Hundreds of years of experience within a system made up of sovereign states in competition with each other have taught us that: "Persuasiveness in negotiations depends importantly on the options the negotiator has available or is perceived to have at his or her disposal. Europeans historically associated diplomacy with a balancing of rewards and costs; they have little use for an abstract concept of universal goodwill as a facilitator of diplomacy."[30] Such a different, opposing conception of what is normal originates in our history, that history in which Europe itself was born with "limitations," like recognizing it was impossible to bring back to unity the ancient *christiana respublica*. The highly prized European variety and plurality, to which we lay claim and appreciate today as an extraordinary cultural heritage and which challenges us to construct a daring new institutional structure able to contain it and give it political identity and unity of intent, has its origins in "failure."

This is the main point of noncommunication and political and cultural difference between Europe and America: our history as Europeans was born of a bloody failure; the Americans' history was born from an extraordinary success. It could also be said that paradoxically, although America's problem has always been to be able to think out and build a foreign and international policy that chimed in with this incredible success, recent European history has been characterized with the credit of having managed to transform that original and, for a long time, bloody failure into an extraordinary innovation of politics between states. Underneath these differences on the role of law, political sovereignty, and the role of war, there is a difference in the notion of politics that the United States has to do with something that for us is a distant memory and that we can define the conjunction of moral commitment, political, and military commitment. I would like to clarify one fact: the point is not that America always behaves in this way, nor that it always pursues this model. The point is that to understand American foreign policy and the reasons for disagreement with the Europeans, we need to consider these elements. Frankly speaking, American foreign policy is not only the fruit of interest. In the American idea of politics, above all international politics, there is the premise that politics is a commitment of good against evil; there is the idea that politics is the supreme creative art. In American culture politics is given heroic status, a Greek or Roman idea, so to speak. But there is also a profoundly Christian element, so that politics is what makes us most similar to God, insofar as it characterizes us as human beings and distinguishes us from other living beings. Politics is seen as the capacity to create something out of nothing. Well, such a heroic vision of politics is no longer possible in Europe, because Europe has "moved beyond that" so to speak. It was starting from a conception in many ways "heroic" that we built totalitarianism in Europe: first the Terror of Robespierre and then Communism and Nazi-Fascism. It is not surprising, then, that we Europeans take a step backward when faced with the heroic and almost divine conception of politics, because we have experimented what many have called the maximum form of political quality that has gone "out of control": totalitarianism.

It is in this political vision, rather than in the European legalistic approach, that the sacred notion that the United States has of its own sovereignty is based, according to which it is difficult to hypothesize the bestowal of sovereignty over superior needs. The European heads of state and government have just accomplished a similar advance, through the institutive Treaty of the European Constitution and also by means of a plurality of preceding treaties, all aimed at devolving significant quotas for the individual national sovereignties in a new supranational political institution. In more general terms, the positive perception of mutual limitations of sovereignty in favor of a network of global governance about to be established is widely diffused among a considerable part of public opinion in the old continent. The enthusiasm that greeted the creation of the International Criminal Court bears witness to this. A similar process would not be so easily imaginable in the United States, because there it is not possible to devolve sovereignty: no American president could devolve in favor of who-knows-who United States' sovereignty, for the simple reason that it belongs to the U.S. people; it is not a disposable resource. The words of the declaration delivered to the UN Security Council in January 2000 by Senator Jesse Helmes in his capacity as Chairman of the Senate Foreign Relations Committee, recall those with which Henry Cabot Lodge led the opposition in the American senate on the U.S. entrance to the League of Nations. "The demands of the United States have not changed much since Henry Cabot Lodge laid out his condition for joining the League of Nations 80 years ago: Americans want to ensure that the United States of America remains the sole judge of its own internal affairs, that the United Nations is not allowed to restrict the individual rights of the United States citizens, and that the United States retains sole authority over the deployment of United States forces around the world."[31] As commentators have observed, Henry Cabot Lodge was not an isolationist—far from it. He shared a sincere internationalist predisposition with President Wilson, and led those "internationalist" opponents to the League of Nations. They were not worried about the fact that the United States would have to engage itself in world problems, but "simply opposed the way Wilson intended to engage the world . . . believed that the United States had to preserve a free hand to act abroad, not tie its fate to the whims and interests of others. They charged that the League would trump the Constitution and usurp Congress's power to declare war. The leader of the anti-League internationalist, Republican Senator Henry Cabot Lodge of Massachusetts, went to the heart of the matter when he asked his colleagues: 'Are you willing to put your soldiers and your sailors at the disposition of other nations?' "[32]

The power to declare war directs us immediately to the other big question that divides Europeans from Americans: the acceptability or nonacceptability of the use of force in international politics. Europe and America are increasingly at variance on this point. As was mentioned a short while ago, it could be said that the determination to flee from the inevitability of war, can be seen in some ways at the beginning of the American experience. It then continued to be present, in part, even when America plunged itself into the world through Wilson and Roosevelt's projects and accomplishments. Meanwhile, precisely because of the devastating experience of the two world wars and the decline of the colonial empires, Europe turned against power politics. This is also the expression of the end of its own political power in the international system. During the Afghanistan War, *Le Monde* published an open letter signed by some intellectuals belonging to very different currents of thought and political opinions.

Among these were Michael Novak, Francis Fukuyama, Robert Putnam, Will Marshall, Samuel Huntington, and Michael Walzer. The letter insists clearly on the need and moral imperative of war, inasmuch as "careful moral deliberation teaches us that when facing evil the best response is to put an end to it."[33] It may be that war is not only morally acceptable but also morally necessary to counter ignominious demonstrations of violence and injustice. Today we find ourselves in this situation, and it is the same position substantiated by Tony Blair over the years, the same position expressed in a report drawn up by Kissinger's staff following the attacks on September 11, which simply said that there are basically two ways to resolve the problem of terrorism: one is to try to understand the minds of the terrorists to deduce what kind of defense to set up; the other is to kill all the terrorists and potential terrorists—in short, to eliminate evil, even if it means acting alone: "The United States has reserved the right to use military force unilaterally, without international authorization, and has done so with increasing frequency since the end of the Cold War," which means that "the United States will continue to act unilaterally for purposes it deems necessary, even if its international partners do not agree."[34]

It would seem that Europe and America have followed two different courses that were not necessarily destined to cross in a stable, institutionalized way. And it would have continued like this at length, if it were not for sporadic and unenthusiastic contacts, until two elements decided to give a decisive shove toward drawing the two sides of the Atlantic closer together. The first was the natural expansive capacity of ideas and the principles of democracy within Western culture. This tended to become the most particular characteristic of its political culture in the twentieth century. Prepared by the spreading of the values of liberalism and nationalism during the nineteenth century, the twentieth century saw democracy compete and triumph in establishing itself in the West and become the most distinctive regime. The association between the West and democracy becomes so strong as to cause the latter to be rejected by countries that had recently attained independence, precisely because it was too markedly Western, and so by definition foreign to their own traditions and autochthonic values. Democracy is a concept so inextricably linked to the West as to make it incompatible with a road to originally authentic national independence.

The second element that brought the two sides of the Atlantic together was the interweaving of the two roads on which America and Europe had started out as regards the international arena. In the twentieth century, America's return to the international scene is a natural consequence considering the important level of its development and the expansion of its economic capabilities. But the immediately hegemonic way with which it presents itself is basically forced by American "exceptionalism," and it brings the United States to set itself up as the champion of a notion of international order which is in many ways extraordinarily similar to its internal order. Kagan's theory, that Europe lives in a "Kantian paradise" while America is forced to fight in an international arena of Hobbesian nature, is partly true. He does however omit to include a significant "detail" that is able to explain American politics better than can be done by resorting to the usual image of "international anarchy." The detail is that in the perspective of U.S. foreign policy the idea that America will be safe only when the rest of the world follows its example is a recurring idea.

At the Paris Peace Conference in Versailles in 1919, the attention that was reserved particularly by the Europeans for the stubborn reassertion of the principles of national self-determination and the legitimization of boundary decision-making on predominantly ethnic grounds did not permit the understanding of the really revolutionary aspect of the famous "Fourteen Points" with which Woodrow Wilson called the victorious powers to prepare the order that should result from the end of the First World War: even in the anarchicae international arena it must be possible to pursue and realize a level of justice and democracy that is similar to that desired in the domestic arena. This ambitious objective can be reached provided that the American lesson is heeded.[35] American hegemony, which restores order, democracy, and the market within half of Europe after the Second World War, is not so very different from what inspired Wilson: and it is in this way that Woodrow Wilson and Franklin Delano Roosevelt can be considered two "relay runners" on the same leg. Vice versa, it is the collapse of the first European fusion to try to achieve "order in plurality," that is, to ensure each other by means of the politics of the balance of power, that calls on "the great lord" twice in a quarter of a century to put an end to the recurring German temptations for power and heralding the advent of another hegemony, this time outside Europe.

This is the origin of the political significance of the idea of the West, an extreme synthesis of the relationship between Europe and America, which is founded on two pillars, one very congenial to us Europeans, the other far less so. The first one is seen in the necessarily democratic nature of the West: without democracy there is nothing to bond sufficiently and peacefully hold together what the concept entails. The consequence of this first thesis is that safeguarding democracy in Europe (i.e., on the side of the Atlantic where it had proven to be historically most fragile) is essential for the survival of the West in its entirety. The second pillar is that the concept has shown extraordinary political force since the Western arena was dominated by the United States. Because of the way events have unfolded in recent years, we should ask ourselves if the political meaning of this concept (that we know to be much older in cultural terms) will be able to survive a possible relaxation of American domination. As Europeans, we should ask ourselves if, without the Communist threat and with the intensifying of American unilateralism, it really is "the West" that we are talking about when we say "we members of this political community" even on the understanding that we may suffer temporary disadvantages.[36]

We have mentioned how during the cold war the notion of the West "had crystallized in a new way. It was in opposition not with the East, but with the vision of the world, economy and society of the countries that were described as Communist." America was the link and champion of this West. The end of the Communist regimes and the advancing of the process of European unification now seemed to push Europe again to search for its identity. At the same time, and inconsistently, "the opposition between capitalism and communism, dissolved in the 1980s would seem to be substituted by the opposition between the West and Islam, despite the various forms existing between the West today and the different Islamic states and despite the different political regimes existing within them."[37] This contradiction was exacerbated by the conflict with Iraq, from which many Europeans wanted to renege "politically" to emphasize that it was possible for the West to be defined not only by means of open confrontation with the Islamic world, led or imposed by the United States. For other equally "political" reasons, other Europeans preferred to stay alongside America, fearing that further isolation would have made the choice for "power politics" irreversible, to the detriment of "leadership politics" operated by Washington after September 11.

Quite apart from our own opinion on this most recent Iraqi campaign, there is an obvious paradox. Although the domination of the United States outside the West has the traits of an increasingly aware semi-imperial power, American authority within the West is not so unchallenged; this is not because some other power wishes to take its place (not only in Germany but even in France they are aware of this) but because governments, public opinion, and authorities of all kinds challenge the legitimacy, on the basis of a no-longer concurring assessment of what is in fact in the general interest of the West. It is the so-called paradox of the hegemon, so that the dominant nation within an international political system carries out the role of hegemon and great power. Each hegemonic nation obviously has the material capability to act in a unilateral fashion, but if it does so at the expense of the system as a whole, it risks losing its hegemony, which requires a certain consensus from those on whom it is exercised. There is, thus, a veritable contradiction in the inclination of a great power to act unilaterally in order to follow its own national interests and the desire to preserve long-term stability within the system. After September 11, America seems to have solved the paradox by opting decisively for the role of the great power, to the detriment of that of leader of the West; their decision can in part be comprehended, given that the protection of their own citizens and territory had come to be an absolute priority for the Bush administration.[38]

The question for us Europeans, following the fact that America has increasingly become a "lonely superpower" and less and less the "leader of the West" is very simple: if the colonies in 1776 had to become American because they believed that it was London's politics that prevented them from continuing to be at the same time British subjects and free individuals, is Europe perhaps facing a similar option? Has it reached a similar cross-roads? Following recent American political choices and in order to preserve our freedom, perhaps we should cease to be "citizens" of the West and become first and foremost "Europeans"?

The European Union in Search of Its Identity

The theme of the search for identity on the part of Europe is at the center of the question we have to face to prevent the thoughts on the future of the relationship between Europe and the United States taking on the well-known semblance of a list of pious wishes or else of dreadful scenarios. In the dramatic phase leading up to the recent Iraqi campaign, we witnessed a decidedly unexpected split (its virulence was particularly unexpected) between the most important nations in the European Union. The mass media and more than one interested commentator presented reality in the simplified version of an "American party" (Great Britain, Spain, and Italy) against a "European party" (France and Germany). In truth, it should be said that both sides had the safety and the assertion of a more united

Europe at heart; but certainly neither had any hesitation in acting as they saw fit, shattering the little that had been laboriously achieved in terms of foreign policy and common security. In any case, for the first time two underlying conceptions (completely specular) of European identity were clearly outlined. The first, Blair, Aznar, and Berlusconi's, moved from the premise that European identity in political terms was so fragile as to emerge again only if the stormy Atlantic were transformed into a calm mirror of sea under American hegemony: only this hegemony, forcing the individual sovereignty of European states, permits Europe's common identity to come to the fore, and to prevail over the stronger national identities. The second, Schroeder and Chirac's, assumed that European political identity was already in profile, and that only persistent American hegemony prevented it from emerging in all its might. Draining off, or at least reducing the extent of American hegemony within the "Western sea" is, thus, the necessary premise for a common European identity to be finally established.

If we look at how the situation evolved, it might be said that the supporters of a "weak identity" might have been "a little more right," insofar as those who were under the illusion that they could mobilize the European governments in the name of a challenge to American leadership obtained the result of shattering that little unity of intent and behavior in foreign policy and security that had been achieved in 15 years or so of patient work and of providing a "shore" for those that consider the natural seat of democratic politics to be the "squares" rather than the parliaments. Quite apart from the many " 'sarong' declarations," that tried in attractive, multifarious ways to cover up rifts and failures in the face of a dramatic decisive test for the assertion of its political importance—that is, the choice of war or peace—the European Union suffered a serious split. It split so sensationally as to make it paradoxically legitimate to ask the question that, up until a few years ago, would have sounded senselessly provocative: "will the European Union survive the Second pillar of the Maastricht treaty? Or was it a decisive mistake to demand that we equip ourselves with a common foreign and security policy without having previously solved the problem of the role of national sovereignty?"

In effect, the fact that political military security in Europe was guaranteed through American hegemony made it possible that in the past European national sovereignties were in fact tamed. In this way, the gradual construction of the European Union took place starting from weakened sovereignty that facilitated harmonization. It is no coincidence that, just when American leadership wavers within the West— also because of an excess of unilateralism and shortcomings in communication on Washington's part—contrasting (or at least differing) national interests within the European states reappear, re-endowing the national sovereignties with a large part of their explosive potential. The recent controversy between Germany and Italy regarding the reform of the Security Council is another piece in the same puzzle of discord. The regression to a strictly nationalistic reasoning on Berlin's part is besides anything else a logical contradiction to the claim, supported also by Paris, that the French-German axis is a guarantee of Europeanism within the Union. This is why, quite different from what was possible for the Founding Fathers in their escape from politics, power and the responsibility of exerting it, Europeans must be aware that, not only physical secession nor even political secession between the two sides of the Atlantic can be an answer to the obvious Euro-American tensions. And, in any case, only by remaining anchored to the transatlantic relationship will the Europeans be able to strengthen their common identity, so that it may one day take on a strong, innovative political connotation, just as emerged on July 4, 1776 in Philadelphia.[39] There are no other practicable roads for those who have Europe's political future at heart. Unless Europe is to be connoted as a political identity in which democracy and freedom are "accidents," it is in the interests of "old Europe" to keep the notion of the West alive and kicking, which was the main guarantee against our recurring tendency to be attracted by far more mysterious and hazy enchantments: by the pan-politicism of the last century to the anti-politics of these years.

The existence of a European political space and a European political community is a far more controversial problem than may appear at first glance. Its substance is closely dependent on what we understand by the expression "political community." If we fill the notion with institutional structures, then we may say that a European political community exists. The Union's political space is indeed one of the most densely populated, in terms of institutions, that history has ever produced. On the other hand, as is fairly well known, the fact that many of the most important decisions can only be made with the agreement of all the member states, some with qualified majority, others with the mechanism of co-decision between different Union institutions, and lastly, very few with simple majority; all this makes the vast institutional apparatus even more cumbersome in its mechanics than it is gargantuan in its composition. It is here that the problem of the so-called democratic deficit is collocated; the congestion of institutions, none of which are exclusively responsible for a particular function, meets the fact that as effective decision-making power grows, democratic legitimization becomes more indirect.

To remedy the reality of a political organization founded prevalently on institutions, the opportune, historical decision has been reached to begin a real constituent process founded on two elements: the Charter of Rights ("proclaimed but not adopted" by the Council of Nice) and the Convention, with the task of drawing up the outline of a European Constitution to be subjected to the approval of the member states. At the bottom of these changes lies the clear awareness that, without a warm heart and a genuine common citizenship, Europe cannot become a truly political community. Some important factors play against this: the European institutions are far from the citizens and not given high consideration by public opinion. The democratic deficit of the Union does not seem to be easily resolvable. Its hyper-bureaucratic structure and the absence of structure filled with "mediators and representatives of the common interest" (i.e., a system of parties and associations which is well-structured throughout the continent), makes sure that even a more direct relationship between electorate, parliament, and Commission might end up giving an even greater advantage to those powerful groups that, even now, are the only ones able to receive an effective hearing in the Union. Then again, it is difficult to imagine that this structure, vital for any democracy, could develop when European civil society appears to be so fragmented: consider the variety of languages that makes the formation of a really European system of media or a perfectly European political speech impossible, so that it is not easy to imagine the development of a common public opinion even in the long term. The problem that the Convention tried to resolve by means of the drafting of the so-called European Constitution is that of a structural democratic deficit, so that any further conferment of power to the centre of the Union risked being a step backward not only as regards the ideals of a democracy functioning in an exemplary way, but also regarding the reality of the member states.[40]

The survival of the nation states, which despite increasing difficulties remain the primary object of political loyalty for European citizens is probably the second obstacle for the realization of an effective European political community. Being European, which exists in cultural terms as a differentiation with others (Westerners and non-Westerners), has always coexisted with a plurality of political and institutional orders. This plurality has somehow constituted the idea itself of Europe, from Westphalia to the Treaty of Rome. Today we wonder if European identity will manage to become a shared political identity, even without the endorsement of the Constitutional Treaty.[41] To wonder about the extent to which one may talk about

European political space means going beyond the fact that there is a European institutional scenario, that decisions that determine the lives of Union citizens are made continually, and that a single currency ties a dozen of them together out of 25 member-states. All these institutions and even the single currency seem to have two characteristics. On one hand, they have created more order and reason; on the other, they include a bet on the future of the Union, a bet that risks being a hazard, unless it is not suitably defined.

In very recent times, Europe has shown that it has an extraordinary capacity to face challenges and transform them into opportunities for development. Events in the 1990s forced Europe to come to terms with a completely changed reality from the past decades. First, it was confronted with a scenario in which foreign policy reverted to being no longer or exclusively an exogenous variable. The end of bipolarism, while making the context less stable and predictable, imposed greater activism in foreign policy, returned sovereignty to states, and demanded more responsive powers from them; it also brought to the center of the debate the question of national interest and the correct determination of this. At the same time, however, the spread of globalization showed how the state-national dimension risked being insufficient in its attempt to govern politically such a phenomenon. The European states received a twofold request that urged them to seek greater political integration, but also a stronger national determination as regards foreign policy, which were less and less frozen within the orders established after the Second World War. Not by chance, the institution that best incarnated that situation of big decisive choices made once and for all—NATO—experienced extremely tricky moments after 1989, and these were only overcome with the outbreak of the Balkan crisis and the change of the strategic mission of the Alliance. Anyhow, precisely the Balkan crisis and the failure of Europe to go beyond the simple claim to be autonomous in managing it, show how even in the close vicinity of its own boundaries Europe was not able to cast its own political influence.

Post–cold war Europe was in fact dominated by one problem—as regards the Union—of internal politics: how to absorb the new Germany and how to make sure that the German colossus would not succumb to the recurring dream of a *Sonderweg* toward the east and south-east, a dream that was a nightmare for the survival of the project of unification. That the fear was far from being outlandish, is proven by the fact that the German speed in recognizing Croatia and the other countries born from the dissolution of ex-Yugoslavia, contributed substantially to the degeneration of the situation in the

Balkans. But then again, it is enough to go back over the crucial period of June 1986 to December 1991, to ascertain the close link that existed between the German reunification and the effective launch of procedures aimed at widening and deepening the European Community, transforming it into a Union that would be immediately equipped with a common currency. At the Madrid Summit in June 1989 the political conditions for the launch of the euro were established. Only at the Rome Summit in October 1990, however, did the single currency suddenly pass beyond the project stage, with an as yet unspecified deadline. In the meantime, during the summer of 1989, hundreds of thousands of Germans physically "abandoned" East Germany and reaching the West through Czechoslovakia and Hungary provoked the irreversible crisis for Honecker's regime, the fall of the Wall and the premises for German reunification.

Against this eventuality, Germany's most important European ally, French President François Mitterrand, had flown to Moscow, in the vain attempt to halt the course of history, without managing to do much other than irritate the German Chancellor. United States' pressure and the billions of *Deutschmarks* Helmut Kohl had promised to Mikhail Gorbachev, convincing him to acquiesce to the reality of a unified Germany even though it was a member of NATO, also forced Europe to give its political agreement to the German right to reunification. And there was a particularly important thing: to admit the Eastern Laender to the Union, inasmuch as they were an integral part of one of the member states. At the special meeting organized in Strasbourg in December 1989, Germany's European partners formally accepted its reunification, receiving in exchange Germany's full participation in the euro project. This basically meant an exchange between the *Deutschmark* and the new common currency. At the same time—almost as if they were renewing the conditions, the promises and mutual reassurance of the postwar years—there was general acknowledgment for the need to establish Germany solidly within Europe, by means of the transition from the community to the Union, emphasizing the political nature, which in the previous decade had remained very much in the background. Lastly, it was assured that the German desire and interest to move toward the east to fill the political, economic, and cultural gap left by the Russian withdrawal would be achieved far better, faster, and under conditions of greater security and stability, if it happened within the sphere of Europe. This was the real political premise in the Maastricht Treaty (with its three pillars) and inaugurated a new phase in the European story: a common currency, a deepening of the political ties within the Union, and the widening of its borders.

A peculiar thing that should be mentioned is that the launch of the euro, that is, the thing that may be considered to have been most successful in terms of economic integration and an extremely important factor in contributing to a less unilateral order to the global economic system was accelerated by the worry of European internal politics. It was a barter between Europe and Germany: the former accepted German reunification and its immediate integration in the Union in exchange for the German renunciation of the *Deutschmark* in favor of the euro. Even more peculiar, perhaps, is the fact that since then, Germany does not seem to have recovered from the economic effort borne of the unification, so much so that from 1990 until now it has no longer been one of the alternative engines in the international economy, able to take over from America when it was in difficulty.

Even though it was dictated by the shock of German reunification and the fear of a split in the Franco–German axis without which a united Europe could not exist, the idea of simultaneous widening and deepening of the Union was not only a "defensive" response in the face of an unexpected event, but it was also a courageous response, which permitted the re-launching of the idea of unification by means of a return to the creation of a more political European project. It contributed to promoting a frame for collective security, which would be able to guarantee order to the central-eastern area of the continent from which, for almost half a century, the main threat to Western security had originated. In this sense, the mere launch of the widening of Europe was an objective and undeniable success. Throughout the whole of central Europe, north of the Balkans, the prospect of becoming part of the Union worked as a stabilizing factor for the newly born democratic regimes. In the areas where it was impossible to imagine either the enticing prospect of being admitted to the "club" or the more difficult prospect of having a real common foreign policy, assisted by credible military force, events developed as we know. Today, the process of enlargement has proven to be excessively rigid and extremely fast in its execution. But then again, it would have been a disaster had the schedule not been respected by the Union. Any procrastination would have seriously disappointed the expectations, hopes, and even the emotional energy expended by the people in the candidate states; it would have undermined their still fragile democratic institutions and raised a new intangible wall of resentment within Europe. In short, any delay would have been a political error and a moral defeat.

In the period between the launch of the expansion project and the time it was to be realized, there was another change of scene in

Europe. The calming of the Balkan crisis culminating in the trial of Milosevic, changed the origin of threats to European security. Today, they no longer come from the heart of old Europe, but from outside—from the Mediterranean and the Middle East. This change of scenario does not deprive the expansion project of importance in any way, but it certainly deprives it of an important "environmental resource," insofar as it modifies the governments' priorities and the worries of public opinion that see the problem of security rise to first place, thus soaking up more resources.

For several years now a different scenario has been developing, and it accelerated visibly with September 11, 2001 and its aftermath. It is a scenario where security is no longer predictable but something to conquer and check day by day. On this issue, the nation-states reacquire all their authority, paradoxically accentuated by the fact that the threat to national security may even come from nonstate players (like the terrorist organizations). All of this confers a certain amount of legitimization to their existence. The states cannot be portrayed as if they were old dinosaurs threatened with extinction, substituted by a new "European creature." They are no longer "out of scale" to manage their own national security as in the cold war years, or to control in its own "national way" the social consequences of globalization. They revert to being suitable for confronting the new threats and challenges. Because up until today and until proved otherwise, the states are still the only political authority legitimized by direct democratic vote, entitled to control, and use the security resources in terms of intelligence, military force, investigations, and repression on the part of the police force. Consequently, they are the only depositories of that fundamental element of national interest that has as its objective the security and defense of the political community.

THE EUROPEAN UNION: FROM INSTITUTIONAL SPACE TO GLOBAL POLITICAL PLAYER

The European Union is traversing a veritable identity crisis, and it is a crisis dictated by the fact that the nature of the Union is undergoing great change. Such change is dictated in turn by the "return of politics"— that which was once defined "high politics"—to the European scene. Again the great change comes from outside the Union, its territory, and its highly institutionalized political arena. But yet again, the change that comes from the Hobbesian realm of the anarchicae international political arena, testing the soul and identity of the Kantian Republic that the Union has embodied until now. What has seemed to

be lacking in Europe has been a soul, an identity: this is a decisive factor for the future of the Union, at least as important as its institutional
order. Europe has given a very bad account of itself on this matter in
recent years, years of dramatic choices as regards foreign policy, because
the "identity of a subject—national, pluri-national, or federative—is
measured by its capacity to act as such, above all with relation to the
outside world. It must therefore be acknowledged that the European
Union was absent or not able to take the necessary steps on the big
international issues, just when the integration of men, goods and currency was being created."[42]

The first immense challenge, as we have just seen, came from the
fall of the Soviet Union, from the problem of German reunification
and the collapse of the Communist order in central-eastern Europe.
The Union responded to that challenge with three deeply significant
political reactions: widening, deepening, and the euro. The recent history of these years has taught us that those three responses incorporated three challenges that were to a certain extent similar in caliber to
those that had created them and made them necessary. But these same
years have also clarified beyond any reasonable doubt, that up until
now one of the challenges has indeed been overcome. The euro is a
reality, and an important one at that; it has proven that it is able to survive and assert itself both when the exchange rate against the dollar
floats poorly above the rate of 0.80, and when it soars triumphantly up
to 1.20 and more. It is no coincidence that such a conservative, cir-
cumspect, and realistic country like China retains a sizeable portion of
its reserves in euro, and other countries in Asia are preparing to do
likewise. So, to this extent the euro is such a good reality, that there
are those that forward the hypothesis that the euro will survive even if
there should be a collapse in the processes of widening and deepening
of the Union.

The two other challenges have by no means been overcome. They
have constituted a sort of "up and under" created by a defense that is
in difficulty, put under pressure by the external events that took place
at the end of the 1980s. Now the ball has changed course dramatically
and is plummeting toward the ground; many wonder if the
"European team" will be there to catch it before it bounces, and will
be able to recuperate and above all, whether it is sufficiently close-knit
and well-organized to put it back into play again. There are many
doubts because in the meantime, the Union has been put under severe
stress by an outside world that refused to hear of "leaving Europe in
peace," so that it could concentrate on the historical task of transforming the structure of the "Community of 12" to the "Union of 25."

First we had ten years of Balkan wars: Europe was incapable of resolving a minor conflict, yet with devastating consequences, both from a material and symbolic point of view, right on its own doorstep. Those who have found Donald Rumsfeld, or Paul Wolfowitz's acerbity unbearable, would do well to remember the tough words of the then American Secretary of State Madeleine Albright, when, at Rambouillet, she "dictated" the timings of the intervention in Kosovo to a recalcitrant Europe. Then there was the Iraqi conflict that split Europe completely, just when it was necessary for it to find unity in any way possible. In terms of resources or problems that came from outside, the big difference for the Union between the cold war years and today lies here: in these 15 years no aid has arrived, only challenges, which have been confronted with the necessary courageous pugnacity. Now, however, "the cards must be shown," and there is a considerable risk that they do not have a good enough hand to win, because "the ability to regulate and solve conflicts peaceably, in particular those bordering its own confines, will increasingly become the source of symbolic legitimisation for the Union, while failures on this front will be fatal."[43] The effects of an eventual rejection of the "European Constitution" by important countries like France or a group of average or average–small-sized countries would be devastating.

Pressurized by an outside world that has no intention of respecting the time necessary for the Europeans to win their historical internal match, the Union today must transform itself from the most extreme and refined expression of a political and institutional arena, into something different and much more ambitious. It must become a subject of international politics, with ambitions and responsibilities commensurate with its traditions, economy, and culture. For a long time there has been debate as to whether this implies equipping ourselves with a suitable military tool. Personally, I believe it is the only course open to us. It is, however, above all a technical problem. More difficult to resolve is the political problem of how to prevent the incredible journey that has been accomplished from being frustrated just when we are approaching the most important objective. The issue of the rivalry for political leadership between the great nations of Europe is one of the first to be tackled. It may well be that Robert Kagan's image of Europe as a "Kantian paradise," all legality and rights, hits the nail on the head, with an America forced to live within "the Hobbesian hell," where only the rules of the balance of force or hegemony really count. We cannot refrain from pointing out that precisely in Europe, there is the risk that a conflict will break out again dramatically (not military, of course) for the balance or hegemony in the Union between France, Germany, and Great Britain.

In Europe of the 12 (and then, but to a lesser extent when it became 15) the real political engine in the Union was formed by the Franco-German axis. When France and Germany spoke the same language, when Paris's political *grandeur* and Bonn's economic greatness went hand in hand, the whole of Europe enjoyed good health and was on the move. The moments of weakness of this special continental relationship were seen by all and, rightly so, were considered dangerous for the fate of the Community and then of the Union. The Europe that was born from the ashes of two world wars is built wholly around a simple intuition and a great risk: the realization of peace in Europe through French-German reconciliation. Europe in political terms, from the Treaty of Rome to the Treaty of Maastricht, is this: founded on the neutralization of the bloody frontier of the Rhine so that it will be no longer the main reason for division between Europeans, but the necessary premise for possible political union. In this way, French and German agreement is necessary, indeed crucial.

During the weeks that preceded the war with Iraq, the same agreement is preserved and even strengthened with the challenge of dominant America. And yet, that understanding brings the Union to sensational political failure. The Franco-German axis, the engine for peacemaking, turned into the inertial gearing system that was able to stop the machine. Why? What was it that transformed a traditional strength into a new element of weakness? The answer is at once simple and striking. Today, the European Union can no longer be only or prevalently the maximum institutionalized form in the reconciled European political arena, nor can it settle to be "much less than a unitary nation but much more than a loose grouping of sovereign states" or even "a historic experiment in geopolitical engineering that has proved remarkably effective in erasing the strategic relevance of Europe's national borders" within it, as Kupchan optimistically observes.[44] Today, the Union is called upon to become a political player in the global arena. It is called upon to do this by the external challenges thrown at its space (political and institutional), challenges that the Union itself has constructed over the last 15 years, precisely in order to put it in the condition of being able to confront the global arena. This new Europe is searching for an obscure and different identity. To create it, it must be aware of one thing: the Franco-German axis no longer suffices for a Europe of 25 that has opened itself to the world. The issues of political and military security, the current state of transatlantic relations and the Mediterranean arena are all factors that bring Great Britain's role seriously back into play, and that reopen the need for a "European concert" as a necessary stage before finding the "European soloist."

At the beginning of the twentieth century, the inability to create an effective equilibrium or a satisfactory understanding between the leading players in the "European concert" led to the disaster of a bloody continental civil war, fought in two stages (1914–1918 and 1939–1945). At the end of that new "Thirty Year War," an order emerged in which no European power was among the leading players. Imperial Russia had disappeared, substituted by the Soviet Union, which, in the name of communist ideology, proposed itself as global challenger to the other superpower outside Europe: the United States. In the transition from Tsarist Russia to the Soviet Union, the factors constituting the split were so radical and predominant as to reduce the importance of the fact that the new communist super-power was at least partially, in purely geographic terms, a European power. In its rise from the ashes of the Tzar's empire, Russia had undergone a radical change in nature.

Today, the decline of bipolarism goes parallel with the rise of Europe. But this, too, is a resurrection in which the new elements prevail over those traditional and continuous ones. Europe is no longer the main stage of a war for world power conducted by two merciless rival giants. Nor is it the continent that hosts the greatest number of big powers or the most credible candidates to the future leadership of the world. For the first time in the course of its centuries-old history, starting at least from the decline of the Roman Empire, Europe is "almost united." Or rather, as would be more precise and loaded with significance, Europe is being offered the extraordinary opportunity to become united, and what is more, being able to enrich this dimension of unity of a size, importance, and influence that for the first time might even be projected beyond its boundaries.

EUROPE AND UNITED STATES: A PLURAL WEST

In order to escape from the rampant rhetoric on Europe's radiant future and to disentangle ourselves from the Euro-skepticism that has prevented us from taking immediate advantage of the opportunities that history has offered us (to speed-up and consolidate the European project), it is necessary to start from a full recognition of where we actually stand today. Today, the Europe that is trying to unite in different and heretofore unheard of ways must come to terms with the permanence of the sovereignty of states. Whoever has the project and the ideal at heart for a united Europe, must act in the light of this awareness. This means not only trying to avoid setting the European plan and state sovereignty on an open, inopportune course for collision, but also preventing the continuing contrasts between the various sovereign states, the different national interests, and the member states' particular views of foreign policy from having the result that makes it impossible to further any permanent advance toward greater continental cohesion. It is not enough to detest or condemn the rising of national interest; it is necessary to equip ourselves so that this phenomenon can be managed toward the greater general good of the union of Europe. In a word, we must "exploit" the politics of the states so that it will come to determine common political positions among the European states. In the meantime, it must preserve the community institutions so that they may once again be on hand when times are more propitious.

For this opportunity to be grasped we need first and foremost to extract ourselves from pro-European rhetoric that prevents us from understanding the real situation and to tame it to the general interest. The pro-European rhetoric referred to is the same as that which on the second day of the Athens Summit in 2003, when Europe laboriously and grudgingly made the declaration, pompous as it was useless, that the United Nations should have had a central role in the reconstruction and administration of postwar Iraq. The well-established custom to try to "conceal" the divergences of opinion between the states is Europe's worst vice, and from which it must abstain. As has been observed, "there is nothing strange that in Europe there are different interests and opinions on such a complex issue as the Iraq War and the political and economic future of the area." The same thing happens at the level of nation-states in their own parliaments, that is, within the "institutions where different ideas are pitted against each other, the majority prevails and the government expresses itself with one voice."[45] In Europe these institutions do not exist, and the Convention has had to refrain from ferrying common foreign and security policy from the foggy, stagnant Sargasso Sea of the unanimous vote, to the open, stormy ocean, tossed by the relentless, dynamic winds of politics represented by a majority vote.

It is up to all of us to decide whether we want our answer to the "difficulties of the times" to consist of weeping and wailing, because a foreign and security policy that binds the European states has not become concrete in an institutional way (which would have coincided with an increase in the power of Euro-bureaucracy). It will all depend on our political determination and on the significance of the issue in question whether we permit Malta or Cyprus or Belgium to block collective decisions that regard European security. The alternative route is to realize that at the moment it is not possible to find agreement on the "institutionalisation of procedures" of determination of European political objectives. Starting from this, it is possible to concentrate our efforts, so that from time to time, through patient work that continues to strive for the "greatest mediation attainable," the attempt is made to reach a consensus on "common political positions" and on "shared objectives" at least on the part of the six largest countries in the Union. It would have been sheer arrogance to subject the Union institutions to the task of defining and implementing common objectives, without basic political agreement between the member states: perhaps it would have been useful for those who develop as a strategy the increasing of the Commission's bargaining power, but damaging for the safeguarding of the institutions that have been created.

Left to themselves or treated only with the tools of irritating Euro-rhetoric, it is difficult to see how disharmony can be restored, disharmony that so often sees Great Britain on one side and France and Germany on the other (as long as the Berlin-Paris axis survives). There are historical, geographical, political, and cultural reasons that make British opposition to the possible creation of a Franco-German hegemony on the continent even more radical and less "manageable" than a split of the Rhine. It is true that French and German disagreement was what characterized bloodily the history of Europe between 1870 and 1945; it is also true that in order to put an end to this historical dispute, the idea for a united Europe was born. But it would be dangerous to forget that the opposition from London to any form of continental hegemony has lasted for at least three centuries. To this should be added that since 1945, but in fact even at the beginning of the twentieth century, Great Britain founded its own security policy by consolidating that special relationship with the United States, and it is unrealistic that it would consent to disconcert this relationship even more so in the name of a Europe, which is perhaps more united but is discerned as being dominated by Berlin or Paris

At the same time, as the attempt is gradually made to outline the essential structure of the confrontation that it is necessary to defuse, the result will inevitably be that there is a reduction in the number of players with the designation of a continental party as opposed to an insular party, in a banal revival of old geopolitics. Just as we proceed encouragingly toward a more cohesive Union, we must, rather, not lose the fortunate factor of "plurality within diversity." This is not only an inheritance from our continent or its most characteristic trait—inasmuch as "Europe's true hallmark is not weakness but diversity"[46]—but it is also its soul. In fact, we should try to see if, by using this precise asset, exploiting it as an opportunity, we can find a way of extricating ourselves from this unyielding confrontation. It is a question of acting wisely and with determination, in order to create that team game that at the moment is not only the only possible solution for overcoming internal divisions and resuming the process of integration with vigor, but also to renew and preserve the dialogue with the United States that can bring Washington back to the terrain of shared decisions.

The history of Europe can, yet again, come to our aid. In 1914, it was the reduction in the game of European powers to an increasingly restricted confrontation between two well-defined formations (Triple Understanding and Triple Alliance) that led to conflict and the end of the continent. Today, we must avoid making the same mistake, and reinstate in the match even those "minor" states that could both reassure London about the fact that a more united Europe would not be dominated by France and Germany, and also the latter, that a Great Britain freed from its own historical fears, would cease to be the usual old obstacle on the path to greater unity. To this end, an increase in the number of players, that is, the dilution of possible contention to two in a pluri-dimensional match, in which several positions try to compensate for each other and arrange themselves so that they create a dynamic balance, could be the winning move. One of the reasons for the good functioning of the so-called "European concert" for a large part of the nineteenth century lay precisely in the fact that it saw the participation of minor powers alongside the obviously "great" powers of the day. This enlarged composition served the purpose of preventing contrasts between two or three important players being resolved with continual "duels" that would be capable of jeopardizing the structure of the system. Today, forewarned of the inadequacy of the French-German axis, and with continual proof of the ever-recurring collision course that this axis and Great Britain insist on taking, it would be opportune that the most populous countries in the Union put themselves at the service of the common cause, to prevent the return of "great politics" on the European stage from producing constant tension between Great Britain, France, and Germany.

Italy, Spain, and Poland, if they are able to refrain from being ensnared in respective rivalry, which would damage all three, have good reason to aspire to performing a decisive role both in contributing to the establishment of a common vision of "European national interests," and in permitting an outcome which is open to more cooperative solutions that would be possible with a revival of the "three-a-side match" between the greater partners. Even though they differ widely, all these average-sized powers have characteristics that make their roles particularly interesting. Of the six founding members of the

European Community, Italy is the one that has been most stoically loyal to the United States, even after the end of the cold war and under both center-Left (Prodi, D'Alema) and center-Right governments (Berlusconi). Its interest in the Mediterranean, which is the fruit of both a long historical tradition and its objective geographical position, makes it act as natural guarantor for the fact that in its race to the east and north-east, the Union will not segregate this sea and its coasts from its political agenda. Such consideration would be a particularly important sign that the EU had finally reached a new awareness, that the security of the Mediterranean and the success of the peace process in the Middle East must not be renounced. In conclusion, this would mean that the EU renounced that attitude of isolationism from the outside world that has made international efforts so sporadic and unreliable.

In the years following the long isolation that Franco's regime had enforced, Spain has shown increasing interest and remarkable activism in foreign policy. Having strong traditional ties with the Muslim world and a consolidated network of relationships with Latin America, today Madrid can put this heritage at the service of a common foreign policy. In the years of the Aznar government, it seemed as if Spain managed to forget that anti-Americanism that dated back to the Hispanic-American War in 1898, proving to be a faithful ally and an important interlocutor for the United States. The Zapatero government has taken a different course, more banal in some ways, and not without its staunch critics. However, for a Europe that wishes to open up the game of entering the Latin-American market, and which thus accepts to compete commercially with the United States without wishful thinking of political or military challenges, but also without reverential fear, Spain, possibly with a better leadership than it has at present, is best equipped.

Poland's entrance to this informal European concert seems motivated above all by avoiding reinforcing the unpleasant sensation that in the membership of the Union there are aristocracies dictated by the length of time one has been a member. This requisite, already important in itself, is today particularly relevant after the disdainful accusations leveled by France at those countries that signed the "Document of the 8." It could represent informally all those countries that are entering this phase of enlargement, and thus eliminate any doubts about "division A" and "division B" countries. Poland is, moreover, in a very similar position to Spain when it became a member: it is a young highly populated country, with a recently privatized economy and is of considerable international broadmindedness, with a skilled workforce and contained costs. Its geographical position close to Germany and at the gateway to the large markets of Eastern Europe, would lead us to believe in an even swifter development. After all, Poland was fundamental in the Ukraine crisis of 2004–2005. The European Union seemed incapable of taking a decisive position in the contest between the ruling Prime Minister Viktor Yanukovich backed by the Russians and the opposition candidate Viktor Yushenko. On that occasion, the Franco-German gear-box was stuck for fear of displeasing Moscow, the third partner in the stormy "Paris–Berlin–Moscow" axis. Warsaw, for its geographical proximity and the strong ties with the Ukraine and having greater knowledge of the situation, managed to take the situation in hand, until the Union made its voice heard clearly and decisively, in support of the emerging democracy. This was one of the first examples where the "plural, composite" nature of the Union proved to be a decisive factor toward a concrete success.

As has already been said, Europe was built in a setting where security was guaranteed by the ally, America, where there was no objective space for any differences of opinion with America regarding Europe's vital interests and where the threat was posed by Soviet communism: a common enemy that brought the threat from within Europe itself. Of course, in those same years there were quarrels that were even quite bitter: just think of the Vietnam War. But these disagreements happened on remote stages, where European countries had no specific interests that could feel threatened by American initiatives they did not share. Today, the situation has radically changed: there can be strong differences of opinion and interests between Europeans and Americans even on the question of security. Some American decisions on this issue may even be seen as liable to make Europe less secure, because the consequences have an impact on the safety of the continent. Finally, the threat now comes from various sides and is not localized on the old continent. So, while Europe may lose importance in the eyes of America (at least in the short term and regarding security), it finds itself having to reckon with its weakness in terms of its capacity for defense and foreign policy. It then ends up wavering between the will to distinguish itself from its powerful ally and the awareness that the Euro-Atlantic relationship is fundamental, especially for Europe, which "does not have resources, army and arms industries in common; it does not have suitable, effective institutional tools nor does it have a doctrine or common security policy."[47]

It is quite customary to underline the aspects of civil influence that seem to characterize the Union itself, or its will to propose itself as the champion of a peace-loving civilizing mission, pursued this time "by example." This European copy of "American exceptionalism," faded and very much out of time, in which Europe puts itself forward as the "maximum institutional objective" of dilution of national sovereignty is really quite unbearable.

It is true that alongside the "challenge of globalisation" and the "impact of the single currency," the "memory of war"[48] is one of the unifying forces that contributes to making us typically European, within the wider Western context. Those who rightly remind us of this by underlining that, although "liberal democracy is the form of government that is most committed to maintaining peace, the citizens must accept the possibility of going to war against anti-democratic powers, if they really take democracy seriously and wish to preserve its future."[49] Undeniably, the excessively illusory and literal version of "Europe as a civil power" contributed to this, along with a certain lack of clarity and ability to create the political requirements—even before institutional ones—as well as the lack of common foreign and security policy. It is as if we could aspire to having an international role only thanks to the agreements of cooperation and association, aid for development or integration, thus "renouncing a priori deciding for war or peace, and carrying out only indispensable interventions."[50]

Europe may even be a sort of Kantian paradise, regulated by laws and not by force, but it is right to make some qualifications. In the first place it must be highlighted that all this continues to be possible as long as someone else takes on the "dirty work" of maintaining the security of the system. Europe has chosen to supply the world with the example of a "shared sovereignty" being respectful of other sovereignties, including adversary sovereignties, when they show they are willing to compromise, deter, and negotiate. But for this strategy to be, credible, it "requires Europe not to repudiate the use of force entirely, and that it should be sufficiently capable of exercising it to cooperate with the United States, possibly even to do so without its help. Otherwise, there is a risk that the dialogue between 'the arrogance of power' and 'the arrogance of impotence' could develop into confrontation or even divorce."[51] Second, when Europe pursues its own objectives of economic power, it does so with the same unscrupulousness and "arrogance" of the United States, given that the Europeans well know that globalization is guaranteed by the political and military power of the United States. In the third place, as regards the refusal to take up arms, the very recent past of colonialism and the destruction of other cultures come to mind: Europe still in the guise of "civilizer should be considered with a certain fear, above all by those populations that have experienced the "delights" of European colonialism at first hand.

The attempt to build a European political identity that is strong and spendable in foreign policy certainly appears very difficult, but it is just as decisive. Until now, Europe has not been able to create a foreign policy without it being "integrationist," and it is no coincidence that it has found itself in difficulty when the integration charter for admission to the Union was not feasible immediately (as in the case of ex-Yugoslavia) or was postponed for too long (as in the case of Turkey). It seems that Europe's only strategy in confronting the challenge of international politics has basically consisted of transforming foreign policy issues into internal policies, including neighboring countries within its boundaries and giving up the idea of creating a veritable doctrine, which is able to lead its (important) presence on the global chess-board, and determining European national interest. The history of the United States, the friendly rival with whom mutual difficulties seem to increase, gives us an enlightening example. For over a century, during which the United States was completely absorbed with moving its frontiers toward the West, it was essentially absent from the international political scene. Its only development in foreign policy—the Monroe doctrine—was little more than a conceptual shield, behind which its own territorial expansion could be carried out, and its own continental leadership consolidated. Today the risk that Europe runs is to let itself be almost exclusively absorbed over the next ten years by the effort of consolidating the moving of its frontier eastward. As a result, it will be hard to find the necessary resources to play a united role on the global political scene. And yet, it is in Europe's interest to renounce this isolationist attitude and decide to shoulder its part of the responsibility in governing an international political system that must, first and foremost, be rebuilt as a unit.

To this end, the ostensible quest for splitting up Western unity is not only useless, it is also detrimental. All too often it is underlined on the other side of the Atlantic that America has no need of allies like the European countries. There is a cry for a new "Pacific route," which is more important and strategic for the United States than the glorious but dusty transatlantic solidarity. A breakdown in institutionalized relations and cooperation between Europe and the United States would be damaging for both partners. Europe still needs the United States to defend itself from threats that continue to increase and are more expensive and difficult to combat. The United States still needs its European allies in order to provide (political) legitimacy to its own hegemony, and also to fight the global threat of transnational terrorism. Any exclusively national strategy is inadequate, even if implemented by a superpower like the United States. America knows well that it cannot send the Marines to Milan to arrest suspects of terrorist activities, or bomb Riyadh just because there is the suspicion that Al Qaeda terrorists are hidden there. Nor can it get information by force from Russia. It is on this issue that the "United States now needs lots of things from lots of governments. This is a potential boon to cooperation between the United States and other states."[52]

If the United States has in these years succumbed to the temptation of overestimating the use of force, Europe has too often seemed to underestimate it, as if it wishes to flee from the tragic reality of international politics. So, from time to time, to defend and promote good, it is necessary to oppose evil, even if it means fighting it. In its own interest, the Americans must discard satisfied unilateralism—of which Robert Kagan is the most popular exponent—which does not befit them, nor does it do them credit and it goes against their interests. They must forge again a "common U.S.–European approach to confront the most pressing issues of the day . . . Unilateralism and ad hoc coalitions will not be good enough." As far as Europe is concerned, it must acknowledge the fact that the "threat we face is a common one . . . It must stop seeking to define its identity and role in the world in contradistinction to that of America."[53] America cannot disengage itself from the world and withdraw into splendid isolation, which no longer exists. It has the most extraordinary opportunity to be able to choose whether to do it or not, on its own conditions and in its own time, or whether to wait for problems to break out into conflict in the ways and at the time dictated by its enemies. "The choice is between the United States against the world or a United States with the world, in which America accords the same respect to other countries that it does to its own citizens drawn from so many other lands. That, truly, would be a worthy goal."[54] Assuming that the Europeans and Americans perceive that they are different (now and again it seems they do so extremely hastily), we cannot lose consciousness to the fact that the common denomination of belonging to the West, makes them more "similar" compared to their relationship with non-Westerners. As was highlighted by the Italian Foreign Minister, Gianfranco Fini, America and Europe are different in history, tradition, and culture. But these differences must not be confused with the differences of opinion on concrete political and economic issues that can be reassembled by the will and political capacity of the two parties. It would be "wrong to belittle the divergences, since there have been even sensational moments of misunderstanding on a series of important topics: on the legitimacy of the death penalty; the Kyoto Protocol; the International Criminal Court; America's perception of the significance of the growth of European defence policy; what can determine the growth of European support in NATO in the nature itself of the military alliance yesterday and the political and military alliance today. But these differences should be observed realistically and with a sense of proportion, knowing that what units Europe to the United States today—not yesterday and not twenty years ago—is far more important than the differences of opinion that can be established by some dossiers."[55] Moreover, there are interests of a far greater bearing that unite Europeans and Americans: "Americans and Europeans broadly share the same democratic, liberal aspirations for their societies and for the rest of the world. They have common interests in an open international trading and communications system, ready access to world energy supplies, halting the proliferation of weapons of mass destruction, preventing humanitarian tragedies, and containing a small group of dangerous states that do not respect human rights and are hostile to these common Western values and interests."[56] Europeans, in particular, have to find a new way to define a common position towards the U.S. As the period between 2002 and 2003 has demonstrated, the "attempt to unite Europe around a rival policy to the United States ended up splitting Europe down the middle", and the "neo-Gaullist vision of a unipolar Europe in a multipolar world ended with a multipolar Europe in a still unipolar world". On the other hand Euro-Atlanticism, a "policy aimed at uniting the West ended up helping to split it more sharply".[57] Above all, Europeans and Americans hold firmly to the belief that the transatlantic relationship, the friendship between Europe and the United States continues to be the architrave of democratic peace and the security of the West, both of which are necessary conditions for world peace and global stability. Let us conclude these pages with the words of appeal launched by 17 European figures (from Giuliano Amato to Helmut Schmidt, from Raymond Barre to Felipe Gonzalez to Valery Giscard d'Estaing) in favor of the indispensable alliance between Europe and America: "Our values and our fundamental political objectives are shared by the United States. No important problem in the world can be resolved without the joint efforts of the United States and Europe; no problem is unsolvable when we confront it together . . . North America and Europe are depositories of democracy and freedom. Together they will be able to share these values with the rest of the world. By uniting our forces we further strengthen the stability of the international community and defend the dignity of all human beings."[58]

NOTES

I FROM THE END OF HISTORY TO THE END OF THE WORLD

1. For the most part, with the sole exception of Ceausescu's Rumania where paradoxically the "revolution" brings the second and third lines of Communist party ranks.
2. See Francis Fukuyama, "The End of History?," originally published in *The National Interest*, Summer, 1989, republished in *America and the World. Debating the New Shape of International Politics*, A Council on Foreign Relations Book, New York 2002, pp. 1–28, here quot. p. 11.
3. Ibid., p. 21.
4. On the concept of "constitutional order," see G. John Ikenberry, *After Victory. Institutions, Strategic Restraint, and the Rebuilding of Order After Major Wars*, Princeton University Press, Princeton 2001, pp. 29–44.
5. Craig Kennedy and Marshall M. Bouton, "The Real Trans-Atlantic Gap," in *Foreign Policy*, October/November 2002, pp. 66–74, here quot. p. 70.
6. Michael J. Cox, *Are Europeans from Venus and Americans from Mars? Transatlantic Relations from 9:11 to Iraq*, paper presented to 44th ISA Annual Convention, Portland, Oregon, February 25–March 1, 2003, p. 20.
7. See Raymond Aron, *Paix et guerre entre les nations*, Calmann-Lévy, Paris 1962.
8. See Hedley Bull, *The Anarchical Society. A Study of Order in World Politics*, Macmillan, London 1997, here quot. p. 111.
9. See Giorgio Carnevali, *Nazionalismo o federalismo. I dilemmi alla fine del secolo*, UTET, Torino 1996, p. 11.
10. See Carlo Galli, "Spazio e politica nell'età globale," in *Filosofia Politica*, XIV, 2000, n. 3, pp. 357–378, here quot. p. 367.
11. At the end of October 2005 more than 2,000 American soldiers have been killed, whereas 199 allied (27 Italian) and 3,400 Iraqi policemen and Iraqi security forces had fallen at the hands of terrorists. On December 21, 2004, in the attack on the military base in Mosul, 19 Americans, between soldiers and contractors, lost their lives.

12. Samuel H. Huntington, "The Clash of Civilizations," or. publ. in *Foreign Affairs*, Summer, 1993; republished in *America and the World. Debating the New Shape of International Politics*, pp. 43–70, quot. pp. 43 and 50. See also Huntington's book on the same topic *The Clash of Civilizations and the Remaking of World Order*, Simon & Schuster, New York 1996.
13. See Gabriel Kolko, *Another century of War?*, The New Press, New York 2002, p. 138.
14. Ibid., p. 145.
15. See Joseph M. Grieco, *Ie futuro delle relaziomi Transatlantiche*, in *Che differenza può fare un giorno. Guerra pace e sicurezza dopo l'11 settembre*, Vittorio Emanuele Parsi (Ed.), Vita e Pensiero, Milano 2003, pp. 86–100, here quot. p. 88.
16. See John J. Mearshaimer, *The Tragedy of Great Power Poltics*, W.W. Norton & Company, New York, London 2001, p. 401.
17. See Robert Gilpin, *The Challenge of Global Capitalism*, Princeton University Press, Princeton 2000, p. 349.
18. See Charles A. Kupchan, *The End of the American Era. U.S. Foreign Policy and the Geopolitics of the Twenty-First Century*, Alfred A. Knopf, New York 2002, p. XVII.
19. See Michael Hirsch, "Bush and the World," in *Foreign Affairs*, LXXXI, n. 5, September/October 2002, pp. 18–43, here quot. p. 20.
20. See John L. Esposito and John O. Voll, *Islam and the West*, in *Religion in International Relations. The Return from Exile*, Fabio Petito e Pavlos Hatzopoulus (Eds.), Palgrave Macmillan, Houndmills 2003, pp. 237–269, here quot. p. 238.
21. See Joseph S. Nye Jr., *The Paradox of American Power*, Oxford University Press, Oxford 2002, p. 8. On the concept of American leadership, by the same author see also, *Bound to Lead. The Changing Nature of American Power*, Basic Books, New York 1990.
22. See Joseph S. Nye Jr., *The Paradox of American Power*, p. 9.
23. Ibid., p. 17.
24. See Roger Scruton, *The West and the Rest. Globalization and the Terrorist Threat*, Continuum, London 2002, p. 133.
25. See Niall Ferguson, *Colossus. The Price of American Empire*, The Penguin Press, New York 2004, p. 296.
26. See Yoram Schweitzer, Shaul Shay, *The Globalization of Terror. The Challenge of Al-Qaida and the Response of the International Community*, Transaction Publishers, New Brunswick 2003.
27. See Fabio Armao, *La rinascita del privateering: lo Stato e il nuovo mercato della guerra*, in *Guerre globali. Capire i conflitti del XXI secolo*, Angelo D'Orsi (Ed.), Carocci, Roma 2003, pp. 91–101.
28. For a wider reinterpretation of the concept of security see Peter Hough, *Understanding Global Security*, Routledge, London 2004.
29. For the concept of "hegemonic war" see Robert Gilpin, *War and Change in World Politics*, Princeton University Press, Princeton 1981,

particularly, chap. 5. Luigi Bonanate defines "constituent war" as the war "at the end of which the winners (or winner) find themselves in a dominant position over the conquered, on whom they can impose their concept of international politics," with a process "similar to the one that regards the state, which is born of a conflict between social and political forces that dictate the power to dictate the constitution," understood here in the meaning of "material constitution": see Luigi Bonanate, *Storiografia e teoria delle relazioni internazionali*, in *Le relazioni internazionali. Cinque secoli di Storia: 1521–1989*, Luigi Bonanate, Fabio Armao, Francesco Tuccari (Eds.), Bruno Mondadori, Milano 1997, pp. 1–24, here quot. pp. 12 and 14. The concept of "material constitution" dates back to Costantino Mortati, one of the greatest Italian constitutionalists of the 1900s, who was among the constituent fathers in 1948. See Costantino Mortati, *Istituzioni di diritto pubblico*, Cedam, Padova 1969, chap. II. The concept's heuristic capacity is not unanimously accepted by the constitutionalists, because of its vagueness. Material constitution "indicates the concrete constitutional order conceived or created by the political forces or other figures," see Roberto Bin, *Capire la costituzione*, Laterza, Roma-Bari 1998, p. 189, whose criticism, however harsh, to the juridic validity of the concept does not prejudice its use in political science.

30. See Michael Hardt and Antonio Negri, *Empire*, Harvard University Press, Cambridge, London 2000, p. 10.

31. John Ikenberry's book was one of the main sources of inspiration for this book, and the reconstruction of the previous pages summarises Ikenberry's proposal: see G. John Ikenberry, *After Victory*, in particular, see chs 1, 2, 6, and 7. The quotation is from p. 163.

32. See Karl W. Deutsch, et al., *Political Community and the North Atlantic Area: International Organization in the Light of Historical Experience*, Princeton University Press, Princeton 1957.

33. Ted Hopf talks of the Western alliance as an "authoritative alliance," a kind of "collective hegemony . . . with more than a few States combining to create and reproduce the ideological consensus that cements it. The authoritative alliance is closest to Hedley Bull's ideas about international society" rather than as a traditional form of hegemony. See Ted Hopf, *Post–Cold War Allies: The Illusion of Unipolarity*, in *US Allies in a Changing World*, Barry Rubin and Thomas A. Keaney (Eds.), Frank Cass, London 2001, p. 31.

34. John Ikenberry defines intra-Western hegemonic peace as a "constitutional order," emphasising the characters of co-binding and distinguishing it clearly from the "hegemonic order." I prefer to consider the intra-Western order as a variant of the hegemony.

35. On the role of Great Britain in the European order and the world order, see Niall Ferguson, *Empire. The Rise and Demise of the British World Order and the Lessons for Global Power*, Basic Books, New York 2002.

36. See John Lewis Gaddis, *Surprise, Security and the American Experience*, Harvard University Press, Cambridge 2004, p. 54.

37. Suffice to think of the behavior of Athens in the Atticus League during the Peloponnese War, in the fifth century BC.

38. See Vittorio Emanuele Parsi, *Interesse nazionale e globalizzazione. I regimi democratici nelle trasformazioni del sistema post-westfaliano*, Jaca Book, Milano 1998, especially pp. 53–78.

39. The First Gulf War was fought by Iraq and Iran for over ten years, following an attack by Saddam Hussein on the neighboring theocracy in order to assume control of the eastern shore Shatt-el-Arab.

40. It was a coalition of over 50 countries, of which also Italy was part, with a flying squadron of eight Tornado fighterbombers and a naval division.

41. See Walter Russel Mead, *Power, Terror, Peace and War. America's Grand Strategy in a World at Risk*, Alfred A. Knopf, New York 2004, p. 5.

42. See John Lewis Gaddis, *Surprise, Security and the American Experience*, pp. 75–76.

43. See John Lewis Gaddis, *Surprise, Security and the American Experience*, p. 77.

44. See Samuel Huntington, "Why International Primacy Matters," in *International Security*, XVII, n. 4, 1993, pp. 82–83.

45. See Walter Russel Mead, *Power, Terror, Peace and War*, p. 5.

46. See Roger Scruton, *The West and the Rest*, p. 90.

47. See Charles Krauthammer, "The Unipolar Moment," in *Foreign Affairs*, LXX, n. 1, 1991, pp. 23–33, here quot. pp. 32–33.

48. See Andrea Bonanni, "Solo la grande Europa unita bilancerà lo stapotere USA. Intervista a Romano Prodi," in *La Repubblica*, April 19, 2003, p. 11.

49. See Thomas Risse, *U.S. Power in a Liberal Security Community*, in *America Unrivaled. The Future of the Balance of Power*, G. John Ikenberry (Ed.), Cornell University Press, Ithaca 2002, pp. 260–283, here quot. p. 282.

50. See Henry Kissinger, *Does America Need a Foreign Policy? Toward a Diplomacy for the Twenty-First Century*, revised edition, Free Press 2002, p. 34.

51. See William Wohlfort, *The Stability of a Unipolar World*, in "International Security," XXIV, n. 1, 1999, pp. 5–41.

52. For a comparison between quantitative data on the military accounts of the main European countries and the United States, see The International Institute for Strategic Studies, *The Military Balance. 2002–2003*, Oxford University Press, Oxford 2003, pp. 332–337.

53. Ibid.

54. See data supplied by William C. Wohlforth, *U.S. "Strategy in a Unipolar World,"* in *America Unrivaled*, pp. 98–118, especially pp. 104–106.

55. See Niall Ferguson, *Colossus*, p. 151. Curiously, the subtitle in the edition published in Great Britain reads "the rise and fall" of the American Empire.
56. See Samuel H. Huntington, "The Lonely Superpower," in *Foreign Affairs*, LXXVIII, n. 2. March/April 1999 pp. 35–49.
57. See "Remarks by the President at 2002 Graduation Exercise of the United States Military Academy, West Point," New York, republished in President George W. Bush, *West Point Commencement Speech*, in *America and the World*, pp. 364–371, here quot. pp. 366 and 367.
58. See President Abraham Lincoln, *Annual Message to Congress. Concluding Remarks*, Washington, December 1, 1862, http://www.swcivilwar.com/MessagetoCongress.html.
59. See John Lewis Gaddis, *Surprise, Security, and the American Experience*, pp. 17–18. See it also for the distinction between prevention and pre-emption: "Preemption implied military action undertaken to forestall an imminent attack from a hostile State. Prevention implied starting a war to keep such a State from building the capability to attack," pp. 122–123.
60. See John Lewis Gaddis, *Surprise, Security, and the American Experience*, p. 110.
61. Ibid., p. 108.
62. Ibid., p. 109.
63. Ibid., pp. 109–110.
64. See Emanuele Ottolenghi and Guglielmo Verdirame, "Il diritto al primo colpo. Cambia il nemico, bisogna cambiare le regole della guerra. Per salvarle," in *Il Foglio*, March 1, 2003, p. III.
65. See Celeste A. Wallander and Robert O. Keohane, *Risk, Threat, and Security Institutions*, in *Imperfect Unions. Security Institutions over Time and Space*, Helga Hafteendorn, Robert O. Keohane, and Celeste A. Wallander (Eds.), Oxford University Press, Oxford 1999, pp. 21–47.
66. See Stephen M. Walt, "Keeping the World "Off-Balance": Self-Restraint and U.S. Foreign Policy," in *America Unrivaled*, pp. 121–154, here quot. p. 133.
67. See Stephen G. Brooks and William C. Wohlforth, "American Primacy in Perspective," in *Foreign Affairs*, LXXXI, n. 4, July/August 2002, pp. 20–33, here quot. p. 27.
68. For a reflection that differs from the assumption that "any reasonable state would see US primacy as not worth trying to overthrow, as perhaps even beneficial," see John M. Owen IV, "Transnational Liberalism and American Primacy; or, Benignity Is in the Eye of the Beholder," in *America Unrivaled*, pp. 239–259, here quot. p. 240.
69. See G. John Ikenberry, *After Victory*, pp. 252–253.
70. See John M Owen, *Transnational Liberalism and American Primacy*, p. 257.
71. Ibid., pp. 258–259.

72. See Stephen M. Walt, "Keeping the World 'Off-Balance'," in *America Unrivaled*, p. 150.
73. See Anthony Lake, "Defending Missions, Setting Deadlines. Prepared Remarks of Anthony Lake, Assistant to the President for National Security Affairs," in Defense Issues, XI (1996), n. 14, March.
74. See Alain Joxe, *L'empire du chaos*, Editions La Decouverte & Syros, Paris 2002, it. transl. *L'impero del caos. Guerra e pace nel nuovo disordine mondiale*, Santoni, Milano 2004, pp. 164–165.
75. For these figures see Michael G. Vickers, *Revolution deferred: Kosovo and the Transformation of War*, in *War over Kosovo: politics and strategy in a global age*, Andrew J. Bacevich and Eliot A. Cohen (Eds.), Columbia University Press, New York 2001, pp. 189–209.
76. See Michael E. O'Hanlon, "A Flawed Masterpiece," in *Foreign Affairs*, LXXXI, n. 3, May–June 2002, pp. 47–63.
77. For a reconstruction (not impeccable) of anti-Americanism in Italy see Massimo Teodori, *Maledetti americani. Destra, sinistra e cattolici: storia del pregiudizio antiamericano*, Mondadori, Milano 2002. Among the epigones of anti-Americanism from the radical-Right, see Massimo Tarchi, *Contro l'americanismo*, Laterza, Roma-Bari 2004.
78. On Bin Laden and Al Qaeda, see Peter L. Bergen, *Holy War, Inc. Inside the Secret World of Osama bin Laden*, New York Times Books, New York 2001.
79. See Qiao Liang and Wang Xiangsui, *Guerra senza limiti. L'arte della guerra asimmetrica fra terrorismo e globalizzazione*, Libreria Editrice Goriziana, Gorizia 2001, p. 77 (Chinese original edition 1999; English edition, *Unrestricted Warfare: China's Master Plan to Destroy America*, Pan American Publishing 2002).
80. Ibid., p. 78.
81. See Matthew Evangelista, *The Chechen Wars. Will Russia Go the Way of the Soviet Union?*, Brookings Institution Press, Washington, D.C. 2002, p. 186.
82. "Pathological anarchies" emerge, in which "the major threat for a substantial part of a population in a state can come from the State, or rather the regime in power": see Jamie Munn, *Intervention and Collective Justice in the Post-Westphalian System*, in *Human Rights and Military Intervention*, Alexander Moseley and Richard Norman (Eds.), Ashgate, Aldershot 2002, pp. 185–210, here quot. p. 205.
83. See Robert I. Rotberg, "Failed States in a World of Terror," in *Foreign Affairs*, LXXXI (2002), n. 4, pp. 127–140. The author ties the success of the fight against terrorism to the prevention of new *State failures*. See also Stephen M. Walt, "Beyond bin Laden: Reshaping U.S. Foreign Policy," originally published in *International Security*, Winter 2001/2002, republished in *America and the World*, pp. 320–347.
84. See Andrew J. Bacevich, *American Empire. The Realities and Consequences of U.S. Diplomacy*, Harvard University Press, Cambridge,

Mass., 2002, pp. 143–147. On humanitarian intervention see also Chris Brown, *Humanitarian Intervention and International Political Theory*, in *Human Rights and Military Intervention*, pp. 153–169.

85. See Alain Joxe, *L'empire du chaos*, p. 165.

86. According to the United Nations, in 1999, that is, in the middle of the Taliban regime, Afghanistan recorded a peak in its production of opium, it reaching 4,600 tons. In 2004 the production of opium reached 4,200 tons.

87. See Robert Kagan, *Of Paradise and Power. America and Europe in the New Order*, Alfred Knopf, New York 2003.

88. See Bernard Lewis, *What Went Wrong? Western impact and Middle Eastern Response*, Oxford University Press, Oxford 2002, pp. 158–159.

89. See Ali Ahmad Said Esber, "La condanna di noi arabi: il Potere che schiaccia l'Uomo," in *Corriere della Sera*, April 19, 2003, p. 8.

90. See Michael Novak, *"Asymmetrical Warfare" and Just War*, paper presented in Rome on February 10, 2003 p. 4, www.chiesa. espressonline.it.

91. Here is a summary of the most blood-thirsty attacks by Al Qaeda in the world updated on September 11, 2004 and starting from September 11, 2001 (3020 victims): April 11, 2002, Djerba, Tunisia (21); October 12, 2002, Bali, Indonesia (202); November 28, 2002, Mombasa, Kenya (17); May 12, 2003, Ryadh, Saudi Arabia (35); May 16, 2003, Casablanca, Marocco (45); August 5, 2003, Jakarta, Indonesia (12); November 8, 2003, Ryadh, Saudi Arabia (17); November 15 and 20, 2003, Istanbul, Turkey (49); March 11, 2004, Madrid, Spain (191); March 29 and 30, 2004, Tashkent and Bukara, Uzbekistan (13); May 29 and 30, 2003, Al Khobar, Saudi Arabia (22); September 9, 2004, Jakarta, Indonesia (9).

92. See, as general reconstruction of a terrorism map: Mark Juergensmeyer, *Terror in the Mind of God. The Global Rise of Religious Violence*, University of California Press, Los Angeles 2000; Camille Eid, *Osama e i suoi fratelli. Atlante mondiale dell'islam politico*, Pimedit, Milano 2001.

93. See Peter Townsend, *Terrorism. A Very Short Introduction*, Oxford University Press, Oxford 2002, which is deficient on the reconstruction of Islamic fundamentalist terrorism.

94. See Carl Schmitt, *Der Begriff des Politischen. Text von 1932 mit einem Vorwort und drei Corollarien*, Duncker & Humblot, Berlin 1963.

95. See Massimo Franco, *Polvere di spie. Intelligence, misteri ed errori nella caccia a Bin Laden*, Baldini & Castoldi, Milano 2002, pp. 151–152.

96. Wesley A. Clark, *Winning Modern Wars. Iraq, Terrorism, and the American Empire*, Public Affairs, New York 2003, p. 103. A severe criticism of the choice of Iraq as the object of the war on terror comes from the ex– "Tzar of anti-terrorism" Richard A. Clarke, *Against All Enemies. Inside America's War on Terror*, Free Press, New York 2004.

97. As a strong critic of Bush politics observes: "Bush's mistakes are obvious. What is far less obvious is what Europe's alternative strategy should be to squash terrorism. Europe has in fact experienced first-hand Middle Eastern attacks: from the Olympics in Munich in 1972 to the ship 'Achille Lauro' and the massacres in Paris in the 1980s. European governments have more than once answered by placating the terrorists so that they vent their fury elsewhere: a policy made up of little opportunistic stratagems, not of a strategy. In the meantime, in the run-down suburbs of Paris, Madrid, and Milan the dramatic failure of the integration of the Islamic immigrants in European society has created authentic powder-kegs (there is no equivalent in the United States), repositories of frustration and anti-Westernism, ideal terrain for the recruitment of new terrorist unskilled labor. To complete the picture there are years of dubious international business between various European nations (France at the top) and the worst Middle Eastern dictators, Saddam Hussein included, up to the corruption scandal in the United Nations programme 'Oil-for-food': a performance that is every bit as good as the Bush and Halliburton clans' wheeling and deeling." See Federico Rampini, *Tutti gli uomini del presidente. George W. Bush e la nuova destra americana*, Carocci, Roma 2004, p. 165.

98. See Benjamin Barber, *Fear's Empire. War, Terrorism, and Democracy*, W.W. Norton & Company, New York 2003, p. 95.

99. See Roger Scruton, *The West and the Rest*, p. 161.

100. See Fareed Zakaria, *The Future of Freedom. Illiberal Democracy at Home and Abroad*, W.W. Norton Company, New York 2003, p. 138. See also David Frum, Richard Perle, *An End to Evil. How to Win the War on Terror*, Random House, New York 2003.

101. See Laurence R. Iannacone, Massimo Introvigne, *Il mercato dei martiri. L'industria del terrorismo suicida*, Lindau, Torino 2004, p. 96.

2 FORCE, LAW, AND INTERNATIONAL ORDER

1. For the model of a world divided into different subsystems, I elaborated Henry Kissinger's hypothesis proposed in *Does America Need a Foreign Policy?*, pp. 25–26.

2. See Gilles Kepel, *Fitna. Guerre au coeur de l'islam*. Edtions Gallimard, Paris 2004.

3. See Samuel H. Huntington, "*The Clash of Civilizations.*"

4. It is the Islamic origin that is believed to be one of the causes of the brutality that increasingly characterizes Chechen terrorism. The most cruel episode was the school massacre in Beslan, on September 3, 2004: 394 people (156 children) were killed, 448 (248 children) injured, and 260 declared missing. Because of the large number of children involved in the tragedy the press named it "the 9/11 of the children."

5. Every now and again it exceeds in this "adjustment of the local reality," as happened for example in the Ivory Coast, when l'Armé Française caused a massacre among civilians who were demonstrating in front of the French embassy in the Ivory capital.

6. See Angelo Panebianco, *Il potere, lo stato, la libertà. La gracile costituzione della società libera*, Il Mulino, Bologna 2004, p. 282.

7. Michael Hardt and Antonio Negri, *Empire*, p. 17.

8. On the succession of "international order" see Filippo Andreatta, *Alla ricerca dell'ordine mondiale. L'Occidente di fronte alla guerra*, Il Mulino, Bologna 2004.

9. See Gianni Riotta, "La rivolta dei guerrieri del weekend costretti a combattere senza più congedi," in *Corriere della Sera*, September 18, 2004.

10. See Michael E. O'Hanlon, Adriana Lins de Albuquerque, *Iraq Index. Tracking Variables of Reconstruction & Security in Post-Saddam Iraq*, The Brookings Institutions, Washington, www.brookings.edu/ iraqindex.

11. See Ennio Caretto, "Lasceremo l'Iraq prima della pacificazione" and "Bremer e Rumsfeld, autocritica sull'Iraq," in *Corriere della Sera*, September 25, and October 6, 2004 respectively.

12. See Press Briefing by Scott McClellan, The James S. Brady Press Briefing Room, http://www.whitehouse.gov/news/releases/2005/ 01/20050112-7.html#1.

13. See Geminello Preterossi, *L'Occidente contro se stesso*, Laterza, Roma-Bari 2004.

14. See the excellent work, the fruit of many first-hand interviews, by Alberto Simoni, *G.W. Bush e i falchi della democrazia. Viaggio nel mondo dei neoconservatori*, Falzea Editore, Reggio Calabria 2004, p. 230.

15. Alberto Simoni, *G.W. Bush e i falchi della democrazia*, p. 230.

16. Ibid., pp. 231–232.

17. Ibid., p. 232.

18. See Adriana Lins de Albuquerque, Michael E. O'Hanlon, "The State Of Iraq: An Update," in *The New York Times*, November 26, 2004, http://www.brookings.edu/views/op-ed/ohanlon/20041126a.htm.

19. Ibid.

20. All the figures that follow are inevitably in continual tragic evolution. They are only printed here to give an idea of the cost of human lives and the political cost of postwar Iraq. When not specified otherwise, all the data comes from Michael E. O'Hanlon, Adriana Lins de Albuquerque, *Iraq Index*.

21. See Ennio Caretto, "Annan scrive a Bush: non attaccate Falluja," in *Corriere della Sera*, November 6, 2004.

22. See Michael E. O'Hanlon, Adriana Lins de Albuquerque, *Iraq Index*, www.brookings.edu/iraqindex.

23. See Christian Rocca, *Esportare l'America. La rivoluzione democratica dei neoconservatori*, I libri del foglio, Roma 2003, p. 118.

24. See Magdi Allam, "Disinformazione, così l'Egitto ha rimosso la strage di Taba," in *Corriere della Sera*, October 20, 2004.

25. See the declarations published in *La Stampa* and collected by Marcello Molinari, *Condoleeza Rice: "Così vinceremo la pace in Iraq,"* April 15, 2003, p. 3.

26. Declaration reported by Carlo Panella, in the article "Doni alla frontiera," in *Il Foglio*, April 19, 2003, p. 4.

27. See Stephen Zunes, *Tinderbox: U.S. Middle East Policy and the Roots of Terrorism*, Zedbooks, London 2002, p. 96.

28. This and the following declarations by Perle are taken from the article by the "Corriere" correspondent in Washington, Ennio Caretto, "Richard Perle, il superfalco 'Ora andiamo a rovesciare la tirannia del partito di Assad," in *Corriere della Sera*, April 17, 2003, p. 11.

29. Quot. in Gianni Riotta, "Ecco i segni di speranza che il caos non può cancellare," in *Corriere della Sera*, March 19, 2004.

30. Dept. of Defense, Directorate for Information Operations and Reports (DoD DIOR). Quot. in http://nationalpriorities.org/issues/military/iraq/highcost/index.html.

31. What is reproduced here is a re-elaboration of the Italian version of the table published by the *Corriere della Sera* on April 19, 2003, p. 6.

32. According to the data reported by *The World Almanac and Book of Facts 2004*, p. 118 and supplied by the U.S. Dept. of Treasury and the Congressional Budget Office, the 2003 defense budget exceeded 408 million dollars. The data on the American GDP comes from OECD *Main Economic Indicators*, December 2004.

33. For this data, see Patrick Lenain, "Tutti i costi della guerra al terrorismo," in *Il Giornale*, April 19, 2003.

34. See Michael E. O'Hanlon, Adriana Lins de Albuquerque, *Iraq Index*, www.brookings.edu/iraqindex.

35. See Angelo Panebianco, "Democrazia, si può esportare?," in *Corriere della Sera*, April 3, 2003.

36. See Ralf Dahrendorf, "Lo stretto passaggio alla democrazia," in *La Repubblica*, April 17, 2003.

37. See Enzo Bettiza, "Il modello giapponese," in *La Stampa*, April 20, 2003.

38. See Benjamin Barber, *Fear's Empire*, p. 172.

39. Ibid., p. 173.

40. Ibid.

41. See Angelo Panebianco, "Islam, la chance della democrazia," in *Corriere della Sera*, October 8, 2004.

42. See Samuel P. Huntington, *The Third Wave. Democratization in the Late Twentieth Century*, University of Oklahoma Press, Norman 1993, especially chs 1 and 2.

43. See Ernesto Galli della Loggia, *La morte della patria. La crisi dell'idea di nazione tra resistenza, antifascismo e Repubblica*, Laterza, Roma-Bari 1996.

44. See Roger Scruton, *The West and the Rest*, p. IX.
45. See Michael Scott Doran, "Somebody Else's Civil War," in *Foreign Affairs*, LXXXI, n. 1, January/February 2002, pp. 22–42.
46. See Ian Buruma and Avishai Margalit, *Occidentalism. The West in the Eyes of Its Enemies*, The Penguin Press, New York 2004, p. 147.
47. See Ali Ahmad Said Esber, *La condanna di noi arabi*.
48. See Paolo Branca, *Moschee inquiete. Tradizionalisti, innovatori, fondamentalisti nella cultura islamica*, Il Mulino, Bologna 2003.
49. See John L. Esposito, *Unholy War. Terror in the Name of Islam*, Oxford University Press, Oxford 2002, p. 116.
50. Ibid., p. 82.
51. See Enzo Pace, *Perché le religioni scendono in guerra?*, Laterza, Roma-Bari 2004, pp. 134 and 135.
52. See Gilles Kepel, *Jihad. Expansion et décline de l'islamism*, Editions Gallimard, Paris 2000.
53. See John L. Esposito, *Unholy War*, p. 116.
54. See Ali Ahmad Said Esber, *La condanna di noi arabi*.
55. See Bernard Lewis, *What Went Wrong*, p. 159.
56. Ibid., pp. 159–160.
57. See Thomas Carothers, "Promoting democracy and Fighting Terror," in *Foreign Affairs*, LXXXII, n. 1, January/February, pp. 84–97, here quot. p. 93.
58. See Robert Kagan, "One Year After: A Grand Strategy for the West?," in *Survival* XLIV, n. 4, Winter 2002–2003, pp. 135–156, here quot. p. 153.
59. See Laurence R. Iannacone e Massimo Introvigne, *Il mercato dei martiri*, p. 102.
60. See Slavoj Zizek, "L'epoca Oscura della democrazia armata," in *Il Manifesto*, April 15, 2003.
61. See Antonio Polito, "Una cosa di sinistra sulla guerra dell'Iraq," in *Il Riformista*, April 14, 2003.
62. See G. John Ikenberry, "America's Imperial Ambition," in *Foreign Affairs*, LXXXI, n. 5, pp. 44–60, here quot. p. 59.
63. See among others, Steve Smith, "The End of the Unipolar Moment? September 11 and the Future of World Order," in *International Relations*, XVI, n. 2, 2002, pp. 171–183.
64. See Kenneth M. Pollack, *The Threatening Storm. The United States and Iraq: the crisis, the strategy, and the prospects after Saddam*, Random House, New York 2002, p. 423.
65. See Jackie Ashley, "No moving a prime minister whose mind is made up," *The Guardian*, Saturday, March 1, 2003, http://www.guardian.co.uk/guardianpolitics/story/0,,905197,00.html.
66. See Dino Boffo, "Il realismo di un giorno sospirato," in *Avvenire*, April 20, 2003.
67. See "USA: un nuovo 'piano Marshall' per lo sviluppo della regione," in *L'Osservatore Romano*, March 19, 2004.

68. "L'Ulivo" ("The Olive Tree") is the name of the centre–Left political formation, which includes mainly Democratici di Sinistra (ex-communists) and "La Margherita" ("The Daisy") (ex–left-wing Christian Democrats) around Romano Prodi. Prodi is also supported by the Greens, Rifondazione Comunista and the Italian Communists. The opposition to this coalition is the "House for Freedom," led by Silvio Berlusconi, who has a coalition of Forza Italia, Alleanza Nazionale, the UDC (ex–right-wing Christian Democrats), and the Northern League.

69. See Alberto Asor Rosa, *La guerra. Sulle forme attuali della convivenza umana*, Einaudi, Torino 2002, p. 126 e 184. But see also the violently anti-American pamphlet, ultra-simplistic and highly successful among the Italian left-wing, written by Giulietto Chiesa, a *Rifondazione Comunista*'s member of the European Parliament, and a great nostalgist for Stalin's USSR: Giulietto Chiesa, *La guerra infinita*, Feltrinelli, Milano 2002.

70. See Francesco Merlo, "Passioni forti pensieri vuoti. La lunga stagione delle manifestazioni," in *Corriere della Sera*, April 26, 2003.

71. See Salvatore Cannavò, "Un progetto possibile, l'Europa senza guerra," in *Liberazione*, April 17, 2003.

72. See Rina Gagliardi, "Una giornataccia," in *Liberazione*, April 16, 2003.

73. See Loris Campetti, "Folgorati sulla via di Baghdad," in *Il Manifesto*, April 17, 2003.

74. The CGIL is the largest Italian workers' (and pensioners') trade union, once tied organically to the Communist Party and today to the Democratic Left.

75. See Federico Geremicca, "Cofferati: errore incomprensibile quel voto sull'Iraq," in *La Stampa*, April 19, 2003.

76. Quot. in Magdi Allam, "Al Qaeda Colpiamo la Spagna e si ritirerà dall'Iraq," in *Corriere della Sera*, March 15, 2004.

77. On Al Qaeda's network in Milan (to a great extent wiped out by the Judge Stefano Dambruoso) and its ties with Afghan and Iraqi terrorism, see Stefano Dambruoso, with Guido Olimpio, *Milano-Bagdad. Diario di un magistrato in prima linea nella lotta al terrorismo islamico in Italia*, Mondadori, Milano 2004.

78. See the interview with Michaele Walzer conceded to Ennio Caretto, "Michael Walzer: 'Guerra sbagliata. Ma bisogna vincerla.' Il filosofo politico americano: 'Alla sinistra europea dico: andarsene sarebbe considerato il trionfo di al Qaeda'," in *Corriere della Sera*, March 18, 2004. On September 13, 2004 Zapatero is "rewarded" by Chirac and Schroeder who concede a "Showpiece Summit" in Madrid, almost to make amend for the one held in the Azores by Bush, Blair, and Aznar shortly before the conflict.

79. See Angelo Panebianco, "Madrid 2004 o Monaco 1938?," in *Corriere della Sera*, March 16, 2004.

80. *The President's State of the Union Address*, January 29, 2002.
81. On the Manichaean contrasts between realism and utopia, see the ever-topical work by E.H. Carr, *The Twenty Years Crisis, 1919–1939. An Introduction to the Study of International Relations*, Palgrave, Houndmills 2001 (1st ed. 1939), enriched by a forceful introduction by Michael Cox.
82. See Maurizio Viroli, "Walzer 'Non basta dire no alla guerra,' " interview by Michael Walzer in *La Stampa*, March 8, 2003.
83. See Marc Bloch, *Écrits de guerre. 1914–1918*, Masson & Armand Colin Éditeurs, Paris 1997, pp. 119–120.
84. See Angelo Panebianco, *Guerrieri democratici. La democrazia e la politica di potenza*, Il Mulino, Bologna 1997, p. 92.
85. See Ulrich Beck, "Il nuovo ordine mondiale sognato dagli Stati Uniti," in *La Repubblica*, April 16, 2003.
86. See William Blum, *Rogue State, A Guide to the World's Only Superpower*, Zed Books, London 2002.
87. See Michael Hardt and Antonio Negri, *Empire*, p. 18.
88. See John Lloyd, "La sovranità vince sui diritti? Blair ha varcato il Rubicone e detto no," in *Il Riformista*, April 15, 2003.
89. See Luigi Bonanate, *Democrazia tra le nazioni*, Bruno Mondadori, Milano 2001, pp. 50–51.
90. See Filippo Andreatta, *Istituzioni per la pace. Teoria e pratica della sicurezza collettiva da Versailles alla ex Jugoslavia*, Il Mulino, Bologna 2000, p. 276.
91. See Pierre Hassner, "The United States: the empire of force or the force of empire?," *Challiot Papers* n. 52, September 2002, p. 46.
92. See Ulrich Beck, *Il nuovo ordine mondiale sognato dagli Stati Uniti*.
93. See G. John Ikenberry, *After Victory*, p. 273. On the concept of legitimacy in international politics, see Ian Clark, *Legitimacy in International Society*, Oxford University Press, Oxford 2005.
94. Ibid.
95. Ibid.
96. See Edward Kwarka, *The international community, international law, and the United States: three in one, two against one or one and the same?*, in *United States Hegemony and the Foundations of International Law*, Michael Byers and Georg Nolte (Eds.), Cambridge University Press, Cambridge 2003, pp. 25–56, here quot. p. 56.
97. See Robert Kagan, *America & the World: The Crisis of Legitimacy*, The 21st Annual John Bonython Lecture at The Centre for Independent Studies, p. 6, www.cis.org.au/Events/JBL/JBL04.pdf. Argument and recapitulation are developed in Robert Kagan, *American Power and the Crisis of Legitimacy*, Alfred A. Knopf, New York 2004.
98. See Robert Kagan, *America & the World: The Crisis of Legitimacy*, p. 6.
99. See Andreas Paulus, *The influence of the United States on the concept of "International Community,"* in *United States Hegemony and the Foundations of International Law*, pp. 57–90, especially pp. 58–64.

100. See Martti Koskenniemi, *The Gentle Civilizer of Nations. The Rise and fall of International Law 1870–1960*, Cambridge University Press, Cambridge 2001, p. 514.
101. For a complete reconstruction of the concept of interest, see *Il concetto di interesse. Antologia*, Lorenzo Ornaghi (Ed.), Giuffrè, Milano 1984.
102. For critical observations on the consequences of terrorism on sovereignty, see Audrey Kurth Cronin, "Rethinking Soverignty: American Strategy in the Age of Terrorism," in *Survival*, XLIV, n. 2, Summer 2002, pp. 119–139.
103. See William C. Wohlforth, *U.S. Strategy in a Unipolar World*, in *America Unrivaled*, pp. 98–118, here quot. p. 106.
104. See Michael Hardt and Antonio Negri, *Empire*, pp. 12–13.
105. George W. Bush, *Easter and Passover*, President's Radio Address, April 19, 2003.
106. See Aldo Piccato, "Pax Americana e ipocrisia europea. Che cosa c'è dietro al divorzio tra Stati Uniti e Vecchio continente sull'Iraq? William Shawcross invita la UE a disfarsi delle sue 'illusioni opportunistiche'," in *Il Foglio*, April 19, 2003.
107. See Pierre Hassner, *The United States: the empire of force or the force of empire?*, p. 47.
108. See Angelo Panebianco, *Guerrieri democratici*, p. 92.
109. It is the summary of an interesting survey carried out by Umberto De Giovannangeli, "Il futuro dell'ONU nel dialogo USA–Europa. Arlacchi, Bonanate, Cassese e Picco: quattro esperti rispondono alle domande dell'Unità," in *L'Unità*, April 19, 2003.
110. See Michael J. Glennon, *Limits of Law, Prerogatives of Power*, Palgrave, Houndsmill 2002, p. 177.
111. And also Richard Perle, in Maurizio Ricci, "Il futuro dell'ONU. 'Così quel Consiglio non serve.' Il tramonto delle nazioni Unite," in *La Repubblica*. April 18, 2003, p. 13.
112. See. Joseph S. Nye, "La fine dell'ONU? Augurarsela è follia," in *L'Unità*, April 18, 2003, http://www.iht.com/articles/93062. html.
113. See Michael Glennon, "Why the Security Council Failed," in *Foreign Affairs*. LXXXII, n. 3, May/June 2003, pp. 16–35.
114. See Fausto Pocar, "Le Nazioni Unite servono a tutti," in *Il Messaggero*, April 15, 2003.
115. See Marcelo G. Kohen, *The use of force by the United States after the end of the Cold War, and its impact on international law*, in *United States Hegemony and the Foundations of International Law*, pp. 197–231, here quot. pp. 198–199.
116. See Richard Perle, in Maurizio Ricci, *Il futuro dell'ONU*.

3   THE REMAINS OF THE WEST

1. "Mani Pulite" is the code name for the series of investigations on the relationships between the world of business and the political world

carried out between 1992 and 1994 by the Public Prosecutor's Office in Milan. It led to the incrimination for corruption and extortion of a large part of the Italian political class and to a crisis in the party system. The centre–left coalition parties (Christian Democratic Party, Socialist Party, Social democratic Party, Republican Party, and the Liberal Party) were completely defeated along with their leaders. Among these Bettino Craxi, leader of the Socialist Party (PSI) ex–prime minister and one of the most highly appreciated and promising Italian political statesmen, had to repair abroad to escape arrest. In 2004 he died in Tunisia, also because he was not able to have recourse to suitable treatment. Only the Communists and the post-Fascists from the Movimento Sociale Italiano (MSI) survived that revolution, in part because they were far less targeted by the justice investigations and in part because they were objectively far less involved in the phenomenon of corruption, also because they were excluded from national government (both) or local government (MSI). The centre–left coalitions had always been an alternative to the Communist Party. The dissolution of the parties that made up the coalition created a political and representative void in the moderate part of the political front to which Silvio Berlusconi belonged, who then set up his own party, Forza Italia. He was able to gather around him a centre–right alliance made up of Alleanza Nazionale (AN) and the Northern League (Lega Nord). Totally unexpectedly, this formation won the political elections in 1994. In 2000 the centre–right won the political elections again.

2. The dominant subcultures during the years of the so-called First Republic were the Catholic and Communist ones. See Lorenzo Ornaghi and Vittorio Emanuele Parsi, *Lo sguardo corto. Critica alla classe dirigente italiana*, Laterza, Roma-Bari, 2001.

3. On this see Thomas Risse, *Beyond Iraq: Challenges to the Transatlantic Security Community*, paper presented to the American Institute for Contemporary German Studies, Washington D.C., January 24, 2003.

4. See Zbigniew Brzezinski, *The Choice. Global Domination or Global Leadership*, Basic Books, New York 2004, p. 31.

5. See Michael Hirsch, "Bush and the World" in *Foreign Affairs*, LXXX (2002), n. 5, pp. 18–26, here quot. p. 20.

6. See Charles A. Kupchan, "The End of the West," in *The Atlantic online*, November, 2002, pp. 2–3, http://www.theatlantic.com.

7. See Henry Kissinger, *Does America Need a Foreign Policy?*, p. 35.

8. See "Politica internazionale—La dottrina Romano," interview with Sergio Romano by Pialuisa Bianco, in *Il Foglio*, December 14, 2002.

9. See Pierre Hassner, *The United States: the empire of force or the force of empire?*, p. 43.

10. See Ted Galen Carpenter, *A Great Victory?*, in *NATO's Empty Victory. A Postmortem on the Balkan War*, Ted Galen Carpenter (Ed.), Cato Institute, Washington, D.C. 2000, pp. 1–8, here quot p. 7.

11. So argued Donald Rumsfeld on Feruary 20, 2002: "My point of view is that you have to let the mission determine the coalition and not permit the coalition to determine the mission."

12. President Bill Clinton, *Commencement Address at the United States Military Academy in West Point, New York*, May 31, 1997.

13. See Henry Kissinger, *Does America Need a Foreign Policy?*, p. 44.

14. Ibid., p. 44.

15. Ibid., pp. 46–47.

16. On the theme of anti-Americanism in France and in Europe, see Jean-Francois Revel, *L'obsession anti-américaine. Son fonctionnement, ses causes, ses inconséquences*, Plon, Paris 2002.

17. The economic relationship between the United States and the E.U. is particularly rich and complex. Even if "Competition policy and investment issues have also been the subject of many disagreements" it is necessary to consider at least two aspects: "First, Europe and the United States are not each other's main trading partners . . . Second, many EU–US trade disputes are surmountable and, in fact, get resolved through negotiation or adjudication." Otherwise, "If one looks at foreign direct investment (FDI) figures, one sees that close transatlantic economic relations and high levels of interdependence are in fact the rule . . . In sum, the EU–US economic disputes receive a great deal of publicity, but they do not contain the seeds of divorce and dissolution. On the contrary, strong EU–US economics remain one of the pillars of the fundamentally cooperative EU–US strategic relationship": see Chantal de Jonge Oudraat, *The future of US–European relations*, in Thomas G. Weiss, Margaret E. Crahan, and John Goering (Eds.), *Wars on Terrorism and Iraq. Human rights, unilateralism, and US foreign policy*, Routledge, New York and London, 2004, pp. 174–187, here quot. pp. 177 and 178.

18. The timing of events is interesting. On January 22, while the French–German axis in the Security Council is strengthening, it is Donald Rumsfeld on a visit to Prague who launches the slogan of a pro-American "New Europe" as opposed to an anti-American "Old Europe." One week later the "Document of the 8," is published, which marks a clear distancing from this axis. On February 5 it is the turn of the "Declaration of the 10 in Vilnius," in which the countries which are candidates for entrance to the European Union support American politics. On April 29, France, Germany, Belgium, and Luxembourg try to react through the so-called Terveuren Plan, disparagingly defined by its critics "the chocolate alliance."

19. See Gianni Riotta, "The Coming Identity War," in *Foreign Policy*, XVII, September–October 2000, pp. 86–87, here quot. p. 87.

20. Henry Kissinger, *Does America Need a Foreign Policy?*, revised edition, Free Press, New York 2002, p. 33.

21. See Robert Kagan, *Paradise and Power*, Atlantic Books, London 2003, p. 29.
22. Ibid., p. 32.
23. Ibid., p. 31.
24. Quoted in Kori Schake and Klaus Becher, "How America Should Lead," in *Policy Review*, August and September 2002, pp. 3–18, here quot. p. 13.
25. See Ernesto Galli della Loggia, "Europa e America. Il grande freddo," in *Corriere della Sera*, February 23, 2003.
26. See *Renewing the Atlantic Partnership*. *Report of an Independent Task-Force Sponsored by the Council on Foreign Relations*, Council on Foreign Relations, New York 2004.
27. See. Michael J. Glennon, *The United States: democracy, hegemony, and accountability*, in *Democratic Accountability and the Use of Force in International Law*, Charlotte Ku and Harold K. Jacobson (Eds.), Cambridge University Press, Cambridge 2002, pp. 323–345, here quot. p. 334.
28. See Walter Russel Mead, *Power, Terror, Peace and War*, p. 17.
29. Ibid., p. 23.
30. See Henry Kissinger, *Does America Needs a Foreign Policy?*, p. 49.
31. See Jesse Helmes, "Address before the Security Council," in *New York Times*, January 21, 2000.
32. See Ivo H. Daalder and James M. Lidsay, *America Unbound. The Bush Revolution in Foreign Policy*, Brookings Institution Press, Washington D.C. 2003 pp. 7–8.
33. See Institute for American Values, "Lettre d'Amérique, les raisons d'un combat," in *Le Monde*, February 15, 2002.
34. See Michael J. Glennon, *The United States: democracy, hegemony, and accountability*, pp. 344–45.
35. See Ross A. Kennedy, "Woodrow Wilson, World War I, and an American Conception of National Security," in *Diplomatic History*, XXV, n. 1, Winter, 2001, pp. 1–31.
36. See Barbara Henry, *Mito e identità. Contesti di tolleranza*, Edizioni ETS, Pisa 2000, p. 85.
37. For this and the previous quotation, see Rossella Prezzo and Paola Redaelli, *America e Medio Oriente: luoghi del nostro immaginario*, Bruno Mondadori, Milano 2002, pp. 22 and 23.
38. See Bruce Cronin, "The Paradox of Hegemony: America's Ambiguous Relationship with the United Nations," in *European Journal of International Relations*, VIII (2001), n. 1, pp. 103–130.
39. See André Glucksmann, *Ouest contre Ouest*, Plon, Paris 2003.
40. See *La nuova età delle costituzioni. Da una concezione nazionale della democrazia e una prospettiva europea e internazionale*, edited by Lorenzo Ornaghi, Il Mulino, Bologna 2000.

41. This must be ratified by a long series of member-states. In particular Belgium, Denmark, Ireland, and the United Kingdom must submit approval to a referendum. But the failure of the French and Dutch referendums produced serious consequences for the adoption of the constitution.
42. See Massimo Teodori, *L'Europa non è l'America. L'Occidente di fronte al terrorismo*, Mondadori, Milano 2004, p. 26.
43. See Barbara Henry, "L'identità politica europea. Quale ruolo per la Carta dei diritti," in *La Carta dei diritti fondamentali. Verso una Costituzione europea?*, edited by Barbara Henry and Anna Loretoni, *Quaderni Forum*, XVI, n. 2, pp. 41–52, here quot. p. 50.
44. See Charles A. Kupchan, *The End of American Era*, p. 248.
45. See Boris Biancheri, "Europa unita su documenti insignificanti," in *La Stampa*, April 19, 2003.
46. See Timothy Garton Ash's answer to Kagan, "The great divide," in *Prospect*, March 2003, p. 2, http://www.prospect-magazine.co.uk
47. See Gianni Bonvicini, "Ora difesa e sicurezza comuni," in *Il Messaggero*, April 17, 2003.
48. See Furio Cerutti, *Verso l'identità politica egli europei. Un'introduzione*, in *Un'anima per l'Europa. Lessico di un'identità politica*, edited by Furio Cerutti and Enno Rudolph, Edizioni ETS, Pisa 2002, pp. 17–55, here quot. p. 31.
49. See Furio Cerutti, *Pace e guerra nella coscienza europea*, in *Un'anima per l'Europa*, pp. 151–171, here quot. p. 156.
50. Ibid., p. 165.
51. See Pierre Hassner, *The United States*, p. 48.
52. See G. John Ikenberry, *Conclusion. American Unipolarity: The Sources of Persistence and Decline*, in *American Unrivaled*, pp. 284–310, here quot. p. 308.
53. See Ronald D. Asmus and Kenneth M. Pollack, "The New Transatlantic Project. A Response to Robert Kagan," in *Policy Review*, October and November 2002, pp. 3–18, here quot. p. 17.
54. See Robert Harvey, *Global Disorder*, Constable, London 2003, p. 242.
55. See Gianfranco Fini's speech at the conference *Europa e Stati Uniti:un solo Occidente?*, Roma, January 27, 2005, and published in *Quaderno n. 8 del Centro di Orientamento Politico*, pp. 36–44.
56. See Philip H. Gordon, "Bridging the Atlantic Divide," in *Foreign Affairs*, LXXXII, n. 1, January/February 2003, pp. 70–83, here quot. p. 75.
57. See Timothy gartom Ash, *Free world. America Europe and the surprising future of the west*, Random House, New york 2004, pp. 82 and 83.
58. See "Mai contro l'America," in *Corriere della Sera*, June 14, 2003.

BIBLIOGRAPHY

Allam Magdi, "Al Qaeda: Colpiamo la Spagna e si ritirerà dall'Iraq," in *Corriere della Sera*, March 15, 2004.

———, "Disinformazione, così l'Egitto ha rimosso la strage di Taba," in *Corriere della Sera*, October 20, 2004.

Amato Giuliano et al., "Mai contro l'America," in *Corriere della Sera*, June 14, 2003.

Andreatta Filippo, *Alla ricerca dell'ordine mondiale. L'Occidente di fronte alla guerra*, Il Mulino, Bologna 2004.

———, *Istituzioni per la pace. Teoria e pratica della sicurezza collettiva da Versailles alla ex Jugoslavia*, Il Mulino, Bologna 2000.

Armao Fabio, *La rinascita del privateering: lo Stato e il nuovo mercato nella guerra*, in *Guerre globali. Capire i conflitti del XXI secolo*, Angelo D'Orsi (Ed.), Carocci, Roma 2003, pp. 91–101.

Ashley Jackie, "No moving a prime minister whose mind is made up," in *The Guardian*, Saturday, March 1, 2003, http://www.guardian.co.uk/guardianpolitics/story/0,,905197,00.html.

Asmus Ronald D. and Pollack Kenneth M., "The New Transatlantic Project. A Response to Robert Kagan," in *Policy Review*, October and November 2002, pp. 3–18.

Asor Rosa Alberto, *La guerra. Sulle forme attuali della convivenza umana*, Einaudi, Torino 2002.

Bacevich Andrew J., *American Empire. The Realities and Consequences of U.S. Diplomacy*, Harvard University Press, Cambridge, Mass. 2002.

Barber Benjamin, *Fear's Empire. War, Terrorism, and Democracy*, W.W. Norton & Company, New York 2003.

Beck Ulrich, "Il nuovo ordine mondiale sognato dagli Stati Uniti," in *La Repubblica*, April 16, 2003.

Bergen Peter L., *Holy War, Inc. Inside the Secret World of Osama bin Laden*, New York Times Books, New York 2001.

Bettiza Enzo, "Il modello giapponese," in *La Stampa*, April 20, 2003.

Biancheri Boris, "Europa unita su documenti insignificanti," in *La Stampa*, April 19, 2003.

Bianco Pialuisa, "Politica internazionale—La dottrina Romano," in *Il Foglio*, December 14, 2002.

Bin Roberto, *Capire la costituzione*, Laterza, Roma-Bari 1998.

Bloch Marc, *Écrits de guerre. 1914–1918*, Masson & Armand Colin Éditeurs, Paris 1997.

Blum William, *Rogue State, A Guide to the World's Only Superpower*, Zed Books, London 2002.

Boffo Dino, "Il realismo di un giorno sospirato," in *Avvenire*, April 20, 2003.

Bonanate Luigi, *Democrazia tra le nazioni*, Bruno Mondadori, Milano 2001.

———, *Storiografia e teoria delle relazioni internazionali*, in *Le relazioni internazionali. Cinque secoli di Storia: 1521–1989*, Luigi Bonanate, Fabio Armao, and Francesco Tuccari (Eds.), Bruno Mondadori, Milano 1997, pp. 1–24.

Bonanni Andrea, "Solo la grande Europa unita bilancerà lo stapotere USA. Intervista a Romano Prodi," in *La Repubblica*, April 19, 2003.

Bonvicini Gianni, "Ora difesa e sicurezza comuni," in *Il Messaggero*, April 17, 2003.

Branca Paolo, *Moschee inquiete. Tradizionalisti, innovatori, fondamentalisti nella cultura islamica*, Il Mulino, Bologna 2003.

Brooks Stephen G. and Wohlforth William C., "American Primacy in Perspective," in *Foreign Affairs*, LXXXI, n. 4, July/August 2002, pp. 20–33.

Alexander Moseley and Richard Norman (Eds.), *International Political Theory*, in *Human Rights and Military Intervention*, pp. 153–169.

Brzezinski Zbigniew, *The Choice. Global Domination or Global Leadership*, Basic Books, New York 2004.

Buruma Ian and Margalit Avishai, *Occidentalism. The West in the Eyes of Its Enemies*, The Penguin Press, New York 2004.

Bush George W., *Easter and Passover*, President's Radio Address, April 19, 2003.

———, *The President's State of the Union Address*, January 29, 2002.

———, *Remarks by the President at 2002 Graduation Exercise of the United States Military Academy, West Point*, New York, republished in President George W. Bush, *West Point Commencement Speech*, in *America and the World*, pp. 364–371.

Byers Michael and George Nolte (Eds.) *United States Hegemony and the Foundations of International Law*, Cambridge University Press, Cambridge 2003.

Campetti Loris, "Folgorati sulla via di Baghdad," in *Il Manifesto*, April 17, 2003.

Cannavò Salvatore, "Un progetto possibile, l'Europa senza guerra," in *Liberazione*, April 17, 2003.

Caretto Ennio, "Annan scrive a Bush: non attaccate Falluja," in *Corriere della Sera*, November 6, 2004.

———, "Bremer e Rumsfeld, autocritica sull'Iraq," in *Corriere della Sera*, October 6, 2004.

———, "Lasceremo l'Iraq prima della pacificazione" in *Corriere della Sera*, September 25, 2004.

———, "Michael Walzer: 'Guerra sbagliata. Ma bisogna vincerla.' Il filosofo politico americano: 'Alla sinistra europea dico: andarsene sarebbe considerato il trionfo di al Qaeda'," in *Corriere della Sera*, March 18, 2004.

————, "Richard Perle, il superfalco 'Ora andiamo a rovesciare la tirannia del partito di Assad,' " in *Corriere della Sera*, April 17, 2003.

Carothers Thomas, "Promoting Democracy and Fighting Terror," in *Foreign Affairs*, LXXXII, n. 1, January/February, pp. 84–97.

Carpenter Ted Galen, *A Great Victory?*, in *NATO's Empty Victory. A Postmortem on the Balkan War*, Ted Galen Carpenter (Ed.), Cato Institute, Washington, D.C., 2000, pp. 1–8.

Carr E.H., *The Twenty Years Crisis, 1919–1939. An Introduction to the Study of International Relations*, Palgrave, Houndsmill 2001 (ed. or. 1939).

Cerutti Furio, *Verso l'identità politica egli europei. Un'introduzione*, in *Un'anima per l'Europa. Lessico di un'identità politica*, Furio Cerutti and Enno Rudolph (Eds.), Edizioni ETS, Pisa 2002, pp. 17–55.

Chiesa Giulietto, *La guerra infinita*, Feltrinelli, Milano 2002.

Clark Ian, *Legitimacy in International Society*, Oxford University Press, Oxford 2005.

Clark Wesley A., *Winning Modern Wars. Iraq, Terrorism, and the American Empire*, Public Affairs, New York 2003.

Clarke Richard A., *Against All Enemies. Inside America's War on Terror*, Free Press, New York 2004.

Clinton Bill, *President Bill Clinton Commencement Address at the United States Military Academy in West Point, New York*, May 31, 1997.

Council on Foreign Relations, *Renewing the Atlantic Partnership. Report of an Independent Task-Force Sponsored by the Council on Foreign Relations*, New York 2004.

Cronin Audrey Kurth, "Rethinking Sovereignty: American Strategy in the Age of Terrorism," in *Survival*, XLIV, n. 2, Summer 2002, pp. 119–139.

Cronin Bruce, "The Paradox of Hegemony: America's Ambiguous Relationship with the United Nations," in *European Journal of International Relations*, VIII (2001), n. 1, pp. 103–130.

Daalder Ivo H. and Lindsay James M., *America Unbound. The Bush Revolution in Foreign Policy*, Brookings Institution Press, Washington, D.C., 2003.

Dahrendorf Ralf, "Lo stretto passaggio alla democrazia," in *La Repubblica*, April 17, 2003.

Dambruoso Stefano, with Olimpio Guido, *Milano-Bagdad. Diario di un magistrato in prima linea nella lotta al terrorismo islamico in Italia*, Mondadori, Milano 2004.

De Giovannangeli Umberto, "Il futuro dell'ONU nel dialogo USA–Europa. Arlacchi, Bonanate, Cassese e Picco: quattro esperti rispondono alle domande dell'Unità," in *L'Unità*, April 19, 2003.

Dept. of Defense, Directorate for Information Operations and Reports (DoD DIOR). http://nationalpriorities.org/issues/military/iraq/highcost/index.html

Deutsch Karl W. et al., *Political Community and the North Atlantic Area: International Organization in the Light of Historical Experience*, Princeton University Press, Princeton 1957.

Doran Michael Scott, "Somebody Else's Civil War," in *Foreign Affairs*, LXXXI, n. 1, January/February 2002, pp. 22–42.

Eid Camille, *Osama e i suoi fratelli. Atlante mondiale dell'islam politico*, Pimedit, Milano 2001.

Esber, Ali Ahmad Said, "La condanna di noi arabi: il Potere che schiaccia l'Uomo," in *Corriere della Sera*, April 19, 2003.

Esposito John L., *Unholy War. Terror in the Name of Islam*, Oxford University Press, Oxford 2002.

Esposito John L. and Voll John O., *Islam and the West*, in *Religion in International Relations. The Return from Exile*, Fabio Petito e Pavlos Hatzopoulus (Eds.), Palgrave Macmillan, Houndsmill 2003, pp. 237–269.

Evangelista Matthew, *The Chechen Wars. Will Russia Go the Way of the Soviet Union?*, Brookings Institution Press, Washington, D.C., 2002.

Ferguson Niall, *Colossus. The Price of American Empire*, The Penguin Press, New York 2004.

———, *Empire. The Rise and Demise of the British World Order and the Lessons for Global Power*, Basic Books, New York 2002.

Fini Gianfranco, Speech at the conference *Europa e Stati Uniti: un solo Occidente?*, Roma, January 27, 2005, published in *Quaderno n. 8 del Centro di Orientamento Politico*, pp. 36–44.

Foreign Affairs, *America and the World. Debating the New Shape of International Politics*, A Council on Foreign Relations Book, New York 2002.

Franco Massimo, *Polvere di spie. Intelligence, misteri ed errori nella caccia a Bin Laden*, Baldini & Castoldi, Milano 2002.

Frum David, Perle Richard, *An End to Evil. How to Win the War on Terror*, Random House, New York 2003.

Gaddis John Lewis, *Surprise, Security and the American Experience*, Harvard University Press, Cambridge 2004.

Gagliardi Rina, "Una giornataccia," in *Liberazione*, April 16, 2003.

Galli della Loggia Ernesto, "Europa e America. Il grande freddo," in *Corriere della Sera*, February 23, 2003.

———, *La morte della patria. La crisi dell'idea di nazione tra Resistenza, antifascismo e Repubblica*, Laterza, Roma-Bari 1996.

——— "The Great Divide," in *Prospect*, March 2003, http://www.prospect-magazine.co.uk.

Geremicca Federico, "Cofferati: errore incomprensibile quel voto sull'Iraq," in *La Stampa*, April 19, 2003.

Gilpin Robert, *The Challenge of Global Capitalism*, Princeton University Press, Princeton 2000.

———, *War and Change in World Politics*, Princeton University Press, Princeton 1981.

Glennon Michael J., *Limits of Law, Prerogatives of Power*, Palgrave, Houndsmill 2002.

———, *The United States: Democracy, Hegemony, and Accountability*, in *Democratic Accountability and the Use of Force in International Law*, Charlotte Ku and Harold K. Jacobson (Eds.), Cambridge University Press, Cambridge 2002, pp. 323–345.

———, "Why the Security Council Failed," in *Foreign Affairs*. LXXXII, n. 3, May/June 2003, pp. 16–35.

Glucksmann André, *Ouest contre Ouest*, Plon, Paris 2003.

Gordon Philip H., "Bridging the Atlantic Divide," in *Foreign Affairs*, LXXXII, n. 1, January/February 2003, pp. 70–83.

Grieco Joseph M., *The Future of Transatlantic Relations*, in *Che differenza può fare un giorno. Guerra pace e sicurezza dopo l'11 settembre*, Vittorio Emanuele Parsi (Ed.), Vita e Pensiero, Milano 2003, pp. 86–100.

Hardt Michael and Negri Antonio, *Empire*, Harvard University Press, Cambridge, London 2000.

Harvey Robert, *Global Disorder*, Constable, London 2003.

Hassner Pierre, "The United States: The Empire of Force or the Force of Empire?," *Challiot Papers*, n. 52, September 2002.

Helmes Jesse, "Address before the Security Council," in *New York Times*, January 21, 2000.

Henry Barbara, "L'identità politica europea. Quale ruolo per la Carta dei diritti," in *La Carta dei diritti fondamentali. Verso una Costituzione europea?*, Barbara Henry and Anna Loretoni (Eds.), *Quaderni Forum*, XVI, n. 2, pp. 41–52.

———, *Mito e identità. Contesti di tolleranza*, Edizioni ETS, Pisa 2000.

Hirsch Michael, "Bush and the World," in *Foreign Affairs*, LXXXI, n. 5, September/October 2002, pp. 18–43.

Hopf Ted, *Post–Cold War Allies: The Illusion of Unipolarity*, in *US Allies in a Changing World*, Barry Rubin and Thomas A. Keaney (Eds.), Frank Cass, London 2001.

Hough Peter, *Understanding Global Security*, Routledge, London 2004.

Huntington Samuel, "The Lonely Superpower," in *Foreign Affairs*, LXXVIII, n. 2. March/April 1999, pp. 35–49.

———, *The Third Wave. Democratization in the Late Twentieth Century*, University of Oklahoma Press, Norman 1993.

———, "Why International Primacy Matters," in *International Security*, XVII, n. 4, 1993.

Iannacone Laurence R., Introvigne Massimo, *Il mercato dei martiri. L'industria del terrorismo suicida*, Lindau, Torino 2004.

Ikenberry G. John, "America's Imperial Ambition," in *Foreign Affairs*, LXXXI, n. 5, pp. 44–60.

Ikenberry G. John, *Conclusion. American Unipolarity: The Sources of Persistence and Decline*, in *American Unrivaled*, G. John Ikenberry (Ed.), pp. 284–310.

———— (Ed.), *America Unrivaled. The Future of the Balance of Power*, Cornell University Press, Ithaca 2002.

Institute for American Values, "Lettre d'Amérique, les raisons d'un combat," in *Le Monde*, February 15, 2002.

de Jonge Oudraat Chantal, *The Future of* U.S.*–European Relations, Wars on Terrorism and Iraq*, in *Human Rights, Unilateralism, and U.S. foreign policy*, Thomas G. Weiss, Margaret E. Crahan, and John Goering (Eds.), Routledge, New York and London, 2004, pp. 174–187.

Joxe Alain, *L'empire du chaos*, Editions La Decouverte & Syros, Paris 2002, it. transl. *L'impero del caos. Guerra e pace nel nuovo disordine mondiale*, Santoni, Milano 2004.

Juergensmeyer Mark, *Terror in the Mind of God. The Global Rise of Religious Violence*, University of California Press, Los Angeles 2000.

Kagan Robert, *America & the World: The Crisis of Legitimacy*, The 21st Annual John Bonython Lecture at The Centre for Independent Studies, www.cis.org.au/Events/JBL/JBL04.pdf.

————, *American Power and the Crisis of Legitimacy*, Alfred A. Knopf, New York 2004.

————, *Of Paradise and Power. America and Europe in the New Order*, Alfred A. Knopf, New York 2003.

————, "One Year After: A Grand Strategy for the West?," in *Survival*, XLIV, n. 4, Winter 2002–2003, pp. 135–156.

Kennedy Ross A., "Woodrow Wilson, World War I, and an American Conception of National Security," in *Diplomatic History*, XXV, n. 1, Winter 2001, pp. 1–31.

Kepel Gilles, *Fitna. Guerre au coeur de l'islam*. Editions Gallimard, Paris 2004.

————, *Jihad. Expansion et décline de l'islamism*, Editions Gallimard, Paris 2000.

Kissinger Henry, *Does America Need a Foreign Policy? Toward a Diplomacy for the Twenty-First Century*, revised edition, Free Press, New York 2002.

Kolko Gabriel, *Another Century of War?*, The New Press, New York 2002.

Koskenniemi Martti, *The Gentle Civilizer of Nations. The Rise and Fall of International Law 1870–1960*, Cambridge University Press, Cambridge 2001.

Krauthammer Charles, "The Unipolar Moment," in *Foreign Affairs*, LXX, n. 1, 1991, pp. 23–33.

Kupchan Charles A., *The End of the American Era. U.S. Foreign Policy and the Geopolitics of the Twenty-First Century*, Alfred A. Knopf, New York 2002.

————, "The End of the West," in *The Atlantic Online*, November, 2002, pp. 2–3, http://www.theatlantic.com.

Kwarka Edward, *The International Community, International Law, and the United States: Three in One, Two Against One or One and the Same?*, in

United States Hegemony and the Foundations of International Law, Michael Byers and George (Eds.), pp. 25–56.

Lake Anthony, "Defending Missions, Setting Deadlines. Prepared Remarks of Anthony Lake, Assistant to the President for National Security Affairs," in *Defense Issues*, XI, n. 14, March 1996.

Lenain Patrick, "Tutti i costi della guerra al terrorismo," in *Il Giornale*, April 19, 2003.

Lewis Bernard, *What Went Wrong? Western Impact and Middle Eastern Response*, Oxford University Press, Oxford 2002.

Lincoln Abraham, *Annual Message to Congress. Concluding Remarks*, Washington, December 1, 1862, http://www.swcivilwar.com/MessagetoCongress.html.

Lins de Albuquerque Adriana, and O'Hanlon Michael E., "The State Of Iraq: An Update," in *New York Times*, November 26, 2004, http://www.brookings.edu/views/op-ed/ohanlon/20041126a.html.

Lloyd John, "La sovranità vince sui diritti? Blair ha varcato il Rubicone e detto no," in *Il Riformista*, April 15, 2003.

L'Osservatore Romano, "USA: un nuovo 'piano Marshall' per lo sviluppo della regione," March 19, 2004.

McClellan Scott, The James S. Brady Press Briefing Room, http://www.whitehouse.gov/news/releases/2005/01/20050112–7.html#1.

Mead Walter Russel, *Power, Terror, Peace and War. America's Grand Strategy in a World at Risk*, Alfred A. Knopf, New York 2004.

Mearshaimer John J., *The Tragedy of Great Power Politics*, W.W. Norton & Company, New York, London 2001.

Merlo Francesco, "Passioni forti pensieri vuoti. La lunga stagione delle manifestazioni," in *Corriere della Sera*, April 26, 2003.

Molinari Marcello, *Condoleeza Rice: "Così vinceremo la pace in Iraq*," in *La Stampa*, April 15, 2003.

Mortati Costantino, *Istituzioni di diritto pubblico*, Cedam, Padova 1969.

Moseley Alexander and Richard Norman (Eds.), *Human Rights and Military Intervention*, Ashgate, Aldershot 2002.

Munn Jamie, *Intervention and Collective Justice in the Post-Westphalian System*, in *Human Rights and Military Intervention*, Alexander Moseley and Richard Norman (Eds.), pp. 185–210.

Novak Michael, *"Asymmetrical Warfare" and Just War*, paper presented in Rome on February 10, 2003, p. 4, www.chiesa.espressonline.it.

Nye Joseph S. Jr., *Bound to Lead. The Changing Nature of American Power*, Basic Books, New York 1990.

———, *The Paradox of American Power*, Oxford University Press, Oxford 2002.

———, "La fine dell'ONU? Augurarsela è follia," in *L'Unità*, April 18, 2003, http://www.iht.com/articles/93062.html.

O'Hanlon Michael E., "A Flawed Masterpiece," in *Foreign Affairs*, LXXXI, n. 3, May/June 2002, pp. 47–63.

O'Hanlon Michael E., Lins de Albuquerque Adriana, *Iraq Index. Tracking Variables of Reconstruction & Security in Post-Saddam Iraq*, The Brookings Institutions, Washington, www.brookings.edu/iraqindex

OECD, *Main Economic Indicators*, December 2004.

Ornagli Lorenzo (Ed.), *Il concetto di interesse. Antologia*, Giuffrè, Milano 1984.

––––––– (Ed.), *La nuova età delle costituzioni. Da una concezione nazionale della democrazia e una prospettiva europea e internazionale*, Il Mulino, Bologna 2000.

Ornaghi Lorenzo and Vittorio Emanuele Parsi, *Lo sguardo corto. Critica alla classe dirigente italiana*, Laterza, Roma-Bari, 2001.

Ottolenghi Emanuele and Verdirame Guglielmo, "Il diritto al primo colpo. Cambia il nemico, bisogna cambiare le regole della guerra. Per salvarle," in *Il Foglio*, March 1, 2003, p. III.

Owen John M. IV, "Transnational Liberalism and American Primacy; or, Benignity Is in the Eye of the Beholder," in *America Unrivaled* G. John Ikenberry (Ed.), pp. 239–259.

Pace Enzo, *Perché le religioni scendono in guerra?*, Laterza, Roma-Bari 2004.

Panebianco Angelo, "Democrazia, si può esportare?," in *Corriere della Sera*, April 3, 2003.

–––––––, *Guerrieri democratici. La democrazia e la politica di potenza*, Il Mulino, Bologna 1997.

–––––––, "Islam, la chance della democrazia," in *Corriere della Sera*, October 8, 2004.

–––––––, "Madrid 2004 o Monaco 1938?," in *Corriere della Sera*, March 16, 2004.

–––––––, *Il potere, lo stato, la libertà. La gracile costituzione della società libera*, Il Mulino, Bologna 2004.

Panella Carlo, "Doni alla frontiera," in *Il Foglio*, April 19, 2003.

Parsi Vittorio Emanuele, *Interesse nazionale e globalizzazione. I regimi democratici nelle trasformazioni del sistema post-westfaliano*, Jaca Book, Milano 1998.

Paulus Andreas, *The influence of the United States on the concept of "International Community,"* in *United States Hegemony and the Foundations of International Law*, Michel Byers and George Nolte (Eds.), pp. 57–90.

Piccato Aldo, "Pax Americana e ipocrisia europea. Che cosa c'è dietro al divorzio tra Stati Uniti e Vecchio continente sull'Iraq? William Shawcross invita la UE a disfarsi delle sue 'illusioni opportunistiche,' " in *Il Foglio*, April 19, 2003.

Pocar Fausto, "Le Nazioni Unite servono a tutti," in *Il Messaggero*, April 15, 2003.

Polito Antonio, "Una cosa di sinistra sulla guerra dell'Iraq," in *Il Riformista*, April 14, 2003.

Pollack Kenneth M., *The Threatening Storm. The United States and Iraq: The Crisis, the Strategy, and the Prospects after Saddam*, Random House, New York 2002.

Preterossi Geminello, *L'Occidente contro se stesso*, Laterza, Roma-Bari 2004.

Prezzo Rossella and Redaelli Paola, *America e Medio Oriente: luoghi del nostro immaginario*, Bruno Mondadori, Milano 2002.

Qiao Liang and Wang Xiangsui, *Guerra senza limiti. L'arte della guerra asimmetrica fra terrorismo e globalizzazione*, Libreria Editrice Goriziana, Gorizia 2001 (Chinese original edition 1999; English edition: *Unrestricted Warfare: China's Master Plan to Destroy America*, Pan American Publishing 2002).

Rampini Federico, *Tutti gli uomini del presidente. George W. Bush e la nuova destra americana*, Carocci, Roma 2004.

Revel Jean-Francois, *L'obsession anti-américaine. Son fonctionnement, ses causes, ses inconséquences*, Plon, Paris 2002.

Ricci Maurizio, "Il futuro dell'ONU. 'Così quel Consiglio non serve.' Il tramonto delle Nazioni Unite," in *La Repubblica*, April 18, 2003.

Riotta Gianni, "The Coming Identity War," in *Foreign Policy*, XVII, September/October 2000, pp. 86–87.

———, "Ecco i segni di speranza che il caos non può cancellare," in "Corriere della Sera," March 19, 2004.

Riotta Gianni, "La rivolta dei guerrieri del weekend costretti a combattere senza più congedi," in *Corriere della Sera*, September 18, 2004.

Risse Thomas, *Beyond Iraq: Challenges to the Transatlantic Security Community*, paper presented to the American Institute for Contemporary German Studies, Washington D.C., January 24, 2003.

———, *U.S. Power in a Liberal Security Community*, in *America Unrivaled*, G. John Ikenberry (Ed.), pp. 260–283.

Rocca Christian, *Esportare l'America. La rivoluzione democratica dei neoconservatori*, I libri del foglio, Roma 2003.

Rotberg Robert I., "Failed States in a World of Terror," in *Foreign Affairs*, LXXXI (2002), n. 4, pp. 127–140.

Schake Kori and Becher Klaus, "How America Should Lead," in *Policy Review*, August and September 2002, pp. 3–18.

Schmitt Carl, *Der Begriff des Politischen. Text von 1932 mit einem Vorwort und drei Corollarien*, Duncker & Humblot, Berlin 1963.

Schweitzer Yoram and Shaul Shay, *The Globalization of Terror. The Challenge of Al-Qaida and the Response of the International Community*, Transaction Publishers, New Brunswick 2003.

Scruton Roger, *The West and the Rest. Globalization and the Terrorist Threat*, Continuum, London 2002.

Simoni Alberto, *G.W. Bush e i falchi della democrazia. Viaggio nel mondo dei neoconservatori*, Falzea Editore, Reggio Calabria 2004.

Smith Steve, "The End of the Unipolar Moment? September 11 and the Future of World Order," in *International Relations*, XVI, n. 2, 2002, pp. 171–183.

Tarchi Massimo, *Contro l'americanismo*, Laterza, Roma-Bari 2004.

Teodori Massimo, *L'Europa non è l'America. L'Occidente di fronte al terrorismo*, Mondadori, Milano 2004.

———, *Maledetti americani. Destra, sinistra e cattolici: storia del pregiudizio antiamericano*, Mondadori, Milano 2002.

The International Institute for Strategic Studies, *The Military Balance. 2002–2003*, Oxford University Press, Oxford 2003.

The World Almanac and Book of Facts 2004, World Almanac Books, New York 2004.

Townsend Peter, *Terrorism. A Very Short Introduction*, Oxford University Press, Oxford 2002.

Vickers Michael G., *Revolution Deferred: Kosovo and the Transformation of War*, in *War over Kosovo: Politics and Strategy in a Global Age*, Andrew J. Bacevich and Eliot A. Cohen (Eds.), Columbia University Press, New York 2001, pp. 19–209.

Viroli Maurizio, "Walzer 'Non basta dire no alla guerra,' " in *La Stampa*, March 8, 2003.

Wallander Celeste A. and Keohane Robert O., *Risk, Threat, and Security Institutions*, in *Imperfect Unions. Security Institutions over Time and Space*, Helga Hafteendorn, Robert O. Keohane, and Celeste A. Wallander (Eds.), Oxford University Press, Oxford 1999.

Walt Stephen M., "Beyond bin Laden: Reshaping U.S. Foreign Policy," originally published in *International Security*, Winter 2001/2002, republished in *America and the World*, pp. 320–347.

———, "Keeping the World 'Off-Balance': Self-Restraint and U.S. Foreign Policy," in *America Unrivaled*, G. John Ikenberry (Ed.), pp. 121–154.

Wohlfort William C., *The Stability of a Unipolar World*, in "International Security," XXIV, n. 1, 1999, pp. 5–41.

———, "U.S. Strategy in a Unipolar World," in *America Unrivaled*, G. John Ikenberry (Ed.), pp. 98–118.

Zakaria Fareed, *The Future of Freedom. Illiberal Democracy at Home and Abroad*, W.W. Norton & Company, New York 2003.

Zizek Slavoj, "L'epoca Oscura della democrazia armata," in *Il Manifesto*, April 15, 2003.

Zunes Stephen, *Tinderbox: U.S. Middle East Policy and the Roots of Terrorism*, Zed Books, London 2002.

INDEX

Abrams, Elliot, 116
Abu Ghraib, 53, 77
Abu Mazen (Mahmoud Abbas), 78
Adams, John Quincy, 35
Afghanistan
    invasion and occupation by
        USSR, 42
    Taliban regime, 43, 47, 48, 56,
        91, 144
    War (2001), 13, 17, 36, 41, 44,
        50, 54, 57, 61, 78, 86, 87,
        101, 105, 127
Al Arabiya, 74, 77
Albright, Madeleine, 6, 8, 157
Algeria, 48, 91
Al Jazeera, 74, 77
Allawi, Ayad, 72
Allen, Woody, 75
Allied Force, 41
Al Qaeda, 21, 37, 43, 45, 48,
    52, 59, 69, 91, 104, 105,
    135, 167
Amato, Giuliano, 168
Amin Dada, Idi, 45
Annan, Kofi, 73, 122
apolarity, 20
Arafat, Yasser, 78
Arendt, Hannah, 52
Armed Islamic Group, 91
Aron, Raymond, 14, 17
Asor Rosa, Alberto, 102
Aspin, Leslie (Les), 41
Ataturk, Kemal, 90
Australia, 83

Austro-Hungarian Empire, 54
Aznar, José Maria, 104, 149

Bahout, Joseph, 81
Baldoni, Enzo, 77
Barber, Benjamin, 57, 86
Barre, Raymond, 168
Barre, Mohamed Siad, 46
BBC, 76
Beck, Ulrich, 109
Belgium, 160
Berlin Wall, 13, 21
    fall of (1989), 11, 15, 154
Berlusconi, Silvio, 149, 163
Betchel Co., 82
Bigley, Ken, 77
bin Laden, Osama, 15, 17, 19,
    41–43, 48, 54, 91, 101
Bismarck, Otto von, 62
Blair, Tony, 75–76, 97–98, 106,
    128, 145, 149
Bloch, Marc, 107
Bokassa, Jean Bédel, 45
Bonanate, Luigi, 117
Bonaparte, Napoleon I, 87, 130
Bosnia, 58, 91, 95, 110, 111, 121,
    130, 131
Branca, Paolo, 90
Bremen, Paul, 69, 80
Brezhnev, Leonid, 47
Buddha, 48
Bulgaria, 132
Bull, Hedley, 165
Buruma, Ian, 89

Bush George, 28, 32, 101, 121
Bush, George W, 3–4, 7–8, 34–36,
    43, 57, 71, 73, 76, 78, 80, 82,
    85, 93, 96–97, 105, 107,
    110–111, 129–135, 141, 148

Cabot Lodge, Henry, 144
Cambodia, 121
Carter, Jimmy, 116
Cassese, Antonio, 117
Central Africa, 45, 101
Chechnya, 44, 91, 101, 119, 132
Cheney, Dick, 34, 82
China
    and Afghanistan war, 47
    as American challenger 18, 67
    cultural revolution, 52
    military expenditure, 32
    in a multipolar world, 6, 7, 38, 63
    and principle of sovereignty, 44
    and the UN system, 117, 118
    as a political-economic great
        power, 21, 22, 24, 156
Chirac, Jacques, 82, 101, 105, 128,
    134, 149
CIA, 42
Clark, Wesley, 54
Clausewitz, Carl von 52
client-state, 27, 40, 41, 46, 65, 66,
    78
Clinton, Bill, 4, 8, 28–29,
    39–40, 46, 48, 56, 110, 121,
    129, 132
CNN, 46
Cofferati, Sergio, 103
Congo/Zaire, 47
Cook, Robin, 98
Croatia, 152
Cyprus, 160
Czechoslovakie, 153
Czech Republic, 132

Dahrendorf, Ralph, 85
D'Alema, Massimo, 163
Damocles, 87
De Gaulle, Charles, 33

democratization of Arab world,
    84–97
Desert Fox, 41
Desert Storm, 28, 41, 46
Desert Strike, 41
Deutsch, Karl, 25
Duelfer, Charles, 69

East Timor, 121
Egypt, 33, 64, 77, 78, 91, 92, 122
Eisenhower, Dwight, 137
Esber, Ali Ahmad Said, 50, 89, 93
Esposito, John L., 91
Ethiopia, 46
European Union
    as American rival, 3, 8, 31, 67,
        103
    divisions, 134, 149–158,
        161–166
    enlargement/expansion/widening,
        14, 17, 31, 132, 146,
        153–156, 163, 166
    isolationism, 8, 164
    nature of, 21, 134, 149, 158,
        164, 166
    and UN, 25, 123

Fartusi, Mohammad, 86
Ferguson, Niall, 20, 33
Fini, Gianfranco, 167
Fisk, Robert, 75
France 50, 63
    in Africa, 65
    ambitions of balancing the U.S.,
        37, 128, 133, 134, 138, 147
    and EU, 6, 123, 148, 157, 158,
        161, 162, 164
    and Germany axis, 4, 62, 128, 148,
        157, 158, 161, 162, 164
    grandeur, 101, 105, 128, 158
    and NATO, 33
    military expenditure, 32, 83
    revolutionary and Napoleon's, 26,
        33, 51
    in the Second World War, 141
    and the UN system, 107, 117, 123

Franco, Francisco, 163
Fukuyama, Francis, 11–13, 15, 145
Fulbright, William, 165

Gaddis, John Lewis, 26, 35–36
Galli della Loggia, Ernesto, 87
Germany
  and the concert of Europe, 26
  and EU, 148, 152, 153, 154,
    157, 158, 161, 162, 164
  first unification (1870), 19
  and France, 4, 37, 62, 105, 128,
    138, 148, 157, 158, 161,
    162, 164
  as a landpower, 33
  military expenditure, 32, 83
  and Nazism, 52
  and post-Nazism democratization,
    84, 85, 87, 88, 89
  and Russia, 37, 38
  in the Second World War, 70, 80,
    106
  and the UN system 122, 150
  and the U.S. in the Iraqi crisis,
    61–63, 82, 128, 133, 138,
    147
Gilpin, Robert, 18, 26
Giscard d'Estaing, Valéry, 168
Glennon, Michael, 118–119
Gonzalez, Felipe, 168
Gorbachev, Mikhail, 28, 42, 153
Gramsci, Antonio, 20
Great Britain/United Kingdom
  and the concert of Europe, 5, 26
  and EU, 148, 157, 158, 161, 162
  and Germany, 63, 106, 107
  hegemony, 25–26, 31, 33
  and Iraqi War, 16, 76, 98, 104, 134
  military expenditure, 32, 83
  in the Second World War, 141
  and the UN system, 106, 117
Grieco, Joe, 18
Guantanamo, 36, 53

Hajjaji (al-), Najat, 119
Halliburton Co., 82

Hamas, 91
Hardt, Michael, 22–23, 114
Hariri, Rafik, 81
Hassad (al), Bashar, 81
Hassner, Pierre, 130
Hegel, Friedrich, 42,
hegemonic peace, 24–27, 32, 109,
  115, 171
hegemonic war 22
Helmes, Jesse, 144
Hezbollah, 81
Hitler, Adolf, 105
Hobbes, Thomas, 51
Honecker, Erich, 153
Hungary, 132, 153
Huntington, Samuel, 15, 29, 64,
  145
Hussein, Saddam, 15, 55, 68–73,
  75–79, 82–83, 85, 89–90,
  97–98, 103–105, 107, 125,
  134–135, 138
Hutton, Brian lord Hutton, 76

Ikenberry, G. John, 13, 24, 38, 112,
  118
India, 38, 63, 65, 95, 117, 122
Indonesia, 65
Iran, 43, 47, 64, 73, 78, 79, 81, 82,
  90, 92, 101, 136
Islamic fundamentalism, 12, 15, 48,
  49, 58, 65, 67, 89
Islamic Jihad, 91
Israel 64, 77, 78, 79, 81, 141
  –Palestine conflict, 51, 79, 100
Italy 84
  in the Coalition Forces in Iraq
    (2003-) 69, 74, 77, 79
  and domestic terrorism (in the
    1970s), 55
  and EU, 148, 162, 163
  foreign policy after the Second
    World War, 126–127
  and the "French-German axis," 63
  and the Iraqi War, 125, 134, 167
  pro-peace movement, 98–106
  and Restore Hope Operation, 46

Italy—*continued*
  in the Second World War, 70,
    80, 87
  and the UN system, 119, 122,
    150
Ivory Coast, 47, 101

Japan
  in the American hegemony, 24,
    25, 38, 66
  as an Asian power, 63
  as a democracy, 8
  democratization after the Second
    World War, 84, 85, 86,
    88, 89
  in the Second World War,
    70, 84
  and the UN system, 118, 122,
    140
  military expenditure, 32
Jospin, Lionel 99

Kagan, Robert, 1, 49, 93,
    113, 116, 137, 146, 157,
    167
Kant, Immanuel, 51
Karzai, Hamid, 86
Kashmir, 91, 95
Kazakhstan, 65
Kellog, Brown, & Root Co., 82
Kenya 42, 48
Keohane, Robert, 37
Kerry, John, 76
Khalilzad, Zalmay, 116
Kissinger, Henry, 19, 31, 44,
    63–64, 116, 130, 133,
    135, 145
Klein, Naomi, 23
Kohl, Helmut, 62, 153
Korea, 18, 52
Korean War, 83, 84
Kosovo, 6–8, 31, 41, 58, 61,
    91, 95, 110, 111, 121, 131,
    157
Krauthammer, Charles, 30
Kristol, William, 116

Kupchan, Charles, 19, 129–
    130, 158
Kyrgyzstan, 48

Lafontaine, Oskar, 99
Lake, Antony, 40, 47
Laos, 119
Lebanon, 56
Lewis, Bernard, 50, 93
Liang, Quiao, 42
Libby, Lewis, 116
Liberia, 47
Libya, 56, 77, 80, 81, 95
Lincoln, Abraham, 34
Luxemburg, Rosa, 96

MacArthur, Douglas, 88
Malaysia, 65
Malta, 160
Margalit, Avishai, 89
Marshall, George, 71, 110
Marshall, Will, 145
Mazzini, Giuseppe, 96
Mearsheimer, John, 18
Menghistu, Hailé Mariam, 46
Merlo, Francesco, 102
McCrystal, Stanley, 75
Milosevic, Slobodan, 6, 155
Mitterrand, François, 153
Monroe doctrine, 18, 140, 166
multilateral/multilateralism, 1–9,
    18, 115, 130–131
Mussolini, Benito, 87

NAFTA, 19
NATO, 32, 33, 36–38, 42,
    43, 61, 62, 83, 110, 122,
    126, 127, 131–133, 140,
    152, 153
Negri, Antonio, 22–23, 114
neo-conservatives 30, 119
  influence, 8, 70, 71, 72, 81,
    93, 116
  war, 70–72
new world order, 28, 33, 99, 111,
    115, 119, 122

Nixon, Richard, 44
Novak, Michael, 50, 145
Nye, Joseph S. Jr., 19–20, 56, 119

OECD, 82

Pakistan, 43, 46, 47, 48, 64, 65, 119
Panebianco, Angelo, 65, 84, 86
Perle, Richard, 81–82, 116, 118, 122
Philippines, 65, 72
Poland, 62, 63, 85, 132, 134, 135, 162, 163, 164
Polito, Antonio, 97
Pollack, Kenneth, 98
Pol Pot, 52
Powell, Colin, 34, 121, 133
pre-emptive war, 34, 35, 36, 57
preventive war, 26, 33, 42, 56, 57, 98
Princip, Gavrilo, 54
Prodi, Romano, 31, 105, 128, 134, 163
Putin, Vladimir, 6, 44, 101
Putnam, Robert, 145

Quattrocchi, Fabrizio, 77

Rapallo Treaty (1920), 62
Reagan, Ronald, 56, 81–82, 121, 141
Restore Hope, 46–47
Rice, Condoleeza, 4, 34, 80, 133
Robespierre, Maximilien, 51, 143
Romano, Sergio, 130
Roosevelt, Delano Franklin, 71, 113, 144, 146
Roosevelt, Theodore, 140
Ruini, Camillo, 100
Rumsfeld, Donald, 34, 49, 69–72, 77, 97, 111, 116, 133, 138, 155
Russia
   in Asia, 63, 65, 66
   and EU enlargement, 153

and Germany, 62, 164
and Iraqi War (2003), 7, 133
in Middle East, 78
military expenditure, 32
and multipolarism, 6, 26, 28, 37, 38, 164
and NATO enlargement, 132
and terrorism threat, 44, 47, 48
and the UN system, 118
and the U.S., 44, 82, 133, 167
Russian Empire
   and the concert of Europe, 26, 159
   and the War with Japan (1905), 140
Rwanda, 47, 95, 110, 111

Sahaf (al-), 75
Saint Just, Louis-Antoine, 51
Saudi Arabia, 33, 43, 59, 64, 77, 78, 91, 92
Schmidt, Helmut, 168
Schmitt, Carl, 17, 53, 111
Schroeder, Gerhard, 61–62, 101
Schultz, George, 82
Scott McClellan, Bianca, 69
Scruton, Roger, 30, 58
Secularization, 94–95
Sellers, Peter, 75,
Sharon, Ariel, 78
Shelton, Hugh, 137
Shinrikyo, Aum, 42
Silla, 51
soft power, 19–20, 56
Somalia, 46, 47, 95, 110, 11, 121
sovereignty
   in an age of terror, 38, 43, 44, 56
   and EU, 21, 149, 152, 158–160, 165
   and failed states, 44–47
   and globalization, 23
   hanging, 27
   limited, 27
   principle of, 3, 14, 68, 94–95, 107, 109–115
   and religion, 17, 94, 114
   restoration, 36

sovereignty—*continued*
in the UN system, 117, 121
U.S. concept of, 131, 137,
141–144, 150
Spain
and the war in Iraq, 74, 104, 105,
134, 148
and EU, 162, 163
Sri Lanka, 95
Straw, Jack, 74–75

Tajikistan, 65
terrorism
definition of, 52
goals, 52
Islamic,12, 15, 19, 44, 58, 67
of State, 51–52
Tomaizi (al-), Mazen, 74
Turkey, 73, 78, 90, 91, 166
Turkish (Ottoman) Empire, 12, 17,
49, 94

Uganda, 45, 47
Ukraine, 62, 164
UN, 28, 36, 43, 46, 47, 69,
73, 76
unilateral/unilaterarlism, 1–9, 26,
31, 35, 45, 61, 97, 98, 109,
111, 123, 131, 142, 145–149,
154, 164, 167
U.S.
doctrine of the use of force,
40–41, 57
as empire, 22–23, 66, 67
–Germany relations, 61–63
grand strategy, 13, 16, 19, 23, 24
and Gulf War (1990–91) 28, 29
hegemony, 1, 2, 4, 7, 29–33,
36–39, 61–68, 77, 109–115,
118, 119, 138, 146–149.
157, 161, 166
and the multiple challenge to it,
17–21
leadership, 15, 29, 33, 36, 38, 55,
78, 97, 141, 149, 159

military expenditure/force, 30–32
and NATO, 33
and terrorists threats, 34, 36, 43,
50, 54, 55, 56, 57
unipolar moment, 30–31
USS Cole, 48
USSR
and Afghanistan occupation, 91
born of, 159
fall of, 11, 12, 13, 14, 17, 22, 42,
43, 156
and Gulf War (1990–91), 28
and Italian Communist Party,
125
and Italy, 87, 126
and the UN system, 36, 17, 107,
120
–U.S. rivalry, 3, 18, 24–27, 30,
37, 40, 45, 46, 47, 51, 55,
138, 164
Uzbekistan, 44, 65

Vedrine, Hubert, 110
Vienna
Congress of (1815), 87
siege of (1683), 12, 94
Vietnam War, 84, 164

Wall, Peter, 75
Wallander, Celeste, 37
Walt, Stephen, 37
Walzer, Michael, 104,
106, 145
war on terror, 15, 44, 50, 55, 57,
105, 112, 129, 132
Washington, George, 139–140
Weinberger, Caspar, 82
Westphalia
legacy, 17, 45, 64, 94,
111–115, 151
Treaty of (1648), 13,
17, 94
Wilson, Woodrow, 113, 116,
144, 146
Wohlforth, William, 32

Wolfowitz, Paul, 34, 116, 157
World Bank, 84
Xiangsui, Wang, 42

Yanukovich, Viktor, 164
Yeltsin, Boris, 6, 28

Yugoslavia, 13, 117, 131, 152, 166
Yushenko, Viktor, 164

Zapatero, Luis Rodriguez,
    104–105, 163
Zunes, Stephen, 81